# Consumer Equality

**Recent Titles in**
**Racism in American Institutions**
*Brian D. Behnken, Series Editor*

The Color of Politics: Racism in the American Political Arena Today
*Chris Danielson*

How Do Hurricane Katrina's Winds Blow? Racism in 21st-Century
New Orleans
*Liza Lugo, JD*

Out of Bounds: Racism and the Black Athlete
*Lori Latrice Martin, Editor*

Color behind Bars: Racism in the U.S. Prison System
Volume 1: Historical and Contemporary Issues of Race and Ethnicity in
the American Prison System
Volume 2: Public Policy Influence(s) toward a Racial/Ethnic American
Prison System
*Scott Wm. Bowman, Editor*

White Sports/Black Sports: Racial Disparities in Athletic Programs
*Lori Latrice Martin*

Racism in American Popular Media: From Aunt Jemima to the
Frito Bandito
*Brian D. Behnken and Gregory D. Smithers*

Voting Rights under Fire: The Continuing Struggle for People of Color
*Donathan L. Brown and Michael Clemons*

The Race Controversy in American Education
*Lillian Dowdell Drakeford, PhD, Editor*

How Racism and Sexism Killed Traditional Media: Why the Future of
Journalism Depends on Women and People of Color
*Joshunda Sanders*

The School to Prison Pipeline: Education, Discipline, and Racialized
Double Standards
*Nancy A. Heitzeg*

# Consumer Equality

## Race and the American Marketplace

GERALDINE ROSA HENDERSON,
ANNE-MARIE HAKSTIAN, AND
JEROME D. WILLIAMS

Racism in American Institutions
*Brian D. Behnken, Series Editor*

PRAEGER™

An Imprint of ABC-CLIO, LLC
Santa Barbara, California • Denver, Colorado

**Library of Congress Cataloging-in-Publication Data**

Names: Henderson, Geraldine R. (Geraldine Rosa), 1963– author. |
    Hakstian, Anne-Marie, author. | Williams, Jerome D., 1947– author.
Title: Consumer equality : race and the American marketplace / Geraldine Rosa
    Henderson, Anne-Marie Hakstian, and Jerome D. Williams.
Description: Santa Barbara, California : Praeger, [2016] | Series: Racism in
    American institutions | Includes index.
Identifiers: LCCN 2016019565 (print) | LCCN 2016031005 (ebook) |
    ISBN 9781440833762 (alk. paper) | ISBN 9781440833779 (ebook)
Subjects: LCSH: Consumers—United States. | Minority consumers—United States. |
    Racism—United States | Marketing—Social aspects—United States. | Customer
    relations—United States.
Classification: LCC HC110.C6 H425 2016 (print) | LCC HC110.C6 (ebook) |
    DDC 339.4/708900973—dc23
LC record available at https://lccn.loc.gov/2016019565

ISBN: 978-1-4408-3376-2
EISBN: 978-1-4408-3377-9

20 19 18 17 16    1 2 3 4 5

This book is also available as an eBook.

Praeger
An Imprint of ABC-CLIO, LLC

ABC-CLIO, LLC
130 Cremona Drive, P.O. Box 1911
Santa Barbara, California 93116-1911
www.abc-clio.com

This book is printed on acid-free paper ∞

Manufactured in the United States of America

# Contents

*Series Foreword*     vii

*Preface*     ix

*Acknowledgments*     xiii

*Introduction*     xvii

1. The History of Marketplace Discrimination and Consumer Inequality     1

2. From Stereotyping to Differential Treatment     11

3. Annoyance vs. Avoidance     31

4. The Business Case for Marketplace Diversity     55

5. Legal Protection     75

6. Consumer Racial Profiling and Shoplifting     91

7. Criminal Suspicion Cases     105

8. Mundane Consumption     123

9. Special Occasions of Marketplace Discrimination     135

10. Rx for Success: A Multicultural Plan That Strengthens the Marketplace     147

11. How to Help     167

*Index*     181

# Series Foreword

*Consumer Equality* is the first book in Praeger series, *Racism in American Institutions* (RAI), to explore economic inequality and the practice of "shopping while black or brown." The RAI series examines the ways in which racism has become, and remains, a part of the fabric of many American institutions. For example, while the United States may have done away with overtly racist acts such as extralegal lynching, racism still affects many of America's established institutions from police departments to corporate offices. Schools may not be legally segregated, and yet many districts are not integrated. Prisons are another example, when one considers the racist policies within the legal and penal systems that account for so many people of color behind bars. This open-ended series of one-volume works examines the problem of racism in established American institutions. Each book in the RAI Series traces the prevalence of racism within a particular institution throughout the history of the United States and explores the problem in that institution today, looking at ways in which the institution has attempted to rectify racism, but also the ways in which it has not.

In *Consumer Equality*, Geraldine Rosa Henderson, Anne-Marie Hakstian, and Jerome D. Williams examine the heretofore unexplored phenomenon of consumer inequality. They show that while racist inequities have plagued communities of color for generations, consumer inequality has gone relatively unnoticed. Most especially is the problem of "shopping while black or brown," a type of racial profiling that African Americans, Latino/as, and other ethnic communities encounter with great frequency in the American marketplace. *Consumer Equality* explores a variety of real-life incidences of racism in the marketplace. It also analyzes a host of lawsuits filed by consumers against companies that utilize racist practices in their business operations. The book also includes an important section on how business can reduce instances of consumer racism, particularly through the use of new organizing frameworks designed to establish legitimate consumer equality. Multidisciplinary and far reaching, *Consumer Equality* offers a thorough historical overview of market inequality, a contemporary focus on present day issues, and critical analysis of consumer inequality in American society.

The authors of *Consumer Equality* are all recognized experts in the field. Geraldine Rosa Henderson, an associate professor of marketing at Loyola University, Chicago, has written numerous works on marketplace diversity, branding and marketing, and consumer networks. Anne-Marie Hakstian is a professor of business at Salem State University. She has published many articles on marketplace discrimination and jury bias in market discrimination cases. Jerome D. Williams is provost and executive vice chancellor at Rutgers University. His published work includes studies on marketing to multicultural consumers, Internet privacy issues, and public health communication. Taken together, the three authors of *Consumer Equality* have an amazing breadth of academic and administrative experience, nearly 200 total publications, and multiple degrees. They have produced a thoroughly authoritative book.

Brian D. Behnken
Iowa State University
Ames, Iowa

# Preface

Ask any cultural observer if they have heard of "shopping while black or brown," and it is likely that they have not. Yet, racial profiling is a recurring topic of discussion due to extensive media coverage of incidents involving police officers who are accused of enforcing laws differently based on the race or ethnicity of individuals. Most recently, the deaths of Eric Garner (NYC), Michael Brown (Ferguson, MO), Trayvon Martin (Florida), and Tamir Rice (Ohio) have heightened and reignited the national conversation about race and law enforcement and have challenged the notion that America is a postracial society. However, in the wake of recent incidents involving Barneys' and Macy's customers who were stopped and accused of credit or debit card fraud after they purchased high-end items, an important and intriguing question presented itself: do racial profiling and other forms of race discrimination occur in the marketplace?

*Consumer Equality* is the first book to elucidate the inequalities that exist in the American marketplace. This book incorporates a wide array of real-life cases, the analysis of lawsuits filed against companies by consumers, and the application of newly developed organizing frameworks easily employable by all parties invested in establishing legitimate consumer equality. It offers a vivid, thorough historical, contemporary, and critical examination of consumer inequality and marketplace discrimination in American society. It is our hope that this book will awaken public awareness of the problem of consumer inequality.

While many are familiar with tragic events such as those that have occurred outside of the marketplace, fewer are as familiar with similar tragic events in the marketplace. In fact, retail security guards have shot and killed people of color who they suspected of shoplifting. For example, John Crawford, an African-American man, was killed at a Walmart store in Ohio and several people of color have been killed by off-duty officers working as Dillard's security guards.[1] Arguably, these documented tragedies are not everyday occurrences but they are part of an overall issue of racial bias in retail settings. Historically, retailers have often failed to provide a welcoming shopping environment for consumers of color. Empirical research and consumer self-reports of consumers provide evidence that people of color are treated unfairly in the marketplace on a regular basis.

*Consumer Equality* also is highly relevant for the general consumer public given the current refocusing of attention on the broader issue of racial profiling in department stores. For example, recent allegations of racial profiling at stores in Manhattan were the impetus for a "Customer Bill of Rights" whose goal was to provide knowledge to customers about their civil rights to protect them from "shop and frisk" practices.

This broader audience includes anyone who feels discriminated against or seeks quality information about discriminatory behavior on the part of marketers and the mistreatment of customers in the marketplace. We hope that Americans who are unaware of the phenomenon of marketplace discrimination will be intrigued and unsettled that such a practice is taking place. We feel that anyone who has been affected by marketplace discrimination, whether marginalized or nonmarginalized, should benefit by our analysis of this topic.

While we acknowledge that there have been significant advances in racial equality on many fronts in society, such as employment and housing, we also note that marketplace discrimination continues to operate under the radar of most American cultural, educational, and media institutions. We paint a picture of the contemporary American marketplace in which consumer discrimination remains an unresolved, pressing, and complex issue.

We should also point out that this book is not just about directing attention to a problem. It's also about finding solutions. We provide clear direction about how to address the problem of marketplace discrimination and understand its significance in the face of increasingly diverse consumer demographics, tastes, and behavior. Both policy makers and corporate executives should find our proposed solutions both viable and practical for identifying, analyzing, and ultimately eliminating, or at least minimizing, consumer inequality in the marketplace. Our main argument is that everyone should receive equal access and equal treatment in businesses open to the public.

Consumer inequality, marketplace discrimination, and consumer racial profiling are contemporary and important topics. As authors, we felt that these topics required further and continued examination. As readers of our book, we hope you will look at these topics from a different perspective than most Americans have considered before—thereby accomplishing our goal of providing a fresh and innovative contribution to the public debate.

## Brief Overview and Organization of this Book

This book is organized into three major sections:

1. Introductory Section—A History and Contextualization of Consumer Inequality

   Six chapters on history of marketplace discrimination and consumer inequality, terminology and definitions on stereotyping and consumer differential treatment, a framework for analysis of legal cases involving consumer differential treatment, the business case for inclusion, laws that protect consumers from racial discrimination, consumer racial profiling, and shoplifting.
2. Analysis of Cases Section—Consumer Strategy in the Courts

   Three chapters on case narratives and analysis of legal cases classified as criminal suspicion cases, mundane consumption cases, and special occasions of marketplace discrimination cases.
3. Prescriptive Section—How to Promote the Profitability of Consumer Equality

   Two chapters on prescriptive measures for marketers focusing on profitability of consumer equality and recommendations for the research community, legal community, and consumers.

## Note

1. Downing, 2004.

## Reference

Downing, Margaret. 2004. "A Closer Look at Dillard's." *Houston Press,* January 8.

# Acknowledgments

The seeds for bringing this book to fruition were planted over many years, first through our personal life experiences and later through our academic life experiences. We describe in the Introduction the paths that each of us took to arrive at our collaboration in producing this work. Many individuals played key roles in helping us to nurture various ideas for this book and who provided support, including financially, physically, emotionally, and spiritually. We are deeply indebted to all those who lifted our spirits along this journey. Without the encouragement of family members, friends, colleagues, and our students, we would not have been able to take the steps that led to the publication of this volume.

As we approached the end of our journey, there were several individuals to whom we are especially indebted. Our production manager, Susan Lynn, was the taskmaster who worked diligently to keep us on schedule. Although at times she had to prod us, sometimes "kicking and screaming," she was unrelenting, and for that we are grateful. Praeger Senior Acquisition Editor, Kim Kennedy White, was instrumental in helping us to navigate through the writing, editing, and production processes. Although we were not always as punctual as we would have liked in meeting manuscript and production deadlines, she always displayed a patient and positive attitude throughout the process, and for that we are grateful. Our research consultants, Zachary Yvaire and Kurt Fowler, put in countless hours of background research, transcriptions, and data analysis. Our copy editor Shirley Smoot was indispensable in assisting us to turn the sometimes stilted and formal writing style, to which we were accustomed as academics, into language that would appeal to a broader audience. Although the time constraints we subjected her to often were "last minute" and "we need it yesterday," she never complained and always delivered, and for that we are grateful. Without the support of these three individuals, we would have had a much more difficult time in bringing this volume to fruition. They certainly deserve special recognition.

There are many others, too numerous to mention, who supported us along the way. These include our professional, academic colleagues, who provided much helpful feedback on many of our ideas presented at professional conferences, and in academic journals, and which is reflected in the final product. We also are thankful to them for their own ideas and scholarship on consumer inequality and marketplace discrimination, as we have tried to incorporate as much of this scholarship as possible in our book and give due credit. We also wish to thank our many students, who often were the "testing ground" for many of the ideas and concepts in the book, as we discussed them in class, and especially to our graduate students, who at times assisted us with the research that formed the basis of the book. Also, we wish to thank our respective institutions for all their financial and administrative support and for allowing us to pursue this book as a scholarly achievement that brings recognition to our respective schools, namely, Loyola University Chicago, Salem State University, and Rutgers University-Newark.

The authors also would like to express the following personal notes of thanks and acknowledgments:

Gerri first gives all thanks and glory to God for allowing the words to come forth and be placed on the pages of this book. She would like to thank her mother, Eleanor A. Wilcher (1937–2011), her stepfather, George E. Wilcher (1930–2011), and her father, Bill L. Henderson (1929–2013), for their collective gifts of intellectual curiosity, social consciousness, and spirituality. Thank you to Marcus Alexis (1932–2009) for being such an amazing mentor and trailblazer in marketplace diversity research. Thanks to colleagues Nakeisha Ferguson, Akon Ekpo, Sonya A. Grier, and Vanessa Gail Perry for providing examples of marketplace discrimination and being sounding boards for early thoughts. Thanks to her two research assistants, Jazz and Prez, for being ever present inspirations and calming agents during particularly high times of stress. Thanks to her amazing coauthors, Anne-Marie and Jerome, for their knowledge, patience, and tolerance. Lastly, thank you to her friends, Lauren D. McCadney, Paula Yates, and Kathleen Scovel, for understanding every time that she said that she couldn't hang out with them because she was working on this book!

Anne-Marie appreciates the support of her partner, Shauna, who creates a loving and supportive environment conducive to completing this project and to raising their daughter, Mira. She is indebted to her parents for instilling in her a love of learning. Her friends and family members have been understanding of her need to focus on her research for a very long time.

They have waited patiently for her to be "done" and she owes them special thanks for that. Anne-Marie is grateful for the guidance and friendship of Stephen Lichtenstein, former chairperson of the law department at Bentley University. Steve recognized her passion for teaching and encouraged her to be herself. Finally, she cannot overstate her admiration for Jerome Williams whose personal and professional guidance are greatly appreciated. Her collaboration with him over the years has been extremely gratifying.

Jerome is especially thankful for the loving support of his wife, Lillian, of 48 years who was a beacon of light and encouragement and provided the moral, emotional, and spiritual compass in his life to keep him focused, especially during times when he needed to be uplifted. He also thanks all of his children, Denean, Derek, Daniel, Dante, and Dachia, and their spouses and children, for always willingly accepting the family sacrifices that sometimes had to be made to accommodate his working on this book. Jerome deeply appreciates all the support from his mother-in-law, Florence B. Harrison, as she always provided encouragement for his academic achievements and endeavors, going all the way back to his days as an undergraduate student at the University of Pennsylvania in the 1960s. Finally, Jerome dedicates this book in memory of three people who were instrumental in touching and shaping his life: his parents, Jerome J. and Gloria E. Williams, and his father-in-law, Charles R. Harrison.

# Introduction

*Our Respective Journey as Authors in Arriving at Writing this Book—Three Different Paths All Leading to the Same Place*

As authors, the three of us represent diverse backgrounds in terms of race/ethnicity, gender, nationality, age, and academic discipline. Therefore, our views on discrimination have been shaped by our individual, personal life experiences, and the national cultures and subcultures in which we grew up. However, despite our diverse starting points in being exposed to and experiencing discrimination, each of us has taken a different path that eventually led us to converge in a collaborative effort to write this book. Below, each of us tells our respective story about the journey we've each taken and the experiences that influenced our respective thinking along the way.

## Geraldine Rosa Henderson

While still a doctoral student at Northwestern University, I was excited about the opening of the new Blockbuster Music Store on Sherman Avenue. During the first week of its opening, I walked to the store in the middle of a big snowfall. I had on a big, hooded parka, hat, gloves, and boots. As I entered the store, I removed my hood and immediately was approached by a person who greeted me, welcomed me to the store, and asked me if there was anything that they could do for me during my stay there. I thanked them and said: "No, I am fine for now." I walked a few more steps when another sales associate approached me and asked the same question. I replied in the same manner as I had previously. I took a few more steps and yet a third person approached me with a similar line and I again replied in kind. However, at this point, I was getting a little annoyed with how many times I was "greeted" before I was even able to really get into the store. The main reason I had gone to the store was to buy some new headphones which is a high-ticket item for a record store. I saw the display on the far wall of the store. I continued in that direction when a fourth person offered assistance. At this point, my annoyance turned to anger that I was being harassed and fear about being followed in the store. I no longer felt safe or welcome there and so I turned around and left, never to return.

I walked immediately to my doctoral student office, which was a shared bullpen space for approximately 20 students. Still shaken by my experience at Blockbuster Music, I asked if any other doctoral students had been to the then-new Blockbuster Music store. One student exclaimed, "Yes, I've been there. They are great. They were very attentive and helpful." I was surprised that our experiences at the store had been so different. This woman was very close to me in age. We were also from neighboring suburbs of Cleveland, Ohio, and wore very similar parkas. One difference was that I am black and she is white. I concluded that our race meant that we had very different collective memories regarding the treatment of shoppers in stores. Although we may have been treated in much the same way during our visit to the Blockbuster Music store, we interpreted the sales associates' behavior in very different ways.

My first experience with overt marketplace discrimination occurred during my second year as a faculty member at The Fuqua School of Business at Duke University. There was an incident on campus in which laptop computers were being stolen from faculty offices. A sketch of the alleged suspect was posted at various places on campus including the business school. One day, a young black man named Calvin Harding was walking around or near the business school in an athletic training suit when he was reported to campus police. A graduate student at the business school identified Mr. Harding as fitting the description of the laptop computer thief.[1] When the police arrived and asked him for identification, he said:

> I'm a student here. I don't have my ID with me but it's at my desk. I just ran down to get something for my boss. But if you just take me back up to the office, I can show you where and with whom I work.

Instead of accompanying Mr. Harding to his office to verify his identity, the campus police detained him and told him to "shut up if you are just going to lie." They kept him in custody for an extended period of time before they corroborated his story. As details of the incident became known to the university community, we learned that Harding had been identified and detained simply because he was a young black male. An investigation revealed that the officers involved in Mr. Harding's stop did not follow proper procedure but concluded that there was no evidence that race was a motivating factor in their actions.

The president of the university, Nan Keohane, penned a letter of apology to Mr. Harding in the Duke Chronicle newspaper but failed to mention any connection of race with the incident. Although there were only a few African-American faculty members at Duke at that time, almost all of us signed an open letter to President Keohane to dig deeper and do more. We asked that she reconsider both the treatment of Calvin Harding and the punishment of those involved including the graduate student who first reported Harding as the laptop thief. President Keohane's response was to meet with each of us individually. Ultimately, the officers were suspended but that situation left an indelible impression upon faculty, staff, and students for years to come.

For my part, I continue to try to reconcile how a student who was paying $24,000 a year for tuition was confused for a laptop computer thief. Although some people might not characterize Calvin Harding as a "customer," his experience is one that most African Americans experience in the marketplace. Clearly the Duke University community did not do its best for Calvin Harding that day in April, 1997. It is my hope that through this book, marketers and other stakeholders will understand that marketplace discrimination exists and that it is painful and damaging to all parties involved. Fortunately, it can be avoided with the proper training in processes and procedures.

## Anne-Marie Hakstian

Growing up in Montreal, Canada, during the 1970s meant that my formative years were shaped by the language wars between francophone and anglophone Canadians. The social and political turmoil caused many English speakers to flee the province of Quebec fearing that their livelihoods were at stake when the Parti Quebecois was elected based on its campaign promises to make French the only official language and the dominant language of business and government in the province. It was shocking to me when several of my elementary schoolmates disappeared suddenly. In my bicultural home, both my French-Canadian mother and my English-Canadian father supported the federalists rather than the separatists who wished to achieve independence from the rest of Canada. As the Parti Quebecois implemented its new language laws, my siblings and I felt safe because we were bilingual. That is not to say that the animosity and resentment underlying the sociopolitical changes did not affect me. In fact, the opposite is true. Against this French versus English backdrop, I was an outsider. Among my English-speaking friends, I was seen as "the French girl" and when I played with friends who spoke French, I was considered "l'Anglaise." I believe these circumstances sensitized me to the experience of being "other."

When I came to the United States as an 18-year-old university student, I was not aware of the history of this country that has left a deep divide between blacks and whites. I quickly learned about the domination of whites over others of different racial and ethnic backgrounds. As I have come to understand the grievances of African Americans, I am fascinated that they are so similar to those of French Canadians: a lack of respect for people with a distinctive identity, a lack of understanding of the ways in which culture and history affect perceptions, a failure to recognize the need for self-determination. In both cases, the competition between the groups is viewed as a zero-sum game: if one community wins, the other loses.

Eventually, after graduating from George Washington University Law School, I did equal employment opportunity (EEO) work with federal government agencies. As an EEO investigator, I interviewed agency employees and managers to discover whether individuals had been treated unfairly due to their membership in a particular protected group. That work took me across the country from small towns in the Sierra Nevada and western North Carolina to Denver, Colorado, and Chicago, Illinois. I visited U.S. Forest Service ranger stations, Food Service Inspection Services sites, and FBI facilities. The common denominator was that people who felt that they were poorly treated had lost their motivation to work hard as well as confidence in themselves. I was amazed to witness the physical stress and emotional turmoil experienced by wonderful people across the country because of ineffective management. In addition, I observed suffering among others besides the individuals who believed they were being mistreated: supervisors and managers dealt with the angst of being investigated, the fear of possible repercussions, and low morale among employees in the complainant's workplace.

A few years later, at an academic conference, I heard Dr. Jerome Williams present his research about multicultural marketing. His presentation included a slide on which he had listed a handful of legal cases involving African-American customers who had sued retail establishments for discriminating against them. Because I had never heard of this type of litigation by customers against commercial establishments, I was intrigued.

I felt compelled to research those cases and to educate myself about the laws under which the plaintiffs had articulated legal claims. It was disheartening to learn of the ineffectiveness of existing law in terms of providing redress to people who are mistreated when they are attempting to spend their hard-earned money. This began my personal investigation on the issue of consumer discrimination that eventually led to a professional research stream.

Whenever possible, I have asked friends, colleagues, and acquaintances of color whether they have experienced discrimination while shopping. The answer is always yes. It never ceases to amaze me—although it shouldn't—that the answer is always yes. What often differs is how the individual handles the situation. Some have explained they don't have time to deal with these "minor inconveniences." Others make daily decisions about the value of bringing discriminatory service to the attention of store personnel or service providers. Still others are resigned to the reality of life as a person of color in America today. As a white person, I have never experienced this type of microaggression. As such, it is difficult to truly understand the shame and the emotional pain that people of color know too well. Research now shows that these "small" incidents cause real damage over time.

One of the few stories I heard about my father's upbringing in lily-white British Columbia, Canada, involved the mother of one of his classmates who did not allow my father to enter her home. When the other boys went inside for lemonade and cookies, my dad was told to wait outside. When my dad told us the story, he explained to my siblings and me that his friend's mother did not want him in her house because his father was Armenian. I know that incident left a scar that my father has lived with throughout his life and I can only imagine the damage that occurs when these occurrences happen on a regular basis. I hope that my work will help to decrease the extent to which this type of hurt occurs.

## Jerome D. Williams

How far have we come? How much progress has been made in eradicating discrimination in this country? As an African American whose life has spanned the "Jim Crow" era prior to the passage of Civil Right legislation, with its manifestations of overt forms of segregation and prejudice, to an era when the first black president was elected, I frequently ask myself the question "Is the glass half empty, or is the glass half-full?" As an academic, my primary focus, and that of this book, is examining progress in the marketplace in particular. While I've witnessed tremendous progress in terms of race relations over the past several decades, including progress in housing, employment, and education, the harsh reality is that there still is much to be achieved especially in the marketplace.

In presenting my work across the country, I frequently relate a story about an incident that was the most significant event in propelling me into researching marketplace discrimination. The year was 1987 and I had just joined the faculty at Penn State University, my first academic job after completing my PhD. My wife and I were shopping with our children at the local mall in State College, Pennsylvania, a small university town. Three of our sons went off to shop on their own. When we were ready to leave, my wife and I couldn't find them, so we stopped by the mall's central administration to ask for assistance in finding them. To our surprise, we found our sons sitting there in the office. They were being detained on suspicion of shoplifting. We inquired what they had shoplifted and were further surprised that the security guard had detained them based solely on the fact that all three were wearing new shirts—shirts that my wife had purchased for them the day before which they were wearing for the first time.

Although the matter was quickly resolved with the mall management issuing an apology to us, what piqued my scholarly curiosity was the reaction of my faculty colleagues when I discussed the incident with them. My colleagues—all of whom were white—failed to consider the possibility that the mistreatment of my children had anything to do with their race, whereas I was fully convinced that it did. Of course, it wasn't until years later that I came across the academic literature and theories and found support for what was just a supposition at the time of the incident at the mall: that people of different races respond differently to incidents of marketplace discrimination.

A few years after the incident at the mall, I came across a news article that really caught my attention. It was the first really big case involving consumer racial profiling that grabbed national attention. Interestingly, that case involved three African-American teenagers who were stopped in an Eddie Bauer store for suspicion of shoplifting. Why did store security detain them? They were wearing new shirts! Whereas I received an apology when my sons were mistreated, the three young men sued Eddie Bauer and were awarded two million dollars! At that point, I began documenting every case of marketplace discrimination and consumer racial profiling that I could find and that eventually led to my collaboration with Anne-Marie Hakstian and Geraldine Rosa Henderson in a stream of research that has spanned

15 years and culminated in many scholarly articles, OP-ED pieces, general-interest nonacademic pieces, and this book.

If the truth be told though, my whole academic life, beginning from the time I was a doctoral student, has been spent trying to find answers to questions related to issues of social injustice and how marketing might offer solutions. Much of my early research examined the impact of race and inequities in the marketplace. Some examples are discrimination in housing manifested by racially exclusive real estate advertising, discrimination through targeted marketing of alcohol and tobacco products, and discrimination in marketing alcohol products using pricing strategies in ethnic minority neighborhoods. However, my interest in race and inequalities has not been confined to marketplace phenomena—it extends to society as a whole. As an African American, I frequently have been "one of a few" or the "only one": in my high-school graduating class, my experience as an undergraduate and as a graduate student (I was the only African American in the whole country to receive a PhD in Marketing in 1986), in my first job working for a major corporation (General Electric Company), at almost every institution where I have been on the faculty. In so many of these situations, my racial/ethnic background played a pivotal role in how I was treated—admittedly sometimes to my advantage, but not in most instances. There were so many encounters in my life where race had played a significant part, that I really was driven to see how I could use this research to make this world a better place, not just in the marketplace but in society in general. I truly believe that the many incidents I have encountered in the marketplace and in society in general, and the many incidents of consumer inequality that many others have experienced, as we have documented in this book, can serve as "teachable moments," an opportunity for us to do better.

When I think of the inequitable treatment I experienced due to my race, the example that stands out in my mind occurred when I was a child and was transferring to a new school. Although the incident didn't have much of an impact on my thinking about race and inequality at the time, as I got older and reflected on what happened, I really began to appreciate how different my life might have been. Growing up in the inner city of Philadelphia, I didn't think very much about being "black," let alone about being a black consumer. Everyone around me was black—my classmates, my teachers, my neighbors, the customers in the stores where my parents shopped, and even the employees in those stores. My parents moved to Levittown in suburban Philadelphia when I was in fourth grade, looking for a better environment in which to raise their children. They told me that the schools were going to be a lot harder than what I was used to so I braced myself for this new "multicolored" world.

I was surprised that all of my classmates were black and the new school was a breeze. I had been placed in the special education track without any testing, as was done with most of the children whose families lived in this particular community. All of the black families in this school district lived in the segregated section of Levittown called Bloomsdale because of laws prohibiting them from purchasing homes in Levittown proper. Parents protested and eventually I, along with other black children, was transferred into regular classes. Interestingly, at least two scholars whom I met after joining the Rutgers faculty have written books about Bloomsdale and similar nearby communities of black residents who had moved there from the inner city of Philadelphia.

I often wonder what would have happened to me and my childhood friends if our parents had not stepped up to right this social injustice and we had not been transferred. What I know is what happened as a result of the transfer. As one story reported, "In the 1960s and 1970s, the sons and daughters of Bloomsdale became doctors and lawyers, Ivy League graduates and professional athletes in what seemed like uncommon numbers for a community of only about 1,500 people."[2]

I would be remiss if I didn't mention the very first encounter I had with Gerri Henderson, one of my coauthors on this book. About 25 years ago, she and several other African-American doctoral students at Northwestern University, had arranged to invite me as a seminar presenter. They wanted to increase the number of diverse faculty members to interact with the doctoral students. I was standing outside the Omni Orrington Hotel in downtown Evanston waiting for her to pick me up and drive me over to the Kellogg School of Management. Because we hadn't met face-to-face yet, I was paying particular attention to everyone who was pulling up to the hotel to make sure I didn't miss her. Standing there in my long, camel-colored coat, I was astounded when a white female hotel guest arrived, abruptly exited her car, handed me her keys, told me she was going inside to register, and asked me to park her car. When Gerri arrived a few minutes later, I was still standing there holding the lady's car keys trying to figure out what to do. Gerri couldn't tell if I was the distinguished guest speaker she was expecting to pick up or the bell hop who was parking cars.

I mention this particular incident because of the recent unfortunate incident involving James Blake, once the No. 4 ranked tennis player in the world. He was waiting outside for a car to pick him up and take him to the U.S. Open tennis tournament where he was scheduled to do corporate appearances. An undercover plainclothes NYPD officer rushed Blake, threw him to the ground, handcuffed him and led him away. The officer's explanation for assaulting Blake was that it was a case of mistaken identity related to a sting operation. When I read about incidents such as this one and many others we have documented in our 15 years of research on marketplace discrimination, I come back to the question: "How far have we come?" There's no doubt, that as a society we have come a long way in terms of race relations, in the marketplace, and in society, in general. However, after reading our book, perhaps you will agree with us that the answer is: Not far enough!

## Notes

1. Kauffman, 1997.
2. Sokolove, 1986.

## References

Kauffman, Susan. 1997. "Duke Arrest Controversy Still Simmers." *The News & Observer*, May 15.

Sokolove, Michael. 1986. "Crack City': Good Town Gone Bad. *Philly.com*. August 11.

# Chapter 1

# The History of Marketplace Discrimination and Consumer Inequality

*There are very few African American men in this country who haven't had the experience of being followed when they were shopping in a department store. That includes me.*

—President Barack Obama[1]

In 1873 in the city of Keokuk, Iowa, Emma Coger decided to take the Mississippi River steamer, the SS *Merril*, to return to her home in Quincy, Illinois. A teacher at a school for children of color, Emma Coger was of partial African descent herself. When she first bought her ticket according to the custom and regulations of the steamboat company, Emma was provided only with transportation. A room and meals were not included for her because she was a woman of color.

When the clerk explained the limitations of the ticket, she requested and received a refund. She then requested to pay for first-class service, invoking her right to travel as other first-class passengers, but the clerk refused to sell her the first-class ticket. She later purchased a ticket that entitled her "to meals at an assigned table and first-class cot only." However, the words "This does not include meals," were scrawled on the face of the ticket. Just before dinner, Emma sent her maid to purchase a ticket for a meal, and she returned with a ticket with the words "colored girl" written on it. Emma returned the ticket and got her money back. She then persuaded a white gentleman to purchase a ticket on her behalf. The ticket he purchased did not have any of the previous limitations.

Emma proceeded to the dining room with her new ticket where she sat down at the ladies table, where other women had reserved seats. There, she was told by one of the guards that she needed to leave the table and take her meal in the guard or in the pantry. Emma refused to leave her seat. When the captain of the boat was called and failed to persuade Emma to remove herself, what happened next involved considerable violence. The captain began to physically remove Emma from the table, but Emma knew her rights and wasn't going without a fight. This resulted in a small injury to the captain, a torn table cover, and broken dishes. Later, Ms. Coger sued the steamboat company for $5,000 in damages, and the court awarded her $250. Although she was not the first African American to sue a packet line for denial of first-class service on the upper Mississippi River, Emma Coger was a precursor to the men and women who refused to leave lunch counters of segregated facilities across the country and continued the fight for the rights of African Americans as consumers in the marketplace.

In that same year, Mississippi Representative John R. Lynch traveled to St. Louis, Missouri, to attend a two-day convention along with representatives from 17 states.[2]

The delegates were there to discuss the feasibility of moving the nation's capital from Washington, DC, to St. Louis. At the time, Lynch was a Republican Representative to the Mississippi State House; he arrived at the Planter's Hotel, where he had been told the Mississippi Delegation was to be housed. However, the desk clerk informed him that the delegation was staying at the Saint Nicholas. But the clerk had lied. The Planter's Hotel would not serve Lynch because he was African American.

Lynch then asked his driver to stop at the Southern Hotel, where it took 30 minutes for the owner, Mr. Warner, to come and offer Lynch the opportunity to be the first black man to stay there for a night. Lynch had originally asked permission only to remain in the men's reception area until he could catch his train back to Mississippi. However, Warner insisted that Lynch stay the night. The only caveat: Lynch could not leave his room, even for meals, because Warner was afraid his other customers would leave the establishment if they knew a black man was lodging there. Representative Lynch informed Warner that he was half Irish, hoping that might make a difference. Warner assured Lynch that the next time he visited St. Louis, he would definitely give him a place to stay. Lynch left St. Louis furious and vowed to vote "no" on Missouri's bid to move the nation's capital to St. Louis.

The election of an African-American man as the president of the United States in 2008 and again in 2012 might lead some to believe that stories like those of Emma Coger and John Lynch are simply events from the past. This book attempts to shed light on the reality of race-based discrimination that still exists in the American marketplace. In fact, today, consumers of color are treated differently than white consumers based on their race or ethnicity, resulting in the denial of or degradation in the products and/ or services offered by the merchant. In a retail environment, the denial of goods or services occurs when customers are prevented from participating in consumption experiences. Examples include sales associates refusing to wait on certain customers or refusing to provide them information about goods or services that is available to other customers and store employees denying customers access to the establishment and removing customers from the store.

A degradation of goods or services occurs when customers of color are allowed the opportunity to transact their business but are provided something less—in a variety of possible ways—than white customers receive. Degradation may take many forms: extended waiting periods, required prepayment, and increased surveillance and treatment as a criminal. Both of these concepts will be discussed in greater detail in Chapter 3.

Future business leaders are taught that a business has the best possible chance of maximizing revenue and/or profit when it invests in and commits to engaging consumers in the marketplace to build a relationship. Business students learn about the lifetime value of a customer, customer-relationship management, and customer equity.[3] However, as this book reveals, an increasingly large portion of the potential customer population, people of color, are being treated in anything but an equitable fashion. Instead of being recognized as the valuable assets that they are, shoppers of color are treated as unvalued, unwanted, inconvenient, and second-class citizens who are merely tolerated.

Unfortunately, many senior executives who are not familiar with the day-to-day operations of their businesses are unaware that their employees are treating certain customers unfairly. On any given day, the frontline service providers and even managers are allowing viable customers to walk right out the door. In many cases, they are escorting them out, sometimes in handcuffs and sometimes in body bags, as in the case of John Crawford, who was shopping in a Walmart store in Beavercreek, Ohio, or as has been the case of some alleged shoplifters.[4]

Each industry is limited and prepared to address the issue of consumer inequality in different ways. The first step in eradicating marketplace discrimination is for companies to become aware and knowledgeable about this problem. The goal of this book is to familiarize readers with the diverse histories attached to people of color within the marketplace. Readers will come away with the knowledge and tools to begin to craft industry- and company-specific solutions to address marketplace discrimination. Let's start at the beginning.

## Race in the Colonial American Marketplace

Three distinct racial groups were present in the colonial American marketplace: European colonists, indigenous Americans, and West Africans. At this point in history, the idea of race already existed. Some colonists, particularly the Quakers, felt that indigenous peoples and West Africans were equal to them despite their different cultures. However, many European colonists believed that, as civilized Christians, they were superior to the savage and infidel indigenous people and to the beasts of the world, a category to which West Africans were assigned.[5]

During this era, indigenous communities and colonists exchanged goods and services within a bartering system. Thus, Europeans settlers saw indigenous Americans as participants in the marketplace, either as producers or consumers. Because the indigenous Americans' skin color was lighter than that of the West Africans, they were perceived to be closer to Europeans and thus civilizable. On the other hand, it was generally believed that West Africans were not civilizable. Thus, they did not enter the marketplace as participants, but to be sold as a type of commodity, a labor tool, or "beast of burden."

These early-ascribed roles shaped the types of marketplace exchanges that occurred among members of the three groups. Some of these exchanges resulted in indigenous peoples receiving unequal services in return for land or other goods. As the European colonists' population grew, so did their demand for goods. Indigenous Americans were pressured to supply more goods, and more West Africans were brought to the American colonies to work on the plantations to produce goods. The European settlers' reliance on the bartering economy waned as the modern American marketplace gradually emerged. The marketplace afforded an individual the opportunity to become a consumer, a term which was not applied to purchasers and potential purchasers until the late 19th century, when it was culturally adopted as a role for citizens.[6]

## Race and the Marketplace: From Jim Crow to Civil Rights

After slavery was abolished and blacks began to earn wages, they expected to enter the marketplace to exchange currency for goods and services like white citizens. Unfortunately, they quickly learned the relationship between their treatment as consumers and the color of their skin as they began to experience a new form of marketplace discrimination. Jim Crow policies, established during the 1890s and in effect until the 1960s, required racial segregation in stores, streetcars, buses, public parks, beaches, bathhouses, municipal golf courses, cafeterias, and auditoriums, among other places of public accommodation. During this era, African Americans were excluded from participation in many aspects of society. In some areas, these consumers were not welcome to enter shops owned by whites, let alone purchase goods or services from them. Black customers were excluded entirely from skating rinks, beauty parlors and barber shops, shoe-shine stands, hotels, restaurants, dance halls, and theaters. Other business establishments allowed blacks to buy from them under special conditions. For example, black customers were required to enter through the back door or to sit in the back of the restaurant. The images from these times show the separate water fountains, entry ways, and seating areas that were designated for blacks and whites.

Jim Crow laws were enacted to keep people in "their place" and to prevent them from co-mingling in the marketplace and other public spheres. A person of color who dared to violate one of these laws was punished swiftly and publicly so as to discourage others from doing the same. Some states imposed criminal penalties for violating laws that required separate facilities for blacks and whites. In 1896, the U.S. Supreme Court upheld such a law in *Plessy v. Ferguson*. The statute at issue was a Louisiana law that provided separate railway cars for black and white passengers. Homer Plessy, a 30-year-old shoemaker, was arrested, jailed, and convicted for refusing to leave the "white" car. The Supreme Court, interpreting the 14th amendment's Equal Protection Clause, wrote that it "could not have been intended to abolish distinctions based upon color, or to enforce social, as distinguished from political, equality, or a commingling of the two races upon terms unsatisfactory to either."[7] In 1936, in an attempt to help African Americans navigate the hostile land of Jim Crow, Victor Green created the *Green Book*. The *Green Book* was a guide to restaurants, hotels, and other service providers that were friendly (or at least not hostile to) black travelers.[8]

During the late 1950s and 1960s, people protested these laws and eventually broke down the formal system of segregation and the exclusion of blacks from businesses open to the public. During this period known as the Civil Rights Era, a bus boycott began in Montgomery, Alabama, when Rosa

Parks, an African-American woman, refused to give up her seat on a bus to a white man although blacks were required to do so. Her action sparked a 13-month boycott during which blacks in Montgomery refused to ride the city buses eventually resulting in the Supreme Court ruling that the state law requiring segregated bus service was unconstitutional.

In Greensboro, North Carolina, four African-American students refused to be denied service at the "whites only" lunch counter at Woolworth's. Their act began a protest that eventually inspired student "sit-ins" at lunch counters across the country. George McLaughlin was among the students who joined the "Greensboro Four." He recalls that although they endured threats and harassment by angry whites: "We just kept sitting there. We would line up behind the stools and when one student would get up another would sit down."[9] Five months after the sit-in began, Woolworth's served three black students symbolizing the end of lunch-counter segregation. McLaughlin went on to graduate from Rutgers School of Dental Medicine, where he now serves on the faculty.

Starting in 1961, black and white "Freedom Riders" similarly attempted to integrate facilities at bus terminals from cities in the north to the Deep South. They staged sit-ins at restaurants and tried to use "whites only" restrooms. They faced violent attacks from whites "but also drew international attention to their cause," eventually resulting in the Interstate Commerce Commission issuing regulations prohibiting segregation in interstate transit terminals.[10]

Whites who dared to associate with and empower blacks were not immune from mistreatment. Sandra Adickes was a white school teacher from New York who served as a volunteer teacher at a "Freedom School" for young black children. She sued S. H. Kress & Company, a dime-store chain, for refusing to serve her lunch at its restaurant facilities in Hattiesburg, Mississippi, and for her subsequent arrest—by the Hattiesburg police—upon leaving the store on a charge of vagrancy. The black students she was with were not refused service nor were they arrested. About her experience, she states:

> On August 14, 1964, after a six-week Freedom School session in Hattiesburg, Mississippi, I escorted six Black students: Curtis Duckworth, Gwendolyn Merritt, Carolyn and Diane Moncure, Lavon Reed, and Jimmella Stokes to the Hattiesburg Public Library; there an irate librarian denied their request for library cards and summoned the police chief who came to close the library. We then went to have lunch at the Kress store, but when a waitress

told us she had to serve "the colored, but not the Whites who come in with them." We left. The police car that had been following us stopped; an officer got out and arrested me, and took me to the Hattiesburg jail. Subsequent litigation against Kress for denying me my rights and conspiring in my arrest led to a 1970 Supreme Court decision, *Adickes v. Kress*, in my favor.[11]

We remember these individuals for their courage in the face of injustice, but we rarely think about them as customers who were denied goods or services although they had paid for or were willing and able to pay.

## An Understudied Phenomenon

African Americans are not alone in experiencing marketplace discrimination. In fact, people of color of all backgrounds and ethnicities report similar treatment. Moreover, many individuals are mistreated in the marketplace based not only on race/ethnicity, but also on sexual orientation, physical ability, body shape, age, gender, religion, among others. But the phenomenon of marketplace discrimination is not well understood in large part because it is understudied. However, in this book, we focus on race- and ethnicity-based marketplace discrimination. While thoroughly comprehensive studies of race-based discrimination in other areas—such as employment, housing, lending practices—have been conducted, research on marketplace discrimination is an emerging field. Historically, academics have been limited in attempting to understand issues related to marginalized consumers, and there has been a lack of persistence in researching problems that do not lend themselves to easy solutions.[12] In 1978, Professor Alan Andreasen, a marketing scholar, reprimanded academics for the lack of rigorous and frequent research of public policy issues related to the pervasiveness of racism in the marketplace. He proposed a seven-point research agenda (e.g., family decision-making processes, power relationships in channels of distribution, product and brand beliefs) that essentially served as a call to action for the field.

One of the early studies was an investigation into the treatment of Mexican Americans and African Americans to determine whether they were served fairly by retailers and financial institutions.[13] The researchers discovered that Mexican Americans and African Americans believed that they were not receiving equitable treatment as consumers and strongly supported public policy interventions to increase marketplace fairness.[14] This was one of the first studies to acknowledge ethnic discontent with existing marketing practices. The authors used a theoretical perspective of alienation to frame this discussion based on the work of Erich Fromm, a German social psychologist, sociologist, and philosopher. According to Fromm, alienation refers to a state in which "man does not experience himself as the active bearer of his own powers and richness, but as an impoverished 'thing' dependent on powers outside of himself, unto whom he has projected his living substance."[15] In examining the experiences of Mexican Americans and African Americans, Pruden and Longman observed that the lifestyle of the low-income consumer had been measured by feelings of powerlessness, meaninglessness, anomie, and social isolation. Also, in Fromm's view, the conditions of modern large-scale capitalism alienated consumers from the process of acquisition and consumption of goods. Many of these themes will be revisited in the chapters that follow.

## Consumer Equality in the Modern Era

This book is based on the existence of race-based discrimination in the marketplace and the belief that the marginalization of large numbers of people impacts not only business but also society as a whole. Most people understand that there is something wrong when citizens, wishing to spend their money in retail stores and restaurants are stopped by employees, police, or security personnel just because of their appearance. We know that battles have been fought to guarantee all citizens equal treatment and opportunity in the marketplace. But in a free-market economy, to what extent should businesses be responsible for protecting the civil rights of consumers in the marketplace? This fundamental question gets very little attention, although it affects the daily lives of millions of Americans.

The business sector did not create the problem, but it can positively contribute to the wealth of our nation through a firm, measurable commitment to consumer equality. The first part of the book describes the problem of marketplace discrimination, presents a framework for analyzing it, and presents the business case for diversity. Next, the laws that address this type of discrimination are explained, followed by three chapters containing summaries of lawsuits filed by individuals who believe they were discriminated against as consumers. In the final chapters, recommendations are made for the businesses that wish to be part of the answer, as well as others who believe that marketplace discrimination soon will be history.

## Notes

1. Barack Obama, President. 2013. *Remarks Made by the President on Trayvon Martin.* Remarks presented at the White House, Washington, DC, July 19, 1:33 p.m.
2. Lynch and Franklin, 2008.
3. Rust, Zeithaml, and Lemon, 2000; Blattberg, Getz, and Thomas, 2001; Kumar and Reinartz, 2012.
4. Balko, 2014; Downing, 2004.
5. It should be noted that even at this early time in American history, there were free blacks, some of whom also owned slaves, and many of whom had light complexions that afforded them the ability to navigate marketplaces that perhaps would not have been afforded those with darker complexions (Branchik and Davis, 2009).
6. Strasser, 2003.
7. For an extensive tour of Jim Crow in the marketplace, visit the Jim Crow Museum at Ferris State University founded and curated by David Pilgrim: http://www.ferris.edu/jimcrow/what.htm.
8. Swanson, 2016.
9. Stetler, 2015.
10. The History Channel, 2015.
11. Adickes, 2000.
12. Andreasen, 1993.
13. Sturdivant, 1969.
14. Pruden and Longman, 1972.
15. Fromm, 1962, p. 59.

## References

Adickes, Sandra. 2000. "History Lessons in Hattiesburg." Available at: http://www.crmvet.org/info/hburg.htm. Accessed July 15, 2015.

Andreasen, Alan R. 1993. "Revisiting the Disadvantaged: Old Lessons and New Problems." *Journal of Public Policy & Marketing* 12: 270–275.

Balko, Radley. 2014. "Mass Shooting Hysteria and the Death of John Crawford." *The Washington Post*, September 24.

Blattberg, Robert C., Gary Getz, and Jacquelyn S. Thomas. 2001. *Customer Equity: Building and Managing Relationships as Valuable Assets.* Cambridge, MA: Harvard Business Press.

Branchik, Blaine J. and Judy Foster Davis. 2009. "Marketplace Activism: A History of the African American Elite Market Segment." *Journal of Macromarketing* 29, no. 1 (March): 37–57.

Downing, Margaret. 2004. *A Closer Look at Dillard's.* Houston, TX: Houston Press.

Fromm, Erich. 1962. "Alienation under Capitalism." In *Man Alone: Alienation in Modern Society,* ed. Eric Josephson and Mary Josephson. New York: Dell Publishing Company.

The History Channel. 2015. "Freedom Rides." Available at: http://www.history.com/topics/black-history/freedom-rides. Accessed July 15, 2015.

Kumar, V. and Werner Reinartz. 2012. *Customer Relationship Management: Concept, Strategy, and Tools.* Berlin: Springer-Verlag Science & Business Media.

Lynch, John Roy and John Hope Franklin. 2008. *Reminiscences of an Active Life: The Autobiography of John Roy Lynch.* Oxford, MS: University Press of Mississippi.

Pilgrim, David. "The Jim Crow Museum." Available at: http://www.ferris.edu/jimcrow/what.htm. Accessed July 16, 2015.

Pruden, Henry O. and Douglas S. Longman. 1972. "Race, Alienation, and Consumerism." *Journal of Marketing* 36: 58–63.

Rust, Roland, Valarie Zeithaml, and Kay Lemon. 2000. *Driving Customer Equity: How Customer Lifetime Value Is Reshaping Corporate Strategy.* Boston, MA: Free Press.

Stetler, Carrie. 2015. "Woolworth's Lunch Counter Sit-In Marks Anniversary." *Rutgers Today,* July 20.

Strasser, Susan. 2003. "The Alien Past: Consumer Culture in Historical Perspective." *Journal of Consumer Policy* 26: 375–393.

Sturdivant, F. D. 1969. "Business and the Mexican-American community." *California Management Review* 11: 73–80.

Swanson, Ana. 2016. "The Forgotten Way African Americans Stayed Safe in a Racist America." *The Washington Post,* January 8.

# Chapter 2

# From Stereotyping to Differential Treatment

*I began to worry about racial, religious, and gender discrimination while a graduate student, and used the concept of discrimination coefficients to organize my approach to prejudice and hostility to members of particular groups. . . .*

*It is only through widening of the usual assumptions that it is possible to begin to understand the obstacles to advancement encountered by minorities.*

—Nobel Laureate Gary S. Becker[1]

In 2014, Maurice Bessinger died. He was the owner of Piggie Park BBQ which was touted as the first BBQ drive-thru in the country.[2] Customers came to consume the barbeque by the pound or quart with Carolina Gold, the mustard-based sauce unique to Piggie Park. In addition to the drive-thru, Piggie Park offered parking spots wherein consumers could eat their purchased food. However, not all customers were permitted to use the drive-thru or eat on the premises.

In fact, on August 12, 1964, two black customers pulled into Piggie Park's drive-thru on Sumter Highway in Columbia, South Carolina.[3] A waitress came out, saw the customers' skin color, and immediately went back into the building. Subsequently, a man with an order pad approached their vehicle but also would not take their order. The customers left not knowing whether the decision to not serve them was made by an individual employee or by the company, so the customers sued both the company and Mr. Bessinger.

In court, the plaintiffs proved that all six of the Piggie Park locations denied full and equal service to persons of African descent. The few African Americans who received service did so after placing orders and picking up their purchases at the kitchen window. They were not allowed to stick around to enjoy their BBQ pork and Carolina Gold. In fact, Mr. Bessinger once installed a sign in his restaurant that said: "The law makes us serve niggers, but any money we get from them goes to the Ku Klux Klan."

In 2000, when confronted with the statement that his restaurants had a history of not serving African-American customers, Maurice Bessinger denied it saying:

> We just served them on a segregated basis, like every other restaurant did. What the Blacks didn't realize was that they got the best food, because their dining room was actually in the kitchen.[4]

It doesn't take a discrimination scholar to know that Piggie Park's policies and practices discriminated against African Americans. But in many cases, identifying racism, racist behavior, and race-based discrimination is not a simple matter. Whereas discrimination and segregation were practiced openly during the Jim Crow era, implicit racism is hidden and thus much more difficult to detect.[5] In 2015, few Mr. Bessingers remain. Nevertheless, although people of color experience it daily, most white people do not realize that discriminatory behavior is common in the marketplace.[6]

## Implicit Racism and Unconscious Discrimination

Upon the election of Barack Obama, the first black president, many people believed that the United States had reached a postracial era. That is, because it was possible for a black person to be elected in this country, perhaps racial prejudice had significantly subsided or was eradicated altogether. However, during the years of his administration, the perception is that there have been heightened acts of violence against people of color. Among these was the killing of nine black people as they were worshiping in a church in Charleston, South Carolina, in 2015.[7] The suspect, Dylann Roof, had entered the church for Bible study an hour before murdering those nine people. Like Maurice Bessinger who raised the Confederate flag over his restaurants saying: "I surrounded the city of Columbia with Confederate flags,"[8] Roof had come to embrace the Confederate flag as a symbol for his feelings against an entire race of people.[9] The reaction to Dylann Roof's act was swift and broad with companies like Walmart and amazon.com vowing to stop selling Confederate flags in their stores.[10]

Fortunately, in 2016, acts as heinous as this are few and far between. Today, most Americans consider themselves to be tolerant of others regardless of race or ethnicity. While socially enforced taboos against explicit racism have reduced the obvious expression of prejudice against people of color, forms of implicit racism have replaced it. In other words, modern racism manifests itself in subtle ways. Because of the negative portrayals of blacks and Latinos in culture and mass media, even individuals who espouse egalitarian beliefs may have strong negative associations with black people and implicit preferences for white people. The reason for the inconsistency between explicit and implicit beliefs stems from the mixed messages we receive about race. While we are taught that people of all races are equal, we also learn about the racial traditions in U.S. history. According to Bernard Whitley and Mary Kite (2010), these "two sets of incompatible values conflict with one another, resulting in inconsistent behavior towards members of out-groups."[11]

Psychologists now understand that negative beliefs toward people of color are self-monitored or repressed because they are not generally socially acceptable.[12] Whites who generally avoid interacting with members of other racial and ethnic groups are less likely to discriminate against people of color when they find themselves in interracial situations than when they are interacting solely with other whites. This behavior modification occurs because the appropriate responses are clear and unambiguous if they wish to protect their nonprejudiced self-image. Researchers have found that even the most egalitarian white people may carry internalized racist beliefs that are often based on stereotypes and that express themselves without their awareness.[13] The hostile and negative feelings toward blacks are eventually expressed, but usually in subtle, indirect, and rationalizable ways.[14]

Hodson, Dovidio, and Gaertner conducted a study with white college students as participants to explore the ways in which modern discrimination is expressed. First, they asked the students to respond to survey questions that allowed them to classify them as being high or low on a racial prejudice scale. Next, the participants were tasked with making college admissions decisions about black and white applicants. They were provided with information about the college applicants' college board scores (SATs) and their scholastic achievement through high school. There were no differences between higher-prejudice scoring and lower-prejudice scoring participants when they evaluated the highly qualified applicants, but differences arose for applicants with mixed qualifications. Higher prejudice-scoring participants tended to weigh college board scores unusually low in importance when the black applicant had high college board scores but weak scholastic achievement. They also tended to rank high school achievement lower in importance when black applicants had strong scholastic achievement but weak college board scores. The authors concluded that the higher prejudice-scoring participants weighed application criteria in ways that systematically justified or rationalized discriminating against blacks.[15]

The study's results suggest that subtle discrimination occurs in ways that can be justified on the basis of factors other than race, a process that researchers have referred to as aversive racism which is a form of implicit racism. It tends to manifest itself in "ambiguous" situations when the basis for decision-making is vague. For example, in the context of the marketplace, store employees may not be aware that they are treating customers of color differently than white customers due to unconscious attributions they are making about blacks and Latinos. In other words, the unconscious thoughts and feelings of store employees may contribute to discriminatory behavior against people of color. This is the way in which discrimination manifests itself today.

Another aspect of discrimination that is better understood today is that it can involve seemingly "minor" incidents that occur on a daily basis in addition to major life events like having access to housing or securing employment. These everyday occurrences are known as microaggressions: subtle snubs or dismissive looks, gestures, and tones. Because they often occur outside the conscious awareness of the actor, microaggressions are a manifestation of aversive racism.

## Racial Microaggressions

Racial microaggressions are defined as "brief everyday exchanges that send denigrating messages to people of color because they belong to a racial minority group." They are commonplace verbal or behavioral indignities; they can be intentional or unintentional, and they communicate hostile, derogatory, or negative racial slights and insults. In their book entitled *Microaggressions and Marginality: Manifestation, Dynamics, and Impact,* Derald Wing Sue and his colleagues present a myriad of occasions and contexts in which microaggressions occur.[16] They explain that there are three primary types of microaggressions: microassaults, microinsults, and microinvalidations (see Figure 2.1).

Microassaults are "conscious biased beliefs or attitudes that are held by individuals and intentionally expressed or acted out overtly or covertly toward a marginalized person or socially devalued group."[17] In marketplace settings, microassaults might occur when a sales clerk uses a racial epithet as in the Conoco case that is discussed in Chapter 3. Another example stems from a case that arose in 2012 when Ms. Hammond, an African-American

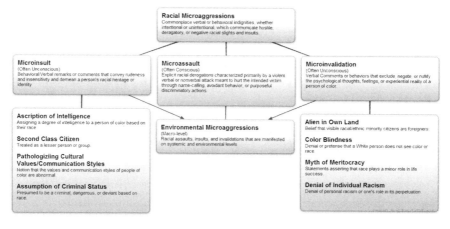

**FIGURE 2.1    Racial Microaggressions**

(*Source:* Sue, Derald Wing, Christina M. Capodilupo, Gina C. Torino, Jennifer M. Bucceri, A.M.B. Holder, Kevin L. Nadal, and Marta Esquilin. 2007. "Racial Micro-Aggressions in Everyday Life: Implications for Clinical Practice." *American Psychologist* 62: 271–286.)

woman in her thirties, and her two young children were Christmas shopping at the Kmart store in Braintree, Massachusetts, a predominantly white suburb of Boston. The white female sales clerk referred to African Americans as "porch monkeys" and commented that African Americans in general are criminals suggesting that Ms. Hammond must be a thief.[18] Yet another example would be a waiter who provided degraded service to black restaurant patrons assuming that all blacks are poor tippers.[19]

Microinsults are often unconscious so the person is not fully aware of the hostility. Assuming that people of color are criminals and therefore placing them under surveillance while they are shopping is an example of a microinsult in the context of a retail setting. Another example is mistaking a customer for a criminal as was the case with Wells Fargo and the rapper Sammie Benson who is also known as Blac Youngsta. Mr. Benson was detained by Atlanta, Georgia, police after Wells Fargo reported a forgery attempt.[20] He was released after he was found to have no part in the criminal activity. Mr. Benson claimed to have been at the bank that day making a withdrawal of $200,000. No one from Wells Fargo apologized to Mr. Benson and a representative for the bank even claimed that he was not an account holder and that he did not enter their bank to make any withdrawals. Mr. Benson later responded via social media. He posted on his Instagram account what appeared to be a letter from Wells Fargo indicating that the bank was closing his account(s) due to a business decision.[21] He also posted a picture of himself at Bank of America with the caption: "Taking My Talents to @BankofAmerica."[22] The topic of suspecting that customers of color are criminals is examined in greater detail in Chapters 3 and 6.

Microinvalidations also occur outside the individual's consciousness. These subconscious or unconscious microaggressions directly attack or deny the experiential realities of socially undervalued groups. Donald Trump's suggestion that Mexico sends only criminals and deviants to the United States is an example of a microinvalidation.[23] In the marketplace, microinvalidations occur every time a person of color's complaint about unfair treatment is ignored. For instance, Manige Osowski staged a protest against Wendy's on October 13, 2015, after finding a racist note inside her daughter's "kids' meal" purchased on October 8, 2015. The note was found on a playing card which was part of a deck that placed inside what should have been a toy packaged with her meal. As soon as Ms. Osowski saw the card with the word "nigga" on it, she immediately returned to the store and confronted the manager. Although the manager did apologize, he offered no explanation for what happened, took the card from Ms. Osowski, ripped it up, and proceeded to provide her with a number for the company's district manager. However, when Ms. Osowski refused to leave until he returned the ripped up card to her, he called the police. Although Wendy's eventually fired the two employees who allegedly placed the note in the meal, the fate of the manager is unknown. Ms. Osowski protested that following week because she did not believe that Wendy's took the incident seriously enough. She wanted Wendy's to send "a formal written apology to [her] family, [institute] comprehensive anti-racism training for employees, and [make] an effort . . . to make amends to [her] daughter."[24]

The difficulty with unconscious behaviors that arise in the marketplace is that service providers are usually surprised that the customer of color has interpreted their behavior as discriminatory because they were not aware of treating the customer differently than white customers. This means that it is challenging to prevent employee behavior that could be perceived as discriminatory by customers of color. Nevertheless, there are ways to raise employees' awareness of the possibility that they have implicit biases that can decrease the likelihood that they will act without first reflecting upon the potential for miscommunication with customers of color. In particular, the Implicit Association Test (IAT) is a tool that can be used for this purpose. It is discussed in Chapter 10.

Another challenge of dealing with racial microaggressions involves identifying and measuring their impacts on people of color. Until recently, this task could be analogized to the near impossibility of diagnosing back pain.[25] Although the physical and mental effects are visible, the underlying causes that lead to them are not. For example, the judge in the case of *Ross v. Schade* that is described below was unwilling to award damages for the plaintiff's humiliation because there was no way of measuring the effect of the racial epithet on him.

The case arose in 1939 when John Ross and his cousin entered the defendant's tavern in New Haven, Connecticut, and ordered sandwiches and beer. The two African Americans were told there were no sandwiches and the beer would be thirty cents a glass. After they drank the beer and paid sixty cents, the waiter took the glasses to the foot rail of the adjacent bar and broke one after the other on the rail in sight of the two men. Mr. Ross and his cousin left the tavern. Five days later, Mr. Ross filed suit claiming an overcharge for the beer and discrimination in treatment. The New Haven Superior Court found that there was sufficient circumstantial evidence upon which to found a reasonable inference that the plaintiff was overcharged by reason of his color. The court held, however, that Mr. Ross's damages must be limited to the overcharge for the beer.

In fact, many people of color are not aware of the psychological and physiological impact that discrimination is causing them. To the extent that people are aware, they may be better able to take charge of the situation. For instance, nationally syndicated talk show news anchor Gwen Ifill gave an interview to *Good Housekeeping* magazine in 2001 in which she described an incident when she was a victim of consumer discrimination in a retail setting. Ms. Ifill had merchandise in her hand and was waiting for assistance from a sales clerk. Both clerks ignored her. After waiting for a long period of time, Ms. Ifill realized that the clerks were not going to wait on her. She put the merchandise down and started to leave but then decided against it.

> I was the only one who was going to be upset. So I turned around and went back and told [the clerks] what they had done. They just stared at me with their jaws open. It wasn't that they had purposely decided not to wait on me—to them I was invisible. I had fit into their profile of someone who was not going to buy their merchandise, so they didn't even see me standing there. It's those kinds of insults that make you crazy.[26]

With that realization, Ms. Ifill was able to take the anger that she was harboring within and release it with a formal complaint to the store manager, so that it did not continue to build up in her and cause long-term psychological and physical damage.

## Psychological Effects of Discrimination on Consumers

Although it has been difficult to quantify the effect of discrimination on an individual in the past, today there is a great deal of research showing that people who are discriminated against experience both psychological and physiological effects.[27] We know that an individual's self-esteem may decrease due to the stress that occurs from internalizing incidents of social devaluation, discrimination, and racism. Robert T. Carter, a nationally known psychologist at Columbia University, specializes in researching the psychological and emotional effects of race discrimination on people of color. Although his focus is not solely on people's experiences with discrimination in retail environments, he includes differential treatment and harassment in those settings among others that he examines.

In one study, Carter and his colleagues found that being followed and observed while shopping caused stress reactions.[28] They determined that a person may respond to the chronic and persistent exposure to racism in many areas of their lives with various forms of emotional, psychological, and physical pains.[29] The detrimental effects of constant vulnerability to racial microaggressions include experiencing emotions ranging from anger, anxiety, confusion, to shame and fear.[30] Due to the collective memory of several generations of people having been exposed to life-threatening violence, having a hypervigilant demeanor has become the norm today. Those findings are consistent with other research, including the U.S. Surgeon General's Report of 2001 and the work of Huynh, Devos, and Dunbar.[31]

According to the Surgeon General, "racism is stressful and compromises the mental health of persons of color."[32] In fact, a study conducted by Huynh and her colleagues found that participants who experienced a higher frequency of perceived discrimination reported higher levels of anxiety and depression. Participants who experienced extreme discrimination, although infrequently, were equally adversely affected.[33] The research team was able to determine that, overall, the frequency of less stressful discrimination was more detrimental to the participants' psychological well-being than fewer high-stress discrimination experiences. Therefore, it is important to examine both the frequency and the stressfulness of each incident of discrimination. Huynh believes these findings will help clinicians treating cultural

minorities who struggle with mental health problems resulting from perceived discrimination.

The most critical factors Carter has identified in maintaining one's
self-esteem and psychological balance are dignity, self-assurance, and
confidence.[34] In his research, Carter uses the Race-Based Traumatic Stress
(RBTS) scale, which has been tested for its psychometric validity to determine whether an individual experiences the symptoms of RBTS injury.[35]
This diagnosis includes humiliation, low self-esteem, generalized anxiety,
and depression, among other conditions and makes it possible for people to seek redress when their symptoms have disabled them to such an
extent that they can no longer fully function on their jobs, for example.
Carter indicates that people deal with racism based on a myriad of factors
including their own individual background and how people in their social
network have influenced how quickly they are able to understand their
experience.

Dr. Carter is often called to testify in cases in which marketplace discrimination has been alleged. His expert opinion includes a description of the
signs and symptoms of the stress that people experience as a direct result
of discriminatory treatment: intrusive thoughts, avoidance behavior, general anxiety, rage, compromised self-worth, feelings of humiliation, hyper-
vigilance, and physiological reactions that indicate they were traumatized
by the experiences. He has concluded that the experiences of consumer
racial profiling and racial harassment are a proximate cause of psychological and emotional harm. Other scholars such as William Goldsby study
what is called the post-traumatic slave syndrome (PTSS).[36] Their research
shows that some people have a better mental and physical capacity to identify, cope with, and move on from the stress of discrimination and racism.
Others, based on the factors previously discussed, may not be able to handle it as well. That results in either physical or mental damage to themselves
and possibly to others.

It is difficult for some people to understand the rioting, the vandalizing
of property, and the looting of stores, which has occurred in reaction to
the killing of young black men—and a child—in 2014 and 2015: Michael
Brown in Ferguson, Missouri; Tamir Rice in Cleveland, Ohio; Eric Garner
in Staten Island, New York; John Crawford who was shot while shopping in
a Walmart Store in Beavercreek, Ohio; and Freddy Gray, who was killed in
the back of a police van in Baltimore, Maryland.[37] Goldsby and others suggest that this behavior is a way for people to process and deal with the legacy of slavery and its manifestations that have been passed down through

generations of their families.[38] Similarly, Cornel West explains that people become nihilistic, thinking that nothing matters and expressing their frustration and despair by destroying whatever is nearest to them.[39] In her book entitled, *The New Jim Crow*, Michelle Alexander also writes about this type of response to marginalization:

> For those Black youth who are constantly followed by the police and shamed by teachers, relatives, and strangers, embracing the stigma of criminality is an act of rebellion—an attempt to carve out a positive identity in a society that offers them little more than scorn, contempt, and constant surveillance.[40]

The notions of RBTS and PTSS are comparable to Post-Traumatic Stress Disorder (PTSD). While people who are diagnosed with PTSD are eligible for treatment through their insurance companies and can qualify for partial disability, RBTS and PTSS have not been recognized in the same way in terms of their diagnostic ability or their treatment. As is the case with PTSD, there are both psychological and physiological effects associated with these syndromes. In the section that follows, the physical effects are discussed.

## Physical Effects of Discrimination on Consumers

The work of Carter and his colleagues is also helpful to doctors in terms of understanding the impact of race-based stress to the physical condition of the body.[41] Many other studies have been conducted that also reveal the nefarious effects of race discrimination on a person's health.[42] For instance, studies published in the *American Journal of Public Health* support the explanation that the psychological stress of experiencing racial discrimination is at least partly responsible for premature and low birthweight babies.[43] Researchers have found that differences in genetics, prenatal care, education, and poverty only partly explain why blacks are three times more likely to deliver very low-birthweight babies (less than 3.3 pounds). For example, a substantial black-white gap persists even among mothers who have college degrees.

Several studies have linked high blood pressure to real-time experiences of stress and discrimination through the use of electronic diaries. The work of psychologist Elizabeth Brondolo, at St. John's University showed that daytime experiences of racism led to elevated nighttime blood pressure, suggesting that the body cannot turn off its stress response.[44] With her colleagues, Vickie Mays, a psychologist and director of the University of California, Los Angeles (UCLA) Center on Research, Education, Training, and Strategic Communication on Minority Health Disparities, is demonstrating that experiences of racial discrimination can trigger the brain for what is known as the fight-or-flight response. This response is regulated by the part of the brain called the amygdala that responds quickly without consulting the cortex, the logical part of the brain. If the fight-or-flight response is triggered over and over again, two things can happen to the brain. First, it can shut down the release of chemicals such as cortisol so that people respond with a kind of numbness. Underproduction of cortisol can result in depression and is linked to asthma, allergies, and rheumatoid arthritis. The fight-or-flight trigger can also fail to shut down, leaving the body in a continuous state of heightened alert. Cortisol readies the body for immediate danger and it takes resources away from some of the body's longer-term resources, such as control of the immune system, while increasing blood pressure and blood sugar levels. If that happens repeatedly over the course of a lifetime, the continual assaults of discrimination can result in a greater vulnerability to infection from a weakened immune system and places the body at greater risk for cardiovascular disease.[45]

Psychologists Matthews, Salomon, Kenyon, and Zhou found in their 2005 study that "unfair treatment and its attribution to race, physical appearance, and peer group were related to elevated ambulatory blood pressure."[46] The study of 334 midlife women published in *Health Psychology* examined links between different kinds of stress and risk factors for heart disease and stroke. Black women who pointed to racism as a source of stress in their lives, the researchers found, developed more plaque in their carotid arteries—an early sign of heart disease—than black women who did not. This was the first report to link hardening of the arteries to racial discrimination. Madeline Drexler, editor of *Harvard Public Health*, writes:

> Collectively, these studies of the racism-health link have tied experiences of discrimination to poorer self-reported health, smoking, low-birth-weight deliveries, depressive symptoms, and especially to cardiovascular effects. In the mid-1980s, scientists began to take advantage of the controlled conditions of the laboratory. When African American volunteers are hooked up to blood-pressure monitors, for example, and then exposed to a racially provocative vignette on tape or TV—such as a White store clerk calling a Black customer a racist epithet—the volunteers' blood pressures rise, their heart rates jump, and they take longer than normal to recover from both reactions.[47]

Although each incident may appear to be relatively minor, because consumer discrimination is repetitive and can be a daily occurrence, it has a cumulative debilitating effect over the course of a person's lifetime. Thus, it is no surprise that victims of marketplace discrimination experience both psychological and/or physical consequences. As mentioned with Gwen Ifill's story above, some people of color develop coping mechanisms to deal with it. In the section below, we discuss coping with race-based discrimination.

## Consumers' Coping Mechanisms

Studies have shown that people of color may attribute a discriminatory act to something they can control—something other than race—as a way of protecting themselves. Victims of marketplace mistreatment may attribute the poor treatment to discrimination only when they are virtually certain that they have been discriminated against.[48] This response is due to the costs associated with such attributions. These financial, psychic, and social costs may prevent stigmatized people from confronting the discrimination they face in their daily lives.[49]

Research conducted by Major, Quinton, and McCoy suggests that minority customers may exhibit more attributional ambiguity than white customers when they experience poor treatment in the marketplace. This means that they are uncertain about whether the treatment they received relates to their own personal merit or whether it reflects social prejudice against their racial or ethnic group as a whole. The researchers identified two opposite perspectives that minority members take: a vigilance perspective means they are highly sensitive to cues of discrimination and over-attribute poor treatment to racism versus a minimization/discounting perspective where minorities are more likely to miss cues of discrimination and under-attribute.[50] One more factor to consider is how strongly the minority customer identifies with his or her racial or ethnic group. For example, individuals who strongly identify with their minority group may be more likely to perceive themselves as victims of discrimination compared with those who have lower group identification and group consciousness.

In the face of discriminatory treatment, typical responses include withdrawal, verbal or physical confrontation, and resigned acceptance. Hirschman, the noted economist, described a similar set of strategies: (a) exit; (b) voice; and (c) loyalty.[51] In the retail context, some individuals stop patronizing the store where they were mistreated and spend their money elsewhere instead. Others shop online to avoid stressful interactions, as demonstrated by Ekpo and her colleagues.[52] Still others try to avoid unfair treatment by showing that they are worthy shoppers.[53] This strategy includes dressing up in the hopes that their appearance will convey the fact that they are both entitled to browse and capable of paying for the items they want.[54] They might buy items they do not want or need just to demonstrate that they are good consumers. Gwen Ifill explained that was her experience as a younger woman until she realized that "it's more powerful to keep the money in my pocket and go shop someplace else."[55]

Reporter Peter Murray recently revealed that a messaging "app" is being used by shop owners in the wealthy neighborhood of Georgetown, to profile customers of color.[56] GroupMe is a messaging app that allows businesses, residents, and police to communicate directly and share photos. The app's intended use is to report suspicious activity in order to protect businesses from shoplifting. However, store employees are reportedly alerting GroupMe users about African-American shoppers who are not engaging in any criminal activity. Unsuspecting black shoppers are being labeled as suspicious with their descriptions and images posted on the app. In response to a story posted on *Gawker* about the use of this technology for profiling, someone commented:

> This is exactly why I refuse to bemoan the demise of brick and mortar establishments. Online shopping is not dehumanizing. Why on earth would anyone pay the commission of someone who thinks you're a criminal because of your skin color? You're either ignored, followed or surreptitiously followed by a phony vendor with a brittle, trying-too-hard to not look uncomfortable smile.[57]

Some research suggests that fear of the consequences of confronting discriminators may keep people of color from taking action when they are dissatisfied with the treatment they receive.[58] Others prefer to address the problem directly with the store manager, and perhaps pursue an informal complaint by writing a letter to the company's corporate office. Some aggrieved individuals bring their complaints to the attention of the Better Business Bureau, their state or local civil rights agency, or even file lawsuits to vindicate their rights. But it can take time for a person to acknowledge, confront, and take steps to seek compensation for unfair treatment.

For businesses seeking to attract and preserve customers of all races, an important question is whether certain types of marketplace interactions lead customers of color to voice their dissatisfaction rather than avoid or ignore them? A review of lawsuits filed against companies accused of discriminating against customers on the basis of race offers a window into the variety of incidents that arise in all sorts of marketplace venues. A classification framework was needed to explore those cases and take into consideration the challenges discussed in this section. That framework is presented in the next chapter.

## Notes

1. Becker, 1993.
2. Monk, 2014; Haire, 2014.
3. *Newman v. Piggie Park Enterprises, Inc.*, 1968.
4. Firestone, 2000.
5. Gaertner and Dovidio, 1986; Dovidio and Gaertner, 2004; Gaertner and Dovidio, 2005. Other researchers such as John B. McConahay and Philomena Essed use terms such as Modern Racism and Everyday Racism, respectively, to account for similar phenomena; McConahay, 1986; Essed, 1991.
6. Ludwig, 2001; Ludwig, 2003.
7. Lamb, 2014; Page, 2014; Stanage, 2013; Brown and Jaffe, 2015.
8. Hitt, 2001.
9. Piston and Strother, 2015.
10. Wang, 2015; Mitchell, 2015.
11. Whitley and Kite, 2010.
12. Richeson and Trawalter, 2005.
13. Gaertner and Dovidio, 1986; Sommers and Ellsworth, 2001, p. 201.
14. Dovidio, Kawakami, and Gaertner, 2002, p. 62; Hodson, Dovidio, and Gaertner, 2002; Eberhardt et al., 2006.
15. Hodson, Dovidio, and Gaertner, 2002.
16. Sue et al., 2007; Ekpo, 2012; Ekpo, Henderson, and Spence, 2013; Sue, 2010.
17. Ibid., p. 7.
18. *Hammond v. Kmart Corp. and Sears Holding Corp.*, 2013.
19. Brewster, Lynn, and Cocroft, 2014.
20. Robertson, 2016.
21. Thompson, 2016.
22. Simmons, 2016.
23. Univision and NBC Universal severed ties to Donald Trump and his Miss Universe/Miss USA pageants. In addition, he has also lost partnerships with Macy's at an estimated loss to him of $50 million; Maglio and Kenneally, 2015; Castillo, 2015.
24. Bertsche, 2015.
25. Contrada et al., 2001.
26. Fifield and O'Shaughnessy, 2001, p. 134.
27. Brown et al., 2000; Clark et al., 1999, p. 805.
28. Carter et al., 2005.

29. Carter, 2006; Carter et al., 2005.
30. Sue et al., 2007, p. 273; Crocker, Cornwell, and Major, 1993; Major et al., 2007.
31. Huynh, Devos, and Dunbar, 2012, p. 26.
32. Mental Health: Culture, Race, and Ethnicity: A Supplement to Mental Health: A Report of the Surgeon General Office of the Surgeon General (U.S.), 2001.
33. Huynh, Devos, and Dunbar, 2012, p. 26.
34. Brown and Mankowski, 199; Gergen, 1971.
35. Carter, 2007, pp. 37–38; Carter et al., 2005.
36. Leary, 2005; Goldsby, 2015.
37. Sanchez and Lawler, 2015; Laughland, Epstein, and Glenza, 2014; Kelly, 2014; Marquez and Almasy, 2015.
38. Goldsby, 2015.
39. West, 1993.
40. Alexander, 2012, p. 171.
41. Barksdale, Farrug, and Harkness, 2009.
42. Lewis et al., 2010.
43. Harrell, Hall, and Taliaferro, 2003; Williams, Neighbors, and Jackson, 2003.
44. Brondolo et al., 2008.
45. Mays, Cochran, and Barnes, 2007, p. 201.
46. Matthews et al., 2005, p. 258.
47. Drexler, 2007.
48. Crockett, Grier, and Williams, 2003.
49. Kaiser and Miller, 2001.
50. Major, Quinton, and McCoy, 2002.
51. Hirschman, 1970.
52. Ekpo, 2012; Ekpo, Henderson, and Spence, 2013; Henderson, Ekpo, and Chenevert, 2012.
53. Folkman, 1984.
54. Lee, 2000.
55. Fifield and O'Shaughnessy, 2001.
56. Murray, 2015.
57. Thompson, 2015.
58. Stangor et al., 2002, p. 69.

# References

Alexander, Michelle. 2012. "The New Jim Crow: Mass Incarceration in the Age of Colorblindness." New York: The New Press, 171.
Barksdale, Debra J., Eugene R. Farrug, and Kimberly Harkness. 2009. "Racial Discrimination and Blood Pressure: Perceptions, Emotions, and Behaviors of Black American Adults." *Issues in Mental Health Nursing* 30: 104–111.

Becker, Gary S. 1993, "Nobel Lecture: The Economic Way of Looking at Behavior." *Journal of Political Economy*: 385–409.

Bertsche, Rachel. 2015. "Racist Note Found in Wendy's Kids Meal." *Yahoo! Parenting*.

Brewster, Zachary W., Michael Lynn, and Shelytia Cocroft. 2014. "Consumer Racial Profiling in US Restaurants: Exploring Subtle Forms of Service Discrimination against Black Diners." *Sociological Forum* 29. Wiley Online Library.

Brondolo, Elizabeth, Daniel J. Libby, and Ellen-Ge Denton. 2008. "Racism and Ambulatory Blood Pressure in a Community Sample." *Psychosomatic Medicine* 70, no. 1: 49–56.

Brown, DeNeen L. and Greg Jaffe. 2015. "Obama Calls for Racial Understanding, Unity as Thousands Mourn S.C. Pastor." *The Washington Post*, June 26.

Brown, Jonathon D. and Tracie A. Mankowski. 1993. "Self-Esteem, Mood, and Self-Evaluation: Changes in Mood and the Way You See You." *Journal of Personality and Social Psychology* 64, no. 3: 421–430.

Carter, Robert T. 2007. "Racism and Psychological and Emotional Injury Recognizing and Assessing Race-Based Traumatic Stress." *The Counseling Psychologist* 35: 13–105.

Carter, Robert T., Forsyth, J. M., Mazzula, S. L., & Williams, B. 2005. "Racial discrimination and race-based traumatic stress: An exploratory investigation." In *Handbook of racial-cultural psychology and counseling: Training and practice,* ed. R. T. Carter, Vol. 2, pp. 447–476. Hoboken, NJ: Wiley.

Castillo, Michelle. 2015. "'Professional Suicide': Donald Trump's Big Mouth Chews Hole in His Wallet." *NBC News*.

Clark, Rodney, Norman B. Anderson, Vernessa R. Clark, and David R. Williams. 1999. "Racism as a Stressor for African Americans: A Biopsychosocial Model." *American Psychologist* 54: 805.

Contrada, Richard J., Richard D. Ashmore, Melvin L. Gary, Elliot Coups, Jill D. Egeth, Andrea Sewell, Kevin Ewell, Tanya M. Goyal, and Valerie Chasse. 2001. "Measures of Ethnicity-Related Stress: Psychometric Properties, Ethnic Group Differences, and Associations with Well-Being." *Journal of Applied Social Psychology* 31, no. 9: 1775–1820.

Crocker, Jennifer, Beth Cornwell, and Brenda Major. 1993. "The Stigma of Overweight: Affective Consequences of Attributional Ambiguity." *Journal of Personality and Social Psychology* 64: 60–70.

Crockett, David, Sonya A. Grier, and Jacqueline A. Williams. 2003. "Coping with Marketplace Discrimination: An Exploration of the Experiences of Black Men." *American Marketing Science Review* 2003, no. 4: 1–21.

Dovidio, John F. and Samuel L. Gaertner. 2004. "Aversive Racism." *Advances in Experimental Social Psychology* 36: 1–52.

Dovidio, John F., Kerry Kawakami, and Samuel L. Gaertner. 2002. "Implicit and Explicit Prejudice and Interracial Interaction." *Journal of Personality and Social Psychology* 82, no. 1: 62.

Drexler, Madeline. 2007. "How Racism Hurts—Literally." *The Boston Globe*, July 15.

Eberhardt, Jennifer L., Paul G. Davies, Valerie J. Purdie-Vaughns, and Sheri Lynn Johnson. 2006. "Looking Deathworthy Perceived Stereotypicality of Black Defendants Predicts Capital-Sentencing Outcomes." *Psychological Science* 17, no. 5: 383–386.

Ekpo, Akon E. 2012. "Transcending Habitus with It: Understanding How Marginalized Consumers Use Information Technology." Dissertation, University of Illinois at Chicago.

Ekpo, Akon E., Geraldine R. Henderson, and Benet DeBerry Spence. 2013. "Subtle Faces of Discrimination: An Exploratory Study of Microaggressions in the Marketplace." In *Chicago Consumer Culture Community*, ed. Kent Grayson and Albert M. Muniz Jr. Chicago, IL: University of Chicago Press.

Essed, Philomena. 1991. *Understanding Everyday Racism: An Interdisciplinary Theory*. Vol. 2. Thousand Oaks, CA: SAGE Series on Race and Ethnic Relations.

Fifield, Adam and Elise O'Shaughnessy. 2001. "Shopping While Black." *Good Housekeeping* November: 129–136.

Firestone, David. 2000. "Sauce Is Boycotted, and Slavery Is the Issue." *The New York Times*, September 29.

Folkman, Susan. 1984. "Personal Control and Stress and Coping Processes: A Theoretical Analysis." *Journal of Personality and Social Psychology* 46, no. 4: 839–852.

Gaertner, Samuel L. and John F. Dovidio. 1986. *The Aversive Form of Racism*. New York: Academic Press.

Gaertner, Samuel L. and John F. Dovidio. 2004. "Aversive Racism." *Advances in Experimental Social Psychology* 36: 1–52.

Gaertner, Samuel L. and John F. Dovidio. 2005. "Understanding and Addressing Contemporary Racism: From Aversive Racism to the Common Ingroup Identity Model." *Journal of Social Issues* 61, no. 3: 615–639.

Gergen, Kenneth J. 1971. *The Concept of Self*. New York: Holt, Rinehart and Winston.

Goldsby, William. 2015. "A Frank Conversation about Race." In *Transformative Consumer Research Conference*, ed. Ronald Paul Hill, Julie L. Ozanne, and Brennan Davis. Villanova, PA: Villanova.

Haire, Chris. 2014. "Maurice Bessinger, BBQ Baron and Unrepentant Racist, Dies." *Charleston City Paper*, Monday, February 24.

*Hammond v. Kmart Corp. and Sears Holding Corp.*, 2013. U.S. Briefs 998, On petition for Writ of Certiorari to the U.S. Court of Appeals for the First Circuit (February 18, 2014).

Harrell, Jules P., Sadiki Hall, and James Taliaferro. 2003. "Physiological Responses to Racism and Discrimination: An Assessment of the Evidence." *American Journal of Public Health* 93, no. 2: 243–248.

Henderson, Geraldine R., Akon E. Ekpo, and Amber Chenevert. 2012. "Shopseeking: Coping with Offline Discrimination Online." In *Chicago Consumer*

*Culture Community*, ed. Kent Grayson and Albert M. Muniz, Jr. Chicago, IL: University of Chicago Press.

Hirschman, Albert O. 1970. *Exit, Voice, and Loyalty.* Cambridge, MA: Harvard University Press.

Hitt, Jack. 2001. "A Confederacy of Sauces." *The New York Times*, August 26.

Hodson, Gordon, John F. Dovidio, and Samuel L. Gaertner. 2002. "Processes in Racial Discrimination: Differential Weighting of Conflicting Information." *Personality and Social Psychology Bulletin* 28, no. 4: 460–471.

Huynh, Que-Lam, Thierry Devos, and Cheyenne M. Dunbar. 2012. "The Psychological Costs of Painless but Recurring Experiences of Racial Discrimination." *Cultural Diversity and Ethnic Minority Psychology* 18: 26.

Kaiser, Cheryl R. and Carol T. Miller. 2001. "Stop Complaining! The Social Costs of Making Attributions to Discrimination." *Personality and Social Psychology Bulletin* 27, no. 2: 254–263.

Kelly, Adrianne. 2014. "Protests Continues in Front of Beavercreek PD over John Crawford Shooting." In WLWT. October 8. Available at: http://www.wlwt.com/news/protests-continues-in-front-of-beavercreek-pd-over-john-crawford-shooting/29022940.

Lamb, Christopher. 2014. "Don't Blame Obama If Race Relations Are Worse During His Presidency." *Huffington Post.* December 23. Available at: http://www.huffingtonpost.com/christopher-lamb/dont-blame-obama-if-race-relations-are-worse-during-his-presidency_b_6356746.html.

Laughland, Oliver, Kayla Epstein, and Jessica Glenza. 2014. "Eric Garner Protests Continue in Cities across America through Second Night." *The Guardian*, December 5.

Leary, Joy DeGruy. 2005. *Post Traumatic Slave Syndrome: America's Legacy of Enduring Injury and Healing.* Portland, OR: Joy DeGruy Publications.

Lee, Jennifer. 2000. "The Salience of Race in Everyday Life Black Customers' Shopping Experiences in Black and White Neighborhoods." *Work and Occupations* 27, no. 3: 353–376.

Lewis, Tené T., Allison E. Aiello, Sue E. Leurgans, and Jeremiah F. Kelly. 2010. "Self-Reported Experiences of Everyday Discrimination Are Associated with Elevated C-Reactive Protein Levels in Older African-American Adults." *Brain, Behavior, and Immunity* 24: 438–443.

Ludwig, Jack. 2001. "Gallup Social Audit on Black/White Relations in the U.S.: Broad Differences between the Views of White and Black Americans about the State of U.S. Race Relations." *Gallup Poll News Service.* Washington, DC. July 11.

Ludwig, Jack. 2003. Blacks and Whites Still Perceive Local Treatment of Blacks Differently. Gallup Poll News Service. Washington, DC. May 27.

Maglio, Tony and Tim Kenneally. 2015. "Donald Trump's $50 Million Mexican Mess: What's the Cost of Calling Immigrants 'Rapists'?" *The Wrap.* July 1. Available at: http://www.thewrap.com/donald-trumps-50-million-mexico-mess-whats-the-cost-of-calling-an-entire-country-rapists/.

Major, Brenda, Cheryl R. Kaiser, Laurie T. O'Brien, and Shannon K. McCoy. 2007. "Perceived Discrimination as Worldview Threat or Worldview Confirmation: Implications for Self-Esteem." *Journal of Personality and Social Psychology* 92: 1068–1086.

Major, Brenda, Wendy J. Quinton, and Shannon K. McCoy. 2002. "Antecedents and Consequences of Attributions to Discrimination: Theoretical and Empirical Advances." In *Advances in Experimental Social Psychology*, ed. P. Zanna Mark, pp. 251–330. New York: Academic Press.

Matthews, Karen A., Kristen Salomon, Karen L. Kenyon, and Fan Zhou. 2005. "Unfair Treatment, Discrimination, and Ambulatory Blood Pressure in Black and White Adolescents." *Health Psychology* 24, no. 3: 258.

Marquez, Miguel and Steve Almasy. 2015. "Freddie Gray Death: Protesters Damage Cars; 12 Arrested." cnn.com. April 25. Available at: http://www.cnn.com/2015/04/25/us/baltimore-freddie-gray-protest/.

Mays, Vicki M., Susan D. Cochran, and Namdi W. Barnes. 2007. "Race, Race-Based Discrimination, and Health Outcomes among African Americans." *Annual Review of Psychology* 58: 201.

McConahay, John B. 1986. "Modern Racism, Ambivalence, and the Modern Racism Scale." In *Prejudice, Discrimination, and Racism*, ed. John F. Dovidio and Samuel L. Gaertner, pp. 91–125. San Diego, CA: Academic Press.

"Mental Health: Culture, Race, and Ethnicity: A Supplement to Mental Health: A Report of the Surgeon General Office of the Surgeon General (U.S.)." 2001. Center for Mental Health Services (US); National Institute of Mental Health (US). Rockville (MD): Substance Abuse and Mental Health Services Administration (US), August.

Mitchell, Garrett. 2015. "Tense Confederate Flag Rally Outside Phoenix Walmart." *USA Today*, July 6.

Monk, John. 2014. "Barbecue Eatery Owner, Segregationist Maurice Bessinger Dies at 83." *The State*, February 24.

Murray, Peter 2015. "Critics Claim Racial Bias in Georgetown Digital Crime Prevention." *The Georgetowner*, August 10.

*Newman v. Piggie Park Enterprises, Inc.* 1968. In 377 F.2d 433 (4th Cir. 1967), 390 U.S. 400, United States Supreme Court.

New York Times/CBSNews. 2015. "Race Relations Poll." July 23.

Page, Clarence. 2014. "Obama's Election Did Not Improve Race Relations." *Chicago Tribune*, September 23.

Piston, Spencer and Logan Strother. 2015. "White Support for the Confederate Flag Really Is About Racism, Not Southern Heritage." *The Washington Post*, July 1.

Richeson, Jennifer A. and Sophie Trawalter. 2005. "Why Do Racial Interactions Impair Executive Function? A Resource Depletion Account." *Interpersonal Relations and Group Processes* 88, no. 6: 934–947.

Robertson, Iyana. 2016. "Wells Fargo Claims Blac Youngsta Does Not Have an Account with the Bank," in *Vibe*.

Sanchez, Raf and David Lawler. 2015. "Ferguson: Timeline of Events since Michael Brown's Death." *The Telegraph*.

Simmons, Ted. 2016. "Blac Youngsta Provides Proof After Wells Fargo Claims He Has No Bank Account." *XXL*.

Sommers, Samuel R. and Phoebe C. Ellsworth. 2001. "White Juror Bias: An Investigation of Prejudice against Black Defendants in the American Courtroom." *Psychology, Public Policy, and Law* 7, no. 1: 201.

Stanage, Niall. 2013. "Black Lawmakers Lament Flaring of Racial Tensions under Obama." *The Hill*. August 26. Available at: http://thehill.com/homenews/news/318601-black-lawmakers-lament-flaring-of-racial-tensions-under-obama.

Stangor, Charles, Janet Swim, and Katherine L. Van Allen. 2002. "Reporting Discrimination in Public and Private Contexts." *Journal of Personality and Social Psychology* 82, no. 1: 69.

Sue, Derald Wing. 2010. *Microaggressions and Marginality: Manifestation, Dynamics, and Impact*. Hoboken, NJ: John Wiley & Sons, 2010.

Sue, Derald Wing, Christina M. Capodilupo, Gina C. Torino, Jennifer M. Bucceri, A.M.B. Holder, Kevin L. Nadal, and Marta Esquilin. 2007. "Racial Micro-Aggressions in Everyday Life: Implications for Clinical Practice." *American Psychologist* 62: 273.

Thompson, Shawnte. 2016. "Update: Wells Fargo Closes Blac Youngsta's Account after Police Incident of Mistaken Identity." *The GED Section by D. L. Hughley*.

Wang, Joy Y. 2015. "Walmart, Sears, and Amazon to Stop Selling Confederate Flag Merchandise." msnbc.com. June 22. Available at: http://www.msnbc.com/msnbc/walmart-stop-selling-confederate-flag-merchandise.

West, Cornel. 1993. *Race Matters*. New York: Vintage Books.

Whitley, Bernard E. and Kite, Mary E. 2010. *The Psychology of Prejudice and Discrimination*. Belmont, CA. Wadsworth.

Williams, David R., Harold W. Neighbors, and James S. Jackson. 2003. "Racial/Ethnic Discrimination and Health: Findings from Community Studies." *American Journal of Public Health* 93, no. 2: 200–208.

# Chapter 3

# Annoyance vs. Avoidance

*As I often say, we have come a long way from the days of slavery, but in 2014, discrimination and inequality still saturate our society in modern ways. Though racism may be less blatant now in many cases, its existence is undeniable.*
—Al Sharpton, President, National Action Network[1]

Robert Johnson is an African-American lawyer, a writer, and a professor at the University of Massachusetts in Boston. When he answered a knock at his door one day in July 2015, he was face-to-face with two police officers who told him to accompany them to the police station regarding a larceny that occurred at Blanchard's Wine and Spirits. Since he had shopped there the previous day, he thought he should help the police in their investigation. At the station, Johnson learned that employees at Blanchard's had identified him as the individual who had stolen twenty bottles of cognac from the store several months earlier. The officers read him his rights and produced a surveillance photograph claiming it showed him stealing from Blanchard's. The photograph of the thief showed a 40-year-old man with no facial hair but Johnson is 66 years old and has a goatee. After the police learned of Johnson's professional standing, their aggressive tone changed and he was allowed to leave the station.

While Johnson believes the incident is a clear case of consumer racial profiling, Blanchard's management claims it was a simple mistake and that the misidentification had nothing to do with Johnson's race. In an interview following the incident, Johnson explained: "It could have been traumatic to someone who didn't know his rights," he said. "I knew if I cooperated with police I would be out of there. But they were on a track to make me one of those statistics—another black man arrested for stealing. It's just routine for them." Johnson described the affront of being suspected and questioned as a failure "to fully recognize the humanity of black people."[2]

Indeed, customers of color experience inequality in the marketplace when they receive either too much or too little attention from store employees. Annoyance discrimination occurs when customers receive too much attention from store personnel. They are repeatedly offered assistance by sales associates, watched closely, and followed around the store. These practices are similar to those of police officers who target blacks and Latinos for enhanced traffic enforcement. In the marketplace, "consumer racial profiling" (CRP) occurs when store security officers or other store personnel follow, stop, question, investigate, and/or arrest customers based on their race or ethnicity rather than their behavior. Like "driving while black," CRP involves being suspected as a criminal.

In contrast, avoidance discrimination takes place when customers are paid too little attention. For example, a sales associate may cause customers of color to wait an inordinately long time for service, treat them rudely, or wait on white customers first. In these situations, customers of color may get the impression that the sales associate and, by extension, the company wishes to avoid serving them and does not want their business.[3]

Compared with employment discrimination that can involve losing the ability to earn a living, for example, consumer discrimination incidents may appear to be relatively insignificant but it is the prevalence of this type of discrimination that can affect its victims, as explained in the previous chapter. Therefore, in studying this phenomenon, it is important to determine how often it occurs. Unfortunately, that is a difficult question to answer because very little research has examined the issue of marketplace discrimination.

A mail survey conducted by Jerome Williams and Thelma Snuggs in 1996 revealed that 86 percent of the households surveyed believed they had been the victims of racial profiling in a retail setting. It is interesting that only 37 percent of African Americans feel as if they have experienced "driving while black," according to one study while a Gallup poll conducted in 1999 reported that 75 percent of black men had experienced CRP of some form or another.[4] Shaun Gabbidon and his colleagues, who have studied the prevalence of consumer racial profiling, found that black respondents were much more likely than whites to report having experienced CRP, and that blacks were significantly more likely than whites to believe that the practice of profiling customers based on their race is widespread.[5] In addition, the news media have reported hundreds of stories in the last 25 years of discrimination and racial profiling against consumers of color.

Another study that attempted to understand the incidence of marketplace inequality relied on examining lawsuits filed by plaintiffs alleging that they were discriminated against based on their race or ethnicity. Harris,

Henderson, and Williams in 2005 analyzed 81 cases in which individuals sued major retailers and other companies in federal courts across the country between 1990 and 2002.[6] This research revealed three primary themes: customers of color experienced differences in the level of goods and services they received compared with white customers; they were subjected to both overt and subtle discrimination; and in many cases, they were treated as potential criminals. In this chapter, the framework developed to analyze these legal cases is described.

The first theme that emerged from the analysis relates to the outcome of the discriminatory behavior. In some cases, discrimination results in an outright denial of goods or services that a customer seeks to buy; in others, consumers suffer a degradation of goods or services. In a retail environment, denial occurs when a store clerk refuses to wait on a customer of color or a sales associate does not provide information about a service that other customers receive, for example. Of course, refusing a customer access to the establishment and removing a customer from the store amounts to an outright denial. In contrast, a degradation of goods or services occurs when customers of color are allowed the opportunity to transact but are provided something less than white customers receive. Examples of degradation include requiring customers of color to wait for extended periods of time, show additional forms of identification when paying for goods or services, pay higher prices or prepay for goods or services. In addition, being subjected to increased surveillance amounts to degradation because many customers experience this type of treatment as harassment. As explained in Chapter 5, the law guarantees a consumer both the right to buy a ticket to get on the bus as well as the right to sit in any seat one chooses.

The second dimension refers to the type of discrimination the customer experiences. In Chapter 2, we saw that "overt" discrimination is obvious and direct while "subtle" discrimination is more ambiguous and indirect. A landmark study by the National Research Council (2004) on measuring racial discrimination included these two components in its definition of discrimination.[7] When customers are faced with blatant and overt discrimination, they can properly attribute the negative treatment to prejudice and intentional discrimination. When there is more ambiguity in the seller's behavior, as in cases of subtle discrimination, social psychologists Brenda Major, Wendy Quinton, and Shannon McCoy found that the customer may not know whether discrimination is the cause of the poor treatment she is receiving.[8] In 2016, racism tends to manifest itself in ways that make it difficult to identify. Therefore, shoppers of color are faced with having to wonder whether their interactions with store personnel are equal to those of white shoppers. Their perceptions of discriminatory treatment can be invalidated as "over-sensitivity" when there is no evidence of overt racial animosity.

Four different categories of cases are created when the two dimensions described earlier are combined: subtle degradation, overt degradation, subtle denial, and overt denial (see Figure 3.1). Subtle degradation of goods or services involves cases where the customers of color did not receive what they expected in a business establishment, but they cannot prove that this treatment was based on their race or ethnicity. In contrast, overt degradation occurs when it is clear that it is because of their race or ethnicity that customers of color received less than white customers. Subtle denial refers to situations in which customers were denied access to goods or services, but they cannot establish with certainty that the reason for the denial is related to their race or ethnicity. Finally, overt denial happens when there is clear evidence that the denial was based the customer's race or ethnicity.

The third dimension that emerged from the analysis, criminal suspicion, alludes to the common misperception that minority consumers engage in more criminal activity than majority consumers. The stereotype of black and brown people as criminals leads people to assume that the majority of shoplifters are people of color although there are no data to support that assumption. Interestingly, in the retail sector, research shows that the majority of shoplifters are middle-aged white women.

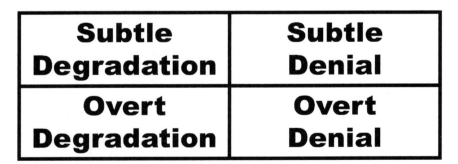

**FIGURE 3.1    Categorization of Discrimination Cases**

(*Source:* Compiled from Harris, Anne-Marie, Geraldine R. Henderson, and Jerome D. Williams. 2005. "Courting Customers: Assessing Consumer Racial Profiling and Other Marketplace Discrimination." *Journal of Public Policy and Marketing, Policy Watch: Commentaries and Viewpoints* 24, no. 1: 163–171.)

We know that law enforcement officers single out—or profile—people of color for increased scrutiny because of their race or ethnicity. The practice of racial profiling was defined by Deborah Ramirez, Jack McDevitt, and Amy Farrell as "any police-initiated practice that relies on race, ethnicity, or national origin rather than the behavior of an individual or information that leads the police to a particular individual who has been identified as being, or having been, engaged in criminal activity."[9] The same phenomenon occurs in stores and other commercial establishments when security officers or sales associates focus their attention on customers based on their race or ethnicity rather than any suspicious behavior on their part.

Widespread recognition of the problem of "driving while black" during the 1990s led several states to pass legislation banning the practice of racial profiling. Many of these laws required police departments to collect data on the race of motorists who are stopped and searched.[10] Some researchers who have analyzed these data have shown that motorists are more likely to be stopped, searched, cited, and arrested if they are black or Latino rather than white.[11] Others have found the opposite or mixed results.[12] Interestingly, the results of some studies suggest that white drivers have a greater propensity to engage in criminal activity than motorists of color. For example, researchers at the Institute on Race and Justice at Northeastern University found that although black and Latino motorists were two and a half times more likely to be searched than white motorists, whites were more likely to be found with contraband. In fact, Farrell et al., in 2003 found that 23.5 percent of white motorists who were searched were found with guns or drugs compared with 17.8 percent of black and Latino motorists.[13]

The same stereotypes that result in increased enforcement of traffic laws for people of color lead store personnel to watch and search people of color when they are shopping. However, understanding the profiling that occurs in the marketplace is challenging due to the lack of available data. Whereas police stops and searches are public information, data on stops and searches that take place in commercial establishments are the private property of those establishments. Unless business owners are willing to share their data, other publicly available information must be used to approximate the treatment of black and brown shoppers compared to white shoppers. Despite the limitations of the data, an analysis of shoplifting and larceny arrests is presented in Chapter 6. For this initial study, a determination was made as to whether criminal suspicion was "present" or "absent" in the cases that were examined.

## Subtle Degradation

Most of the cases fell into this category and involved a wide variety of defendant companies: bar, restaurants, car rental companies, car dealers, entertainment venues, amusement parks, social clubs, fast food/carryout/delivery establishments, food/grocery stores, hair salons, large retail establishments, lodging, small retail establishments, and tobacco producers. In more than two thirds of these cases, the courts decided in favor of the business establishments (see Figure 3.2). Only two cases were decided in favor

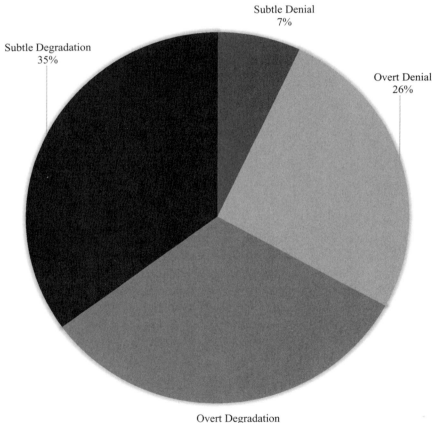

FIGURE 3.2   Common Themes among Cases of Consumer Discrimination

(*Source:* Compiled from Harris, Anne-Marie, Geraldine R. Henderson, and Jerome D. Williams. 2005. "Courting Customers: Assessing Consumer Racial Profiling and Other Marketplace Discrimination." *Journal of Public Policy and Marketing, Policy Watch: Commentaries and Viewpoints* 24, no. 1: 163–171.)

of the customers. This suggests that courts did not believe that the subtle degradation of goods or services occurred because of the race or ethnicity of the customers who filed suit. In one fourth of these cases, the defendant companies settled.

One of the most notorious consumer discrimination cases provides a great illustration of the kind of subtle degradation that many people of color experience when shopping in stores. In that case, Mrs. Hampton was placed under surveillance shortly after entering Dillard's Department Store. She selected her items and paid for them at the checkout counter, where the sales associate gave her a coupon for free cologne. She proceeded to the fragrance counter and attempted to redeem the coupon. At that point, she was stopped by a store security officer and her belongings were searched. As proof that the officer targeted Mrs. Hampton based on her race, her lawyer introduced as evidence the security officer's report which was less than two pages long but made mention of Mrs. Hampton's race 12 times.[14]

The jury found that the store's security officer violated Mrs. Hampton's rights when he harassed her at the fragrance counter and awarded her $1.2 million. The Court of Appeals upheld the jury award finding that, because she was still in the process of redeeming the coupon, the contractual relationship between Mrs. Hampton and Dillard's had not yet concluded when the security officer detained her. Therefore, the store had a contractual duty to allow Mrs. Hampton to complete her transaction by redeeming the coupon. Preventing her from doing so violated her right to make and enforce contracts.

Nevertheless, the court specifically rejected the notion that consumers of all races have the right to a harassment-free shopping experience, explaining that there "must have been interference with a contract beyond the mere expectation of being treated without discrimination while shopping." The U.S. Supreme Court denied Dillard's petition to review this decision.

## Overt Degradation

This category contains the second-highest number of cases (32%) as shown in Figure 3.2. In half of these cases, the court found in favor of the business establishment and close to half (42%) were settled out of court. Despite the overt nature of the discriminatory conduct in these cases, only two cases were decided in favor of the customer. As we will see in Chapter 5, many federal judges do not acknowledge that people of color have valid claims of discrimination unless they experience a complete denial of service.

One example of conduct categorized as overt degradation occurred at a Conoco store in Fort Worth, Texas. Denise Arguello and her father, Alberto Govea, both Latino, stopped to purchase gas and other items on their way to a family picnic. The Conoco employee asked Ms. Arguello for identification when she attempted to pay using her credit card. She refused to accept Ms. Arguello's valid Oklahoma driver's license. During the dispute, Mr. Govea began to feel ill and decided to leave the store to avoid complications to a chronic health problem.[15] Eventually, the employee agreed to complete the transaction but after additional discourse, said to Ms. Arguello: "f—you, you f—ing Iranian Mexican bitch, whatever you are."

The employee then shoved Ms. Arguello's purchases off the counter, gestured obscenely at her and her father, and announced over the store's intercom that they should "go back where you came from, you poor Mexicans . . . you goat-smelling Iranians." When Mr. Govea tried to reenter the store to determine the employee's name, she barred him from doing so. The employee readily agreed that she was discriminating against them. Ms. Arguello and her father attempted to complain to Conoco management, but the company did not respond.

According to the Court of Appeals, none of the conduct alleged in the complaint or proven at trial infringed on the customers' rights. The court found that although the store clerk may have deterred them, she did not prevent them from purchasing the goods they sought from Conoco under the same terms and conditions as white customers. Therefore, Ms. Arguello and her father were not entitled to any relief. The U.S. Supreme Court refused to review the Court of Appeals' decision.

## Subtle Denial

Among the cases that were categorized as involving the subtle denial of goods or services, half were found in favor of the customer. An example of subtle denial of service occurred when Mrs. Murrell, a white woman took her two African-American grandsons and their African-American mother on a weekend trip to the beach. Mrs. Murrell entered the office of the Ocean Mecca Motel while the rest of her family stayed in the car. She checked into the motel for two nights and paid the bill in advance with cash. They then brought their bags into the room and headed for the outdoor pool. Within a few minutes, the desk clerk appeared and demanded that they leave immediately. When the Murrells asked why, the desk clerk said "I want you off my premises now." The desk clerk claimed that he was enforcing the four-person room occupancy limit. The Murrell party consisted of four people and the motel's brochure and website stated that all rooms had between five- and seven-person limits. The clerk initially refused to return 50 dollars claiming it as a room cleaning charge. Mrs. Murrell protested that they had spent less than ten minutes in the room and eventually received a full refund. The trial court found that the Murrells had failed to present sufficient evidence of race discrimination but the Court of Appeals reversed that decision finding the circumstantial evidence to be compelling.[16]

## Overt Denial

This final category contains more than one fourth of all the cases analyzed (see Figure 3.2). More than half of the cases were settled, which is the highest proportion among the four categories. Fewer than 20 percent were found in favor of the business establishment, and the remaining cases were decided in favor of the customer.

This type of prejudicial conduct is exemplified by several lawsuits filed against Denny's Restaurants. One particular case involved a server who forced African-American customers to wait an extraordinarily long time to be seated, made harassing gestures and racially charged, derogatory comments toward them. The waiter refused to serve the customers and told his manager that they could not make him serve "n—." In a similar case, two African-American customers at a different Denny's Restaurant were subjected to racially derogatory comments, refused service, and told to leave the restaurant without receiving their meals. Both cases resulted in confidential out-of-court settlements.[17] Since these lawsuits were filed, Denny's has paid $54 million in damages to settle two class action suits, and has undergone a major restructuring to address these issues. As a result, Denny's has been listed near the top in rankings of the best companies in America for African Americans.[18]

## Criminal Treatment

The analysis revealed that 40 percent of all cases involved allegations that customers of color were treated with suspicion or as if they were criminals. Most of those cases were situations where customers experienced a degradation of goods or services rather than an outright denial. An example is described below.

In this Massachusetts case, a white employee at The Children's Place reported that she was instructed to discriminate against customers of color. For example, her supervisors asked her to follow black and Latino shoppers to prevent them from stealing and to refuse them large shopping bags because they would be used for stealing. She and other sales associates "were told to withhold credit card applications, not to attempt add-on sales with minority customers, nor to inform them of sales or promotions."[19]

The Massachusetts Attorney General's Office sent matched-pair testers to shop at several of The Children's Place stores throughout the state to observe and record customer treatment. The audits showed that black testers were more likely to be followed by store personnel than white testers. When testers made a major credit card purchase, The Children's Place employees were more likely to compare the black tester's receipt signature to his or her credit card signature and to scrutinize the black tester's signature more closely than the white tester's signature. Based on these findings, a settlement was negotiated under which The Children's Place agreed to require training of all employees and to submit to additional testing audits.

The testing audits undertaken by the Massachusetts' Attorney General's Office are the "gold standard" when it comes to measuring discrimination in stores and restaurants. Because they are resource intensive, matched-pair tests are often financially prohibitive. To determine whether a commercial establishment is targeting customers based on their race or ethnicity, loss prevention practitioners and academicians are replicating the methods used in traffic stop studies. Those studies analyze traffic stop data to determine whether law enforcement officers target motorists for enhanced traffic enforcement based on the motorist's race or ethnicity. The researchers compare the proportion of motorists of a particular race who are stopped to the proportion of motorists of that race in the driving population. A similar comparison can be conducted using the shopping population in a particular trade area as the benchmark against which to compare which customers are detained and subjected to a search.

Numerous incidents of consumer racial profiling have received media attention, many of which we discuss in this book. Among the incidents that have resulted in lawsuits, attorneys for the plaintiffs typically retain expert witnesses to analyze data and ascertain to what degree a particular defendant or retail establishment, is targeting certain shoppers for increased surveillance and/or stops for suspicion of shoplifting. For example, in the case of Dillard's Department Stores, lawyer Cletus Ernster of Houston, Texas, has represented more than 100 plaintiffs in lawsuits against the store.[20] To illustrate how consumer racial profiling can be measured, we discuss the methodology used by the expert witness in many of these cases. Specifically, we discuss the expert reports filed with the court in two cases: *Lewis v. Dillard's* and *Anderson and Humphrey v. Dillard's*, both of which are accessible as part of the public record.

First, secondary data is used to assess the percentage of shoppers by race/ethnicity for a particular department store chain or for a particular store location. The expert witness used two types of secondary data sources: (1) consumer surveys, based on two commercial data sources, Mediamark Research Inc. and Scarborough USA+ and (2) U.S. Census Bureau demographic data, from two commercial data sources, The Right Site and Demographics Now. These sources provide several numbers for each racial/ethnic segment for each department store chain (not for the specific store location). Of particular importance are (1) the percentage of all shoppers at a particular department store that are represented by a particular racial/ethnic group, for example, the percent of African Americans that represent all shoppers at Dillard's (12.7% in Table 3.1); (2) the percentage of a particular racial/ethnic group that shops at a particular department store, for example, the percentage of African Americans that shop at Dillard's (16.6% in Table 3.1); and (3) a measure of the performance of a particular racial/ethnic segment in shopping at a particular department store as compared to the total population, for example, the percentage of African Americans who shop at Dillard's compared to the percentage of all shoppers at Dillard's (this is reported as an index number, where 100 means average performance compared to the general population, and numbers below and above 100 mean below and above average compared to the general population—118 in parentheses in Table 3.1).

For example, in Table 3.1, it is readily apparent that white shoppers constitute the majority of Dillard's customers (for comparison purposes, the Table also shows the numbers for Macy's). While the numbers may vary year to year based on the particular survey and the sample, the overall pattern has been the same over the years, that is, the majority of Dillard's shoppers are white. The Table, based on the Scarborough survey, indicates that 72.8 percent of Dillard's shoppers were white in 2002, 12.7 percent were black, and 11.6 percent were Hispanic.

The data in Table 3.2 show that, compared to whites, larger percentages of blacks and Hispanics shop at Dillard's and Macy's. Specifically, while

**TABLE 3.1    Ethnicity and Percent of Customers Who Shop at Dillard's and Macy's**

|            | Dillard's      | Macy's         |
|------------|----------------|----------------|
| White      | 72.8% (99*)    | 64.0% (87*)    |
| Black      | 12.7% (118*)   | 11.5% (106*)   |
| Hispanic   | 11.6% (101*)   | 16.7% (145*)   |

*Source:* Scarborough USA Plus (2004), data accessed directly from Local Market Consumer Insights Report (Spring 2002 Report). Available at: https://www.scarborough.com/, January 25, 2004.

*Index of Performance (See text for explanation of this measure.)

**TABLE 3.2    Percent of Each Ethnic Group Shopping at Dillard's and Macy's**

|            | Dillard's | Macy's |
|------------|-----------|--------|
| White      | 14.0%     | 11.1%  |
| Black      | 16.6%     | 13.5%  |
| Hispanic   | 14.2%     | 18.4%  |

*Source:* Scarborough USA Plus (2004), data accessed directly from Local Market Consumer Insights Report (Spring 2002 Report), accessed at https://www.scarborough.com/, January 25, 2004.

14.0 percent and 11.1 percent of whites shop at Dillard's and Macy's, respectively, 16.6 percent and 13.5 percent of blacks and 14.2 percent and 18.4 percent of Hispanics shop in those stores.

As noted in Tables 3.1 and 3.2, the survey data are for the store chain and not individual stores. To determine the numbers for specific stores, demographic data based on the U.S. Census Bureau for individual store locations is examined. Because of its spatial character, store retailing naturally involves marketing to geographic target markets. Generally, geographic market areas contain consumers that have similar demographic and socioeconomic characteristics. One such characteristic is the racial/ethnic composition of retail customers. Groups of ethnic consumers generally reside in tightly concentrated geographic areas.[21]

According to the typology of shopping center definitions developed by the International Council of Shopping Centers (ICSC), shopping center trade areas can range from 3 miles to 25 miles, or more, depending on the type of shopping center, for example, a neighborhood center versus an outlet center.[22] Typically, this range would represent the area from which 60–80 percent of the center's sales would originate. Therefore, typically 1-, 3-, 5-, 15-, and 25-mile radii are used to assess the demographics of the population surrounding a particular store or shopping center to identify the racial/ethnic composition of that population.

For data in the two expert witness reports examined here, the race/ethnic data come from one of two geodemographic systems (The Right Site and Demographics Now). Both systems rely on data from the 2000 U.S. Census Bureau to forecast demographic statistics for subsequent years. The systems can compute demographic statistics for nonstandard market areas delineated by a fixed radius around a store location and by drive time. For example, it is possible to draw demographic data for a particular Dillard's store from areas with radii of various distances (one mile, three miles, five miles, etc.). This approach relies on the premise that consumers shop in the same general geographic area where they reside. Similarly, it is possible to draw demographic data for a particular Dillard's store based on drive time, for example, 5 minutes, 15 minutes, 25 minutes, etc. This approach to estimating the racial/ethnic composition of shoppers for particular stores is based on the same methodology developed by other researchers.[23]

It should be noted that practitioners also recommended this approach in assessing the occurrence of consumer racial profiling. For example, Mike Magill, the former district security and safety manager for Montgomery Ward and loss prevention director at Longs Drugs, implemented such an approach. He called his method "the demographic test" and used it to detect and prevent discriminatory behavior among his employees. Using U.S. Census Bureau data, he determined the ethnic makeup of the areas where his stores were located. Every three months, he reviewed the arrest and detention records of each store, which were broken down by race, and checked them against the Census data. According to Magill, "If your demographics are ninety percent white and ten percent black, and you're pulling over all blacks, it makes you wonder. The numbers don't lie." Magill required those employees who were responsible for large discrepancies to undergo retraining.[24]

It is interesting to note that this methodology of comparing racial/ethnic demographic data of shoppers with the racial/ethnic data of shoppers who are stopped/detained/arrested, etc., to assess the occurrence of consumer racial profiling was employed in a consumer racial profiling case against

Macy's East in New York by Eliot Spitzer, the state attorney general. According to the *New York Times* story, "Mr. Spitzer's investigation found that most of the people detained at a sampling of Macy's stores around the state were black and Latino, a disproportionately high number when compared with the percentage of blacks and Latinos who shopped at those stores, according to the complaint."[25]

In Tables 3.3 and 3.4, demographic data is provided for the Dillard's store in Tyler, Texas. It is readily apparent that white shoppers constitute the majority of Dillard's customers at this store based on distance radii and drive time. While the numbers may vary from store to store, based on

**TABLE 3.3    Dillard's: Broadway Square Mall, Tyler, Texas, Demographics Based on Radii**

| Description | 1 Mile | 3 Miles | 5 Miles |
|---|---|---|---|
| Population | 7,753 | 52,903 | 87,892 |
| Households | 3,694 | 23,339 | 35,449 |
| Median Household Income ($) | 46,645 | 41,105 | 37,962 |
| White Population | 91.4% | 78.0% | 67.1% |
| Black Population | 4.9% | 16.0% | 21.9% |
| Hispanic Population | 3.3% | 8.7% | 17.5% |

*Source:* DemographicsNow (2004), data accessed directly from DemographicsNow (v. 6.0, 2004 data). Available at: http://www.demographicsnow.com/, January 25, 2004, company now known as Alteryx.

**TABLE 3.4    Dillard's: Broadway Square Mall, Tyler, Texas, Demographics Based on Drive Time**

| Description | 5 Min. | 15 Min. | 25 Min. |
|---|---|---|---|
| Population | 42,907 | 126,641 | 174,891 |
| Households | 18,848 | 49,299 | 68,051 |
| Median Household Income ($) | 41,087 | 39,447 | 40,275 |
| White Population | 78.8% | 67.8% | 71.7% |
| Black Population | 14.7% | 22.1% | 19.6% |
| Hispanic Population | 9.8% | 16.2% | 13.7% |

*Source:* DemographicsNow (2004), data accessed directly from DemographicsNow (v. 6.0, 2004 data). Available at: http://www.demographicsnow.com/, January 25, 2004, company now known as Alteryx.

the demographic composition of the area surrounding a particular store, the overall pattern is the same, that is, the majority of Dillard's shoppers are white. The specific data for the Tyler store indicate that 91.4 percent of the population within a one-mile radius of the Tyler Dillard's store is white, 78.03 percent within a three-mile radius, and 67.1 percent within a five-mile radius. Similarly, the specific data for the Tyler store indicate that 78.8 percent of the population within a five-minute drive time of the Tyler Dillard's store is white, 67.8 percent within a 15-minute drive time, and 71.7 percent within a 25-minute drive time.

The expert witness compared the data above with the data resulting from a review of Dillard's documents detailing surveillance and stops by race. Based on a review and analysis of over 1,300 person-incidents ascertained from incident reports, banning notices, trespass notices, arrest reports, etc., provided by Dillard's, the expert witness concluded that:

> At Dillard's Broadway Square Mall store in Tyler, Texas, there was a significant disparity both in the rate and manner in which minority shoppers were stopped, searched, and detained compared to non-minority shoppers, and this disparity reflected a pattern of consumer racial profiling behavior, i.e., minority shoppers were stopped, searched, and detained more frequently than non-minority shoppers.[26]

Minority shoppers by far represented the majority of individuals who were stopped, searched, detained, and/or arrested, at Dillard's Tyler, Texas, store. These percentages were disproportionate to the percentage of minorities who shopped at Dillard's, based on the secondary data presented earlier. Tables 3.5 and 3.6 provide a summary of this analysis, first for all documented person-incidents over all the years analyzed, and then for the most recent years, year-by-year.

Using the same methodology, the expert witness also presented his analysis in another case: *Anderson and Humphrey v Dillard's* which involved the Dillard's store located at the Oak Court Mall in Memphis, Tennessee. We briefly present the summary of the analysis mainly because the results are even more pronounced than those in the Lewis case. Again, the documents provided by Dillard's consisted mainly of incident reports, banning notices, shoplifting reports, arrest reports, photographs of detainees, police reports, and various other records. To arrive at conclusions that could be drawn from a review of these documents, the expert witness supplemented the methodology described earlier with content analysis methodology, but the process was essentially the same as in the Lewis case.

**TABLE 3.5    Broadway Square Mall Store in Tyler, Texas, Summary of All Documents Reviewed (Includes Incident Reports, Banning Notices, Trespass Notices, Arrest Reports, etc.)**

| | |
|---|---|
| Number of separate document person-incidents* | 1,328 |
| Minorities (black and Hispanic) person-incidents | 742 (55.9%) |
| Nonminorities | 543 (40.9%) |
| Other or race/ethnicity not indicated | 43 (3.2%) |

*A person-incident for purposes of this report is defined as one person for one incident. For example, if two people are stopped during one incident, that is counted as two separate person-incidents. If one person is stopped for two different incidents, that is counted as two separate person-incidents.

*Source:* Authors' Review of Dillard's documents.

*Jannie Lewis v Dillard's, Inc.,* and the Higbee Company, 2005 WL 2877925 (E.D. Texas, 2005), Expert Report and Affidavit.

**TABLE 3.6    Broadway Square Mall Store in Tyler, Texas, by Year: 1996–2003 (Includes Incident Reports, Banning Notices, Trespass Notices, Arrest Reports, etc.)**

| Year | Total | Minority (%) | Nonminority (%) | Other*(%) |
|---|---|---|---|---|
| 1996 | 93 | 54 (58.1) | 39 (41.9) | 0 |
| 1997 | 130 | 86 (66.2) | 44 (33.8) | 0 |
| 1998 | 137 | 76 (55.5) | 43 (31.4) | 18 (13.1) |
| 1999 | 94 | 70 (74.5) | 20 (21.3) | 4 (4.2) |
| 2000 | 80 | 41 (51.3) | 31 (38.8) | 8 (10.0) |
| 2001 | 127 | 74 (58.3) | 47 (37.0) | 6 (4.7) |
| 2002 | 17 | 10 (58.8) | 6 (35.3) | 1 (5.9) |
| 2003 | 20 | 9 (45.0) | 9 (45.5) | 2 (10.0) |

*Other denotes either other races/ethnicities, for example, Asian/Pacific Islander, or race/ethnicity could not be determined, as document did not provide such a designation.

*Source:* Authors' Review of Dillard's documents.

*Jannie Lewis v Dillard's, Inc.,* and the Higbee Company, 2005 WL 2877925 (E.D. Texas, 2005), Expert Report and Affidavit.

Multiple coders were used to analyze the materials. First a training session was conducted to familiarize the coders with the task and to answer any questions. For example, a typical task might involve counting the number of photographs of detainees and then coding each photograph for race/ethnicity. For this kind of content analysis where coders are engaging largely in what is termed in research as manifest content analysis, that is, placing units in categories with only a slight amount of coder judgment necessary for interpreting category assignments, one expects to find fairly high reliability among coders. This is quite different for other types of content analysis, which is termed in research as latent content analysis. This latter type generally requires a significant amount of interpretation by the coder.

A review of Dillard's documents for the Oak Court Mall showed that 95 percent of the 235 people whose race was indicated in the incident reports were African American and only 5 percent were white (see Table 3.7). Therefore, the expert witness concluded that there was a significant disparity in the rate at which African-American shoppers were stopped, searched, and detained compared to white shoppers, and this disparity reflected a pattern of consumer racial profiling behavior, that is, African-American shoppers were stopped, searched, and detained more frequently than white shoppers.

The expert witness also concluded that, at Dillard's Oak Court Mall store in Memphis, African-American shoppers represented a significantly lower percentage of total shoppers compared to the percentage of African-American shoppers who were stopped, searched, and detained. That conclusion was based on U.S. Census Bureau data. The African-American population in Memphis is 61.2 percent. If the Oak Court Mall drew shoppers from the whole of Memphis, and with all things being equal between African Americans and Whites in terms of shopping preference for Dillard's, one would

TABLE 3.7   Summary of Content Analysis of Oak Court Mall Documents

| | |
|---|---|
| Number of Separate Incidents | 235 |
| Number of People Involved in Incidents | 290 |
| Number of People Where Race Indicated | 242 |
| Number of African Americans | 229 |
| Number of Whites | 12 |
| Number of Asians | 1 |
| Percent of People Where Race Is Known | 83.4% (242/290) |
| Percent African American Where Race Is Known | 94.6% (229/242) |
| Percent White Where Race Is Known | 5.0% (12/242) |
| Percent Asian Where Race Is Known | 0.4% (1/242) |

*Source:* Authors' Review of Dillard's documents.

*Natasha Anderson and Shirelle Humphrey v. Dillard's, Inc.*, No. 04-CV-02548-D/P, W.D.Tenn., 2007.

expect at most 61 percent of shoppers in the Oak Court Mall Dillard's to be African American. However, it is unlikely that the Oak Court Mall's trade area extends to the whole of Memphis. Therefore, it is more reasonable to examine the percentage of African-American shoppers within the Oak Court Mall trade area, that is, the area surrounding the Oak Court Mall from which most shoppers are likely to be drawn.

To do so, the expert witness used different radii to determine the demographics of the population based on race/ethnicity surrounding the Oak Court Mall, as shown in Table 3.8. Based on this data, the African-American population within one mile of the Oak Court Mall is less than 2 percent. At the three-mile and five-mile radii, the African-American population is 22 percent and 43 percent, respectively. Even when the radius is extended out to 15 miles, the African-American population does not exceed 50 percent, which is well below the 95 percent figure for the percentage of shoppers who were African American among the 235 Dillard's incident reports.

Finally, the expert witness concluded that the Dillard's Memphis department store at the Oak Court Mall engaged in a pattern of CRP based on an analysis of documents provided by Dillard's that indicates that almost 100 percent (specifically 95%) of all the shoppers where race is known who were stopped, searched, and detained were African American. This compares with an African-American population in the Oak Court Mall trade area that never exceeds 50 percent, even when the trade area is extended up to a 15-mile radius.

The expert witness' reports in both cases clearly quantify the extent of race discrimination in those specific department store locations. Our review of the lawsuits filed across the country illustrates that race and ethnic discrimination remain a vexing problem in the marketplace. We observed that the number of lawsuits filed in federal court alleging marketplace

TABLE 3.8    Oak Court Mall Demographics: Racial Composition of Population Surrounding Mall at One-, Three-, and Five-Mile Radii

| Description | 1 Mile | 3 Miles | 5 Miles | 10 Miles | 15 Miles |
|---|---|---|---|---|---|
| White Population (Race) | 96.9% | 73.8% | 51.6% | 45.6% | 48.9% |
| Black Population (Race) | 1.6% | 22.2% | 43.3% | 50.0% | 47.1% |

*Source:* Easy Analytic Software Inc. (EASI). 2004. Data accessed directly from EASI Census 2000 Reports and Analysis, accessed at www.easidemographics.com, January 25, 2004.

discrimination increased over time which may reflect a greater willingness on the part of people of color to voice their dissatisfaction with poor treatment in business establishments. Business owners and managers may be motivated to take action against marketplace discrimination when they understand that people of color are prevailing in courtrooms across the country. Figure 3.3 shows that decisions were made in favor of the plaintiff in approximately half of the cases of subtle denial. Approximately 60 percent of cases of overt denial resulted in settlement agreements between the plaintiff and the business. As many as 40 percent of the cases of overt degradation and 20 percent of the cases of subtle degradation were settled by the parties.

A settlement between the parties does not necessarily imply that the defendant-merchant would have been found liable for discriminating against the customer of color. It could represent a desire by the company to

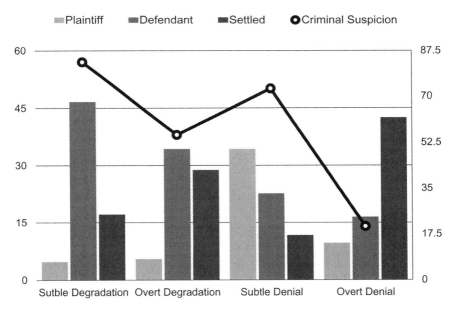

**FIGURE 3.3   Percentage of Cases by Outcome with Criminal Suspicion Overlay**

(*Source:* Compiled from Harris, Anne-Marie, Geraldine R. Henderson, and Jerome D. Williams. 2005. "Courting Customers: Assessing Consumer Racial Profiling and Other Marketplace Discrimination." *Journal of Public Policy and Marketing, Policy Watch: Commentaries and Viewpoints* 24, no. 1: 163–171.)

avoid public attention. The perception among African Americans and other people of color that their money is not valued as highly as that of white customers in certain stores and other establishments—whether it is accurate or not—can have large financial repercussions for those businesses. This point will be examined in greater detail in Chapter 4.

## Notes

1. Sharpton, 2014.
2. Larson, 2015.
3. Harris, 2003; Williams, Henderson, and Hakstian, 2010; Gabbidon, 2003, p. 345; Fitfield and O'Shaughnessy, 2001.
4. Morin and Cottman, 2001, p. A1.
5. Gabbidon and Higgins, 2007; 2008; Jordan, Gabbidon, and Higgins, 2009.
6. Ibid.
7. Blank, Dabady, and Citro, 2004.
8. Major, Quinton, and McCoy, 2002.
9. Ramirez, McDevitt, and Farrell, 2000, p.3.
10. Hakstian, 2013.
11. Examples of such studies include Skolnick, 2007; Engel and Johnson, 2006; Parker et al., 2004.
12. Engel et al., 2003; Smith and Petrocelli, 2001.
13. Farrell et al., 2003.
14. *Hampton v. Dillard's Department Stores,* 2001.
15. *Denise Arguello and Alberta Govea v. Conoco,* 2003.
16. *Murrell v. Ocean Mecca Motel,* 2001.
17. *Charity v. Denny's, Inc.,* 1999; *McCoo v. Denny's,* 2000.
18. Hood 2004; Bean 2003.
19. *Commonwealth of Massachusetts v. The Children's Place Stores, Inc.,* 2000.
20. *USA Today* 2003. Dr. Jerome D. Williams, one of the co-authors of this book, served as the expert witness in many of the cases in which Cletus Ernster was the attorney for the plaintiff. Specifically, Dr. Williams was the expert witness in the two cases discussed in detail in this chapter, namely, *Lewis v. Dillard's* and *Anderson and Humphrey v. Dillard's,* and is referred to as the "expert witness" when discussing the methodology he used in the expert reports. In both cases, counsel for Dillard's hired their own expert witness, who used different methodology and offered testimony to support the defendant's position and to reach conclusions different from those of Dr. Williams.
21. Frey, 1991.
22. International Council of Shopping Centers, 2005.
23. Mulhern and Williams 1995; Mulhern, Williams, and Leone 1998.

24. Fitfield and O'Shaughnessy 2001.

25. Elliott, 2005.

26. *Jannie Lewis v Dillard's, Inc., and the Higbee Company,* 2005 WL 2877925 (E.D. Texas, 2005), Expert Report and Affidavit.

*Natasha Anderson and Shirelle Humphrey v. Dillard's, Inc.,* No. 04-CV-02548-D/P, W.D.Tenn., 2007.

# References

Bean, Linda, 2003. "Legal: What Happened to Diversity's Bad Boys: Texaco, Denny's, Coca-Cola." *DiversityInc.*

Blank, Rebecca M., Marilyn Dabady, and Constance F. Citro, eds. 2004. *Measuring Racial Discrimination: Panel on Methods for Assessing Discrimination,* edited by Committee on National Statistics National Research Council, Division of Behavior and Social Sciences and Education. Washington, DC: The National Academies Press.

*Charity v. Denny's, Inc.,* No. CIV.A.98–0054, 1999 WL 544687 (E.D. La. July 26, 1999).

*Commonwealth of Massachusetts v. The Children's Place Stores, Inc.* (2000). Complaint and Consent Decree, MCD Docket No. 00133755 (December 21).

*Denise Arguello and Alberta Govea v. Conoco, Inc.,* 330 F.3d 355 (5th Cir., 2003).

Elliott, Andrea. 2005. "Macy's Settles Complaint of Racial Profiling for $600,000." *New York Times,* January 14. Available at nytimes.com: http://www.nytimes.com/2005/01/14/nyregion/14macys.html?ei=1&en=f6f4a015fb733fa1&ex=1106722543&pagewanted=print&position=.

Engel, Robin S., Jennifer M. Calnon, Lin Liu, and Richard R. Johnson. 2003. "Project on Police-Citizen Contacts: Year 1 Final Report, May 2002-April 2003." Technical Report prepared for the Pennsylvania State Police. Retrieved from the University of Cincinnati website: http://www.uc.edu/content/dam/uc/ccjr/docs/reports/project_reports/PApolicecitizenscontact0203.pdf.

Engel, Robin S. and Richard Johnson. 2006. "Toward a Better Understanding of Racial and Ethnic Disparities in Search and Seizure Rates." *Journal of Criminal Justice* 34: 605–617.

Farrell, Amy, Dean Jack McDevitt, Shea Cronin, and Erica Pierce. 2003. *Rhode Island Traffic Stop Statistics Act: Final Report.* Boston, MA: Institute on Race and Justice, Northeastern University.

Fifield, Adam and Elise O'Shaughnessy. 2001. "Shopping While Black." *Good Housekeeping* (November): 129–136.

Frey, William H. 1991. "Are Two Americas Emerging?" *Population Today* (October): 6–8.

Gabbidon, Shaun L. 2003. "Racial Profiling by Store Clerks and Security Personnel in Retail Establishments." *Journal of Contemporary Criminal Justice* 19, no. 3: 345–364.

Gabbidon, Shaun L. and George E. Higgins. 2007. "Consumer Racial Profiling and Perceived Victimization: A Phone Survey of Philadelphia Area Residents." *American Journal of Criminal Justice* 32, no. 1–2: 1–11.

Gabbidon, Shaun L. and George E. Higgins. 2008. "Profiling White Americans: Exploring 'Shopping While White.'" *Racial Divide: Race, Ethnicity and Criminal Justice*: 197–209.

Hakstian, Anne-Marie G. 2013. *Racial and Ethnic Profiling in Massachusetts: An Examination of Police Policy and Practice*. Boston: Northeastern University.

*Hampton v. Dillard's Department Stores*, 2001.

Harris, Anne-Marie G. 2003. "Shopping While Black: Applying 42 U.S.C. § 1981 to Cases of Consumer Racial Profiling." *Boston College Third World Law Journal* 23, no. 1: 1–57.

Harris, Anne-Marie, Geraldine R. Henderson, and Jerome D. Williams. 2005. "Courting Customers: Assessing Consumer Racial Profiling and Other Marketplace Discrimination." *Journal of Public Policy and Marketing, Policy Watch: Commentaries and Viewpoints* 24, no. 1: 163–171.

Hood, Ray. 2004. "Perspectives from the Boardroom." In *Symposium on Consumer Racial Profiling*, ed. Jerome D. Williams and Minette Drumwright. Austin, TX.

International Council of Shopping Centers. 2005. Available at http://www.icsc.org/srch/lib/scresources.html. Accessed January 15, 2005.

*Jannie Lewis v Dillard's, Inc., and the Higbee Company*, 2005 WL 2877925 (E.D. Texas, 2005), Expert Report and Affidavit.

Jordan, Kareem L., Shaun L. Gabbidon, and George E. Higgins. 2009. "Exploring the Perceived Extent of and Citizens' Support for Consumer Racial Profiling: Results from a National Poll." *Journal of Criminal Justice* 37, no. 4: 353–359.

Larson, Sandra. 2015. "Shopping While Black? JP Liquor Store Staff Finger UMass Prof. as Perp in Cognac Heist." *The Bay State Banner*, August 5, 10:23 a.m.

"Lawsuits Against Stores Target Racial Profiling." 2003. *USA Today*. Available at: http://usatoday30.usatoday.com/news/nation/2003–06–08-lawsuit-race_x.htm. Accessed January 14, 2016.

Major, Brenda, Wendy J. Quinton, and Shannon K. McCoy. 2002. "Antecedents and Consequences of Attributions to Discrimination: Theoretical and Empirical Advances." In *Advances in Experimental Social Psychology*, ed. P. Zanna Mark. Amsterdam: Elsevier.

*McCoo v. Denny's, Inc.* 2000. WL 156824 (D.Kan., February 11, 2000).

Morin, Richard and Michael H. Cottman. 2001. "Discrimination's Lingering Sting: Minorities Tell of Profiling, Other Bias." *Washington Post*, June 22, A1.

Mulhern, Francis J. and Jerome D. Williams. 1995. "A Comparative Analysis of Shopping Behavior in Hispanic and Non-Hispanic Areas." *Journal of Retailing* 70, no. 3, 231–251.

Mulhern, Francis J., Jerome D. Williams, and Robert P. Leone. 1998. "Variability of Brand Price Elasticities Across retail Stores: Ethnic, Income, and Brand Determinants." *Journal of Retailing* 74, no. 3: 427–446.

*Murrell v. Ocean Mecca Motel, Inc., 262 F.3d 253 (4th Cir., 2001).*

*Natasha Anderson and Shirelle Humphrey v. Dillard's, Inc.*, No. 04-CV-02548-D/P, W.D.Tenn., 2007.

Parker, Karen F., John M. MacDonald, Geoffrey P. Alpert, Michael R. Smith, and Alex Piquero. 2004. "A Contextual Study of Racial Profiling Assessing the Theoretical Rationale for the Study of Racial Profiling at the Local Level." *American Behavioral Scientist* 47, no. 7: 943–962.

Ramirez, Deborah, Jack McDevitt, and Amy Farrell. 2000. *A Resource Guide on Racial Profiling Data Collection Systems: Promising Practices and Lessons Learned.* Washington, DC: U.S. Department of Justice.

Sharpton, Al. 2014. "Racism & Bias: Can We Pause and Be Honest With Ourselves." *The Huffington Post*, May 27, 1:57 p.m.

Skolnick, Jerome H. 2007. "Racial Profiling—Then and Now." *Criminology and Public Policy* 6, no. 1: 65–70.

Smith, Michael R. and Matthew Petrocelli. 2001. "Racial Profiling? A Multivariate Analysis of Police Traffic Stop Data." *Police Quarterly* 4 (March): 4–27.

USA Today. 2003. "Lawsuits against stores target racial profiling." Accessed at http://usatoday30.usatoday.com/news/nation/2003-06-08-lawsuit-race_x.htm, November 20, 2015.

Williams, Jerome D., Geraldine R. Henderson, and Anne-Marie Harris. 2001. "Consumer Racial Profiling: Bigotry Goes to Market," *Crisis*, November/December, 22–24.

# Chapter 4

# The Business Case for Marketplace Diversity

*There is no excuse for the way he was treated. I hope to see him again to personally apologize.*

—Tom Dixon, President of Schwanke-Kasten Jewelers[1]

On October 19, 2015, NBA player, John Henson posted the following on Instagram: "one of the most degrading and racially prejudice [sic] things I've ever experienced in life." The incident he described took place at a high-end jewelry store in the Milwaukee suburb of Whitefish Bay. Henson, a 24-year-old forward who plays for the Milwaukee Bucks, tried to enter the Schwanke-Kasten Jewelers to make a purchase. But employees locked the door, told Henson to go away, and called the police. When the officers arrived, they questioned Henson about his car but they declined the employee's request to stay while Henson shopped.

As more of these incidents are being reported in the media, retailers especially should recognize that subjecting customers to indignities such as consumer racial profiling has a negative impact on their bottom line. Alienating customers in this way translates into a deterrent for these customers to patronize the store, and hence a deterrent for the marketers' increased sales and profits. When racial profiling occurs, victimized consumers are more inclined to take their already significant and growing economic clout elsewhere and transfer their purchasing power and support to those businesses that are truly welcoming to shoppers of all colors.[2]

## The Ethno-Racial Composition of the United States

In 2011, Steve Stoute wrote a book entitled the *Tanning of America: How Hip-Hop Created a Culture That Rewrote the Rules of the New Economy*. As its title suggests, the complexion of America has changed and continues to evolve as indicated by historical census data. That is, as Table 4.1 shows, the change in the population based on ethno-racial background continues to occur. Whites, who were historically the largest ethno-racial group based on absolute numbers and percentages, continue to decrease in numbers relative to others in the population. That is, although the number of white Americans is projected to have increased by 5.1 percent from 2010 to 2019, that percentage increase is lower than the growth expected for African Americans (10.6%) and much lower than Asian Americans (25.2%) and Latinos (24.5%).[3]

When one considers the data presented in Figure 4.1, the picture becomes clearer. Put simply, due to differences in birth rates, immigration rates, and mortality rates, the ethno-racial composition of the United States is on pace for a radical change from what it has been historically. Some states have already become what are called majority-minority states—where the populations of these states is such that more people of color live there than whites.

It is not surprising that companies headquartered in majority-minority states may have a competitive advantage in the long term relative to their counterparts that do not operate in such areas. This potential competitive

**TABLE 4.1    U.S. Population by Ethnicity**

| | In Millions | | | | |
|---|---|---|---|---|---|
| | **1990** | **2000** | **2010** | **2014** | **2019 (Projected)** |
| White | 209.4 | 228.5 | 242.2 | 247.3 | 254.6 |
| | (83.9%) | (81.0%) | (78.3%) | (77.5%) | (76.5%) |
| Black | 30.6 | 35.8 | 40.3 | 42.1 | 44.6 |
| | (12.3%) | (12.7%) | (13.0%) | (13.2%) | (13.4%) |
| Asian | 7.5 | 11.2 | 15.9 | 17.6 | 19.9 |
| | (3.0%) | (4.0%) | (5.2%) | (5.5%) | (6.0%) |
| Hispanic | 22.6 | 35.6 | 50.7 | 55.7 | 63.2 |
| | (9.0%) | (12.6%) | (16.4%) | (17.5%) | (19.0%) |
| Native American | 2.1 | 2.7 | 3.7 | 4.0 | 4.4 |
| | (0.8%) | (1.0%) | (1.2%) | (1.3%) | (1.3%) |
| Total U.S. population | 249.6 | 282.1 | 309.3 | 319.1 | 333 |

*Source:* Table created by authors based on data retrieved from Humphreys, Jeffrey M. "The Multicultural Economy 2014." Selig Center for Economic Growth, Terry College of Business, The University of Georgia, 2014.

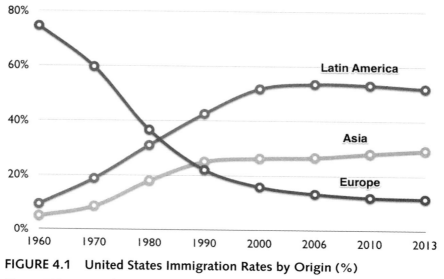

**FIGURE 4.1    United States Immigration Rates by Origin (%)**

(*Source:* U.S. Bureau of the Census.)

advantage arises for such firms inasmuch as they have had more experience employing, manufacturing for, and serving diverse customer sets. In other words, marketers who are not aware of and prepared for the changes in ethno-racial demographics will lose out to those who are. Moreover, considering the earning potential by these individuals both now and in the future, it should be clear that learning about ethnic markets is crucial.

Beyond population demographics, marketers focus on the purchasing power of consumers in each market segment. Purchasing power (also known as spending power or buying power) is defined as:

> the total personal income of residents that is available, after taxes, for spending on virtually everything that they buy, but it does not include dollars that are borrowed or that were saved in previous years.[4]

The fastest-growing group with respect to purchasing power on an absolute basis is the Asian market, but because their base number is smaller, Asian Americans are not having as large of an impact on the marketplace as are Latinos who are growing the fastest on a relative basis (see Table 4.2). Their purchasing power, and associated influence in the marketplace, is already being felt. This purchasing power gets translated into political power, not just in the voting booth during elections, but with respect to sponsorships

TABLE 4.2    Purchasing Power and Growth Rate

| Spending/Purchasing Power 2014 | |
| --- | --- |
| Total United States | $12.6 trillion (76% increase) |
| African Americans | $1.1 trillion (86% increase) |
| Hispanics/Latinos | $1.3 trillion (155% increase) |
| Asians | $770 billion (180% increase) |
| American Indian | $100 billion (149% increase) |
| | $Total (% increase since 2000) |

*Source:* Table created by authors based on data retrieved from Humphreys, Jeffrey M. "The Multicultural Economy 2014." Selig Center for Economic Growth, Terry College of Business, The University of Georgia, 2014.

and advertising and a host of other market-related activities. In 2014, the combined purchasing power of Asians, blacks, and Native Americans was estimated to be $2 trillion, which is equivalent to the tenth largest economy in the world (bigger than India, Canada, or Australia) with respect to gross domestic product.[5] According to the Selig Center, in 2014:

> . . . the $1.3 trillion Hispanic market is larger than the entire economies (2013 GDP measured in U.S. dollars) of all but fifteen countries in the world—smaller than the GDP of Indonesia and larger than the GDP of Turkey.[6]

Even more important than the overall amount of money earned by individuals in each category is how they spend that money. Considering the purchasing power of people of color, it is incumbent upon marketers to recognize the unique needs and wants of these consumer markets. Because of physiological differences such as skin tone or taste preferences and other types of cultural differences, different products and services must be offered. In other words, it should not be assumed that all consumers have the same needs and wants as their white counterparts. For instance, with respect to black consumers, Tom Burrell built one of the largest multicultural advertising agencies based on the unique belief that he instilled in his clients and staff: Black people are not dark-skinned white people, a sentiment that was expressed by academics such as Marcus Alexis and his colleagues in their collective works, *Black Consumer Profiles: Food Purchasing in the Inner City* (1980).[7]

## Economic Spending Patterns of People of Color

Early research on economic spending patterns has been replicated by Alexis and Henderson (1994),[8] the Selig Center, and the Consumer Expenditure Study released by the Bureau of Labor Statistics (BLS).[9] In 2010, the BLS study revealed that there were vast differences in the overall spending pattern of whites, blacks, Asians, and Hispanics. For instance, although Asians had the highest level of income on average, they spent twice as much as others on public transportation. Clearly, they had the money but chose not to spend it on personal transportation (depreciating assets) compared with others. African Americans spend more on personal care items than the average, but less than average on tobacco products. Therefore, depending on the demographic makeup of particular neighborhoods, a local supermarket or drugstore should have a completely different assortment of products available to serve the needs of its customer base. Also, given the racial/ethnic differences in homeownership rates and the fact that homeowners are more likely than renters to make repairs, home-improvement stores may decide not to locate in particular neighborhoods with lower homeownership rates.

In addition, the overall demographic shift and growth in multicultural consumers has had a significant impact on the retail landscape in general, and specifically, department stores. For example, a National Shopping Behavior Study highlights the increasing importance of ethnic minority consumers to department store retailers.[10] In that study, 11 percent of whites, 15 percent of Hispanics, and 18 percent of African Americans reported spending the most at department stores, compared with other retail channels and outlets (e.g., catalogues, the Internet, and other types of retail outlets, such as home furnishing stores, warehouses). Data from the study also indicated that the African-American and Hispanic consumer groups account for 25–30 percent of department store sales. Changes in the shopping behavior of these consumer groups and their purchasing motivations will require department store management to make meaningful changes to their strategies to effectively serve their new customers.

Recognizing these retail purchasing trends is important for retailers that wish to attract younger multicultural shoppers. The National Shopping Behavior Study indicates that overall, the percentage of consumers who named department stores as the place where they spend the most money declined from 15 to 11 percent. However, the percentage of Hispanics and African Americans who identified department stores as the place where they spend the most money outpaces the percentage of whites.[11]

Given the existing levels and projected growth of the purchasing power of consumers of color, it is incumbent upon marketers to avoid "shooting themselves in the foot" by discriminating against and thus alienating consumers of color. For example, sales at one Treasure Cache store fell by more than 50 percent following an incident of consumer discrimination.[12] Dillard's Department store stock underwent a significant drop which some linked to the more than one hundred race-based discrimination lawsuits filed against the retail chain.[13] A Denny's Restaurant poll found that approximately 50 percent of African Americans said they would never eat at Denny's again after negative publicity surrounding a lawsuit—although in a subsequent poll that number fell to 13 percent because of aggressive efforts by Denny's to address discrimination issues.[14]

Beyond merely eliminating discriminatory behaviors and practices that are perceived as exclusionary, marketers must also embrace inclusive practices. They should span the various aspects of a firm's marketing strategies and tactics. Various approaches for marketing to consumers of color involving the 4 Ps, product (service), price, place (distribution), and promotion (advertising), are described along with examples of some fiascos of companies in attempting to do so.

## Product/Service and Discrimination

Problem solving for consumers consists of finding and obtaining the products and services that they need or desire in their life. But consider an African American who cannot find jeans to fit her body, an Asian American who cannot buy gloves that stay on his hands, or a Latina teenager who doesn't understand why "flesh-toned" foundation makes her look like a cartoon character. When internally attributed, these consumers conclude that there must be something wrong with them. The associated long-term emotional impact takes its toll on individual confidence, empowerment, and feelings of inclusion. In turn, these impacts lead to self-imposed limitations on earning potential and leadership opportunities. When externally attributed to negligent or perhaps intentionally discriminatory acts by marketers, these consumers may harbor contempt, alienation, and even anger toward the offending firms.[15]

Consider Levi's Curve ID campaign. After decades of Levi's existing as a company, a brand, and a product, they realized that two different women, both of whom may be a size two and yet, because their bodies are shaped very differently, the jeans they buy would fit very differently. In one case, a woman might have a smaller waist and fuller hips and thighs whereas another woman might have a straighter up and down shape with less of a differential between the waist measurement and the hip measurement. As a result, the woman with the fuller hips and thighs would not be able to wear the size two she found on the store rack without making extreme tailoring modifications to the garment. It became clear to Levi's that certain segments of the marketplace shouldn't always have to make accommodations. Of course, losing business to other brands such as Apple Bottom and FUBU helped Levi's to understand the business case for marketplace inclusion.

In the late 1980s and early 1990s, Hanes Hosiery, the textile company, found that the trend toward casual dress in the workplace was taking a toll on their sales in all of its market segments except for African-American women. Black women tended to spend more than their white female counterparts on hosiery purchases for a number of reasons. First, black women were less likely to dress down for casual day although they were given explicit permission to do so by their employers. Second, in general, black women have fuller hips and thinner ankles than do white women. Therefore, when they buy a pair of pantyhose, they may have a situation where the pantyhose are baggy or saggy down by the ankle. But then when they try to pull the pantyhose up over their thighs and hips, up to their waist, they find that they are unable to do so. So they have to choose between baggy ankles with a larger size or a sagging crotch with a smaller size. Third, for most women, buying hosiery is an exercise in masking imperfections in the appearance of their legs with a skin-tone matching product. However, matching skin tone has long created an interesting, special situation for women of color. The color that was labeled "Nude" assumed that there was a default skin tone. Because "nude" hosiery did not match their skin tone, many women of color bought hosiery to match their outfits rather than their skin to avoid the problem altogether. Once Hanes acknowledged the problem, the company introduced new colors such as "Gentlebrown" and "Barely There" and hired Tina Turner, a new spokesperson for the popular Silk Reflections line. This campaign became iconic and historic and was picked up by many media outlets around the time of its first release,[16] but also years later as a feature of this day in African-American history.[17] These images of Ms. Turner, among others, were among the first to depict an African-American woman as a symbol of beauty for a major advertiser in the United States.

Next, consider the case of black men and their shaving needs. Many black men (among others) have excessively curly hair that tends to form razor bumps called folliculitis barbae when shaved. The hair is pulled by the razor, springs back, and forms a bump just under the skin. This causes a texture problem where the bump was created with potential swelling and pus indicating an infection. When the razor bump is excised, a pigmentation problem may result in permanent scarring especially for those who are subject to keloid scarring. An obvious solution to this problem for many men is to grow out their facial hair. However, the default decorum in the workplace has been for men to wear clean-shaven faces. Thus, if a man with excessively curly facial hair chooses to wear a beard so that he can protect his skin from razor bumps and other irritations, he is seen as violating a workplace norm that has been established by people who have a different physiology.

Because of this, a significant portion of black men use depilatories such as Magic Shave. The problem with depilatories is that they do not actually remove the hair shaft from the follicle, but they can enlarge the pores creating a "crater face." Other black men have considered more permanent solutions such as laser hair removal. However, the refraction of the lasers that are built for the general market do not work very well with individuals with darker skin. The best candidate for laser hair removal has very pale skin and yet very dark hair. Of course, there is much less contrast between the color of the hair and the skin for people of color. Marketers could come to the rescue by creating products that would allow black men to comfortably shave their faces or employers can come to the rescue by giving black men more options so that they do not have to shave their faces.[18]

These issues associated with physiology may also affect the ergonomic design of durables such as automobiles, bicycles, exercise equipment, and office furniture. An example from the realm of computer technology involves Hewlett-Packard (HP), the producer of printers, computers, and monitors. In a highly publicized crisis management situation, HP found itself having to redesign one of its MediaSmart computers that contained a software feature to track an individual's face with its embedded WebCam. The company was forced to respond to a claim that its equipment was racist when two coworkers—Wanda (a white woman) and Desi (a black man)— posted a video on YouTube showing that the monitor followed Wanda's face whenever she appeared in the view but when her colleague Desi appeared, the monitor would stop.[19] After nearly 3 million people viewed the video on YouTube, HP released a statement explaining its software's problems.

> The technology we use is built on standard algorithms that measure the difference in intensity of contrast between the eyes and the upper cheek and nose. We believe that the camera might have difficulty "seeing" contrast in conditions where there is insufficient foreground lighting . . . Everything we do is focused on ensuring that we provide a high-quality experience for all our customers, who are ethnically diverse and live and work around the world. That's why when issues surface, we take them seriously and work hard to understand the root causes. We are working with our partners to learn more.[20]

These marketing hits and misses are indicators of products and services that could attract a large and growing segment of the market that is relatively untapped. Marketers could create a wide diversity of products and services, keeping in mind individual differences in design, branding, and marketing that would serve to maintain the current market share while adding a brand new following of loyal customers.

## Price and Price Discrimination

Although pricing strategy is often overlooked by marketers, it is an essential part of the marketing mix, especially concerning issues related to luxury consumption, price points, and perceptions of value and quality. This is especially true for consumers of color who often have a particularly keen eye for price discrimination and sensitivity to differential pricing. In addition, marketers should understand that many consumers of color also embrace luxury consumption, although this varies along socioeconomic, sociocultural, and socio-geographic lines.

Marcus Alexis and Alan Andreasen and their respective colleagues have conducted research suggesting that people who live in inner cities and in rural areas pay more for products than people who live in suburban areas.[21] The primary reason for the difference in prices is that big-box chain stores that can offer the best pricing are typically located in suburban areas. These merchants make up in sales volume what they lose in profit margin. But inner city and rural consumers who have little or no access to these stores are subject to higher prices which amounts to de facto price discrimination. Of course, a vast majority of blacks, Asians, and Latinos live in either highly urban areas or in rural areas.

In addition, many inner cities are food deserts or food-insecure areas which means that healthy food is not affordable and/or accessible in these areas.[22] The grocery stores that are located in the inner cities often charge higher prices and sell older (and sometimes expired) products. Thus, inner-city dwellers are effectively charged more for products of lower quality than are their counterparts in the suburbs.

Another aspect of pricing strategy that marketers must take into consideration when pursuing multicultural consumers is price sensitivity by different racial/ethnic groups. For example, Mulhern and Williams showed that shoppers in predominantly Latino areas are more prone to purchase store brands, suggesting that they are price sensitive. In another study, Mulhern, Williams, and Leone found that the degree of price sensitivity increased with household income but fell as the proportion of African-American residents increased in a given area.[23,24] Therefore, marketers can alter the price of products and services in different neighborhoods, depending on their racial, ethnic, and sociodemographic make-up, but they should bear in mind that not all consumer segments are equally responsive to changes in prices.

## Place and Retail Redlining

The place in which a consumer may shop for and find products and services is also a very important part of the marketing mix. Retailers provide many important functions such as convenient locations, an assortment of products and services, and other services such as repairs and financing. Whereas it is generally believed that face-to-face interactions are more positively experiential for consumers, the irony is that for many consumers of color, there are many negative experiences in these types of environments. In a now-famous study, Ian Ayres and Peter Siegelman conducted research on car negotiations with black and white, male and female confederates.[25] In their research, they found that although the confederates were the same in every way (age, prepared script, credentials) except race and gender, they received very different outcomes from the car dealerships. The white males were able to purchase the car for the lowest price, followed by the white females, the black females, and finally the black males. This study was conducted with real people but in a fabricated context. However, most of the cases chronicled throughout the remainder of this book detail the real experiences of real people.

A marketplace phenomenon that is getting increasing attention and which is related to location and multicultural consumers is retail redlining.

It occurs when consumers are not served just because they live in particular market areas, typically ones where there is a significantly large population of multicultural consumers. This is a discriminatory practice because the marketer typically does not serve the geographic areas with the same goods and services as in other geographic areas or the marketer charges a higher price for serving those areas. The differential treatment is based on noneconomic criteria such as the racial/ethnic composition of the area, rather than on economic criteria (such as the potential profitability of operating in that area).[26] Consequently, consumers in these redlined areas find themselves vulnerable, because there may be no other retailers willing to serve them or they may be exploited by other, often smaller, retailers who charge higher prices and/or offer inferior goods.

Examples of retail redlining include taxi and food delivery services that refuse to serve certain neighborhoods. This is a discriminatory practice when a marketer does not provide the residents of certain geographic areas with the same goods and services as those who reside elsewhere or when a marketer charges higher prices for serving those areas. The differential treatment is based on the racial or ethnic composition of a particular geographic area, rather than on economic criteria such as the potential profitability of operating there. Though redlining is now illegal in the banking, finance, and insurance industries, it remains a legal practice in the retailing industry. Litigation and lobbying efforts seeking to eradicate redlining in the marketplace are under way. Denver D'Rozario and Jerome D. Williams developed a typology of eight different commonly seen variations of retail redlining and offer a methodology by which this practice can be objectively and empirically tested to determine the presence of retail redlining in given retail areas and neighborhoods.[27] Their methodology involves developing a model based on nine steps that could be used to sort out the merits of the arguments on both sides of any type of retail redlining case. As an example, they illustrate use of the model to assess ongoing charges of retail redlining involving Prince George's county in Maryland. This particular geographic area represents a good example to test the model because there have been consistent allegations against the retailing industry in general, when it compares its retailing portfolio with that of its neighboring counties and cities in the Washington Primary Metropolitan Statistical Area. For example, these allegations suggest that some upscale department stores are not locating in Prince George's County in Maryland but instead locating stores in neighboring Montgomery and Charles counties in Maryland and in Fairfax and Prince William counties in Virginia based on disparities in the demographics of the geographic areas.

One of the ways that consumers of color have tried to get away from discrimination based on treatment in stores or discrimination based on the absence of stores, is by shopping online. Akon Ekpo (2012) and her colleagues write about this phenomenon and suggest that technology such as the Internet (e-commerce) and mobile devices (m-commerce) allow consumers to fulfill their needs in familiar and friendly environments such as their home or workplace. Lindridge, Henderson, and Ekpo (2015) go as far as to describe this as the virtual ethnicity of consumers.[28] However, the same technology that may be used to buy products from marketers with a perception of racial anonymity may also be used as part of the sharing economy to discriminate. For instance, researchers at Harvard Business School have found that Airbnb "requests from guests with distinctively African-American names are roughly 16% less likely to be accepted than identical guests with distinctively White names."[29] As we have written with our coauthor Sophie Evett:

> One of the main differences between in-store and online retailing for consumers of color is that online shopping allows consumers to maintain a certain degree of anonymity in terms of their racial/ethnic background. When a consumer is in a brick and mortar establishment and is interacting with sales and other store personnel, the consumer's race/ethnicity is generally apparent. In one study, May O. Lwin and Jerome Williams suggested that multicultural consumers might find it useful to alter their identities and certain demographic or descriptive information to conceal their racial or ethnic background and thus shield themselves from the type of discriminatory behavior they might encounter in brick and mortar retail environments. For example, online consumers might use the address of a relative who lives in a more ethnically diverse zip code or use a name that sounds less ethnic. In one case, an online job searcher changed one letter in his name, from "Jose" to "Joe" and this had a significant effect on responses to his job applications. This lack of racial anonymity and the fact that a significant percentage of consumers of color feel that they are treated unfairly in stores because of their race underscores the need for brick and mortar retailers to address the problem of marketplace discrimination.[30]

## Promotion and Discrimination in Advertising

Marketers use stereotypes as heuristics in advertising campaigns to convey information in a very short timeframe. Motley, Baker, and Henderson have conducted a great deal of research on the historic depictions that go too far in overgeneralizing and presenting negative characterizations of people of color.[31,32] Many minority customers remember advertising images that promoted grotesque depictions and descriptions of African Americans, Latinos, Asian Americans, and Native Americans. These early advertising images were particularly prevalent between the end of the Civil War (1865) and the passing of Civil Rights Act (1965). Images of African Americans typically revolved around one of several themes: mammy, seductress (Sapphire), smart mouth/loudmouth, Uncle Tom/tragic mulatto, buck, criminal/thief, angry militant, comic buffoons, pickaninny, or poor welfare recipients. Historical depictions of Native Americans have included savages, primitive scalpers, killers, rapists, drunks, gifted with supernatural powers, communing with nature and animals, speaking with one to two syllables, and Indian women as being docile squaws. Latinos have been portrayed as stupid, drunks, comic characters, violent migrants, non-English speaking, low-class servants, round and dirty, seductresses, or strains on the economy/welfare. Asians were depicted as quiet, smart, buffalos with buck teeth, knowing martial arts, docile servants, speaking broken English, dominatrix users, and tech savvy. In more recent times, these hurtful depictions still keep emerging. In 2016, the actress Thandie Newton tweeted to Starbucks regarding their use of a statue for a display of Colombian coffee beans along with a photo of it. Ms. Newton wrote: "Seriously @Starbucks? At the counter—Loin cloth and Safari hat on a black child. Happy New Year circa 19th century." Starbucks issued the following formal statement:

> Serving as a welcoming place for everyone is core to who we are as a company. As we became aware of the offense, we immediately removed the figure from our store. We aim to provide an inclusive environment for all customers and communities in which we serve, and we are working with our partners (employees) to avoid similar incidents from happening in the future. We apologize for the offense caused.[33]

Another modern example is Toyota's ad that ran in 1999 in which the company attempted to contrast the reliability and dependability of the Corolla with a young woman's deadbeat boyfriend who doesn't "get up and go to work in the morning."[34] This attempt at humor fell flat when the ad ran in *Jet* magazine, a weekly magazine targeted at African-American readers. It was viewed by many *Jet* readers as an insulting depiction of African-American males. A letter from the publisher and one from Toyota both ran in a subsequent issue of *Jet* apologizing for the marketing promotion faux pas.

In addition to being depicted in stereotypical ways, people of color are also underrepresented in advertisements. In the early 1960s, black and Latino Americans appeared in only five percent of television commercials. Twenty years later, 26 percent of all television advertising using live actors integrated blacks; however, they appeared principally in large groups and in minor or background roles. Despite greater representation today, people of color continue to be stereotyped in advertising: Blacks as athletes or inner-city dwellers, Latinos with their families, Asian Americans in business settings with technology products. Ross Petty, Anne-Marie Harris, Toni Broaddus, and William Boyd (2003) explained that these stereotyped images can be harmful when they are used to the exclusion of other portrayals because they reinforce cultural racism.[35]

The goal is for marketers to adequately reach and depict multicultural markets without offending a growing group of customers. Williams, Lee,

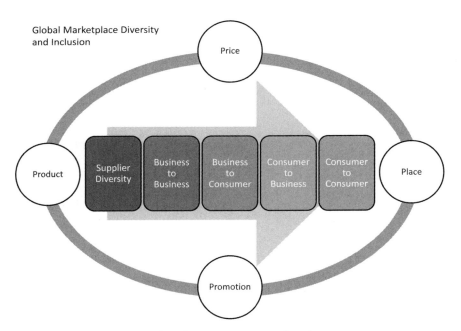

**FIGURE 4.2   Global Marketplace Diversity and Inclusion**

(*Source:* Henderson, Geraldine, and Jerome D. Williams. 2013. "From Exclusion to Inclusion: An Introduction to the Special Issue on Marketplace Diversity and Inclusion." *Journal of Public Policy & Marketing* 32, Special Issue (May): 1–5.)

and Haugtvedt edited an important book entitled *Diversity in Advertising* partly due to the growing importance of the multiethnic consumer and business customer and the fact that firms are increasingly focused on ethnic or multicultural marketing.[36] This book focused on empirical and theoretical work from the fields of marketing and psychology and was a milestone in providing a source of evidence-based research to guide academics and practitioners in developing advertising messages that treat consumers from diverse backgrounds with dignity and respect and that are designed to enhance attitudes toward diversity.

The key to respecting a segment of the marketplace is understanding it. In 1995, R.J. Reynolds believed it was listening and responding to a segment of the market when it developed Uptown cigarettes. Packed filter down to appeal to African-American smokers, the mentholated cigarettes were marketed using a glamorous nightlife image in black magazines. The same year, a small cigarette distributor designed a package for X brand menthol cigarettes using the colors red, green, and black that many people associate with African heritage. In addition, the letter X on the package appeared to connote Spike Lee's movie about Malcolm X.[37] Both companies came under fire for these marketing campaigns. R.J. Reynolds even canceled its plans for Uptown after Louis W. Sullivan, then Secretary of the U.S. Department of Health and Human Services, denounced the marketing of these cigarettes.[38]

A few years later, several tobacco companies including Philip Morris, R.J. Reynolds, Brown & Williamson, Lorillard, and Liggett & Myers found themselves dragged into court by a group of African-American smokers who alleged that they had been encouraged to consume harmful mentholated products in violation of the civil rights laws. The plaintiffs' argument was reminiscent of claims made against alcohol companies for advertising their malt liquor products in low-income predominantly minority neighborhoods in a way that implied their products' elevated alcohol content. In court, the tobacco companies conceded that they intentionally designed certain high-tar, high-nicotine menthol cigarettes to appeal to African-American consumers, that mentholated tobacco products are more harmful to smokers' health than nonmentholated products, and that African Americans account for a significantly greater share of cigarette smokers than their proportion of the U.S. population.

As discussed in Chapter 2, people who experience consumer discrimination react in a variety of ways. One option is to take legal action. The number of lawsuits filed in federal court alleging marketplace discrimination has increased during the past 20 years and companies faced with these charges have financial incentives to avoid the publicity a lawsuit can engender. In the following chapter, we describe the laws protecting consumers from racial discrimination in the marketplace and their effectiveness in doing so.

## Notes

1. Bellware, 2015.
2. Williams, Henderson, and Hakstian, 2014.
3. Selig, 2014.
4. Humphreys, 2014, p. 4.
5. World Bank Social Capital Initiative, 1998.
6. Humphreys, 2014.
7. Glinton, 2015.
8. Alexis, Haines, and Simon, 1980; Alexis, Marcus, and Henderson. 1994.
9. For earlier work in this area, please see Gibson, 1978.
10. Williams, Meyers, and Parker, 2007.
11. Henderson, 2004.
12. Bean, 2001.
13. Kong, 2003; Consumer Ethics Inc., 2013.
14. Hood, 2004.
15. Williams, 2006.
16. Elliott, 1996.
17. Zonyee, 2014.
18. Zax, 2014.
19. See YouTube, https://youtu.be/t4DT3tQqgRM.
20. Albanesius, 2009.
21. Alexis, Haines, and Simon, 1980; Andreasen, 1993.
22. Osorio, Corradini, and Williams, 2013.
23. Mulhern and Williams, 1994.
24. Mulhern, Williams, and Leone, 1998.
25. Ayres, 1991; Ian and Siegelman, 1995.
26. Alwitt and Donley, 1997.
27. D'Rozario and Williams, 2005.
28. Lindridge, Henderson, and Ekpo, 2015; Motley, Carol and Henderson, 2008; Henderson et al., 2013.
29. Edelman, Luca, and Svirsky, 2016; McPhate, 2015.
30. Williams et al., 2015; Lwin and Williams, 2004; Matthews, 2014.
31. Motley, Henderson, and Baker, 2003.

32. Baker, Motley, and Henderson, 2004.
33. Filloon, 2016.
34. See Toyota (1999) in *Jet*. Chicago, IL: Johnson Publishing, January, back cover.
35. Petty et al., 2003.
36. Williams, Lee, and Haugtvedt, 2004.
37. Jackson, 1995, 15A.
38. Schiffman, 1990, B1; Specter, 1990, A4.

## References

Albanesius, Chloe. 2009. "HP Responds to Claim of 'Racist' Webcams." *PC Magazine*, December 22.

Alexis, Marcus and Geraldine R. Henderson. 1994, "The Economic Base of African-American Communities: A Study of Consumption Patterns." *The National Urban League State of Black America*: 51–84.

Alexis, Marcus, George H. Haines, Jr., and Leonard S. Simom. 1980. *Black Consumer Profiles: Food Purchasing in the Inner City*. Ann Arbor, MI: Division of Research, Graduate School of Business Administration, The University of Michigan.

Alwitt, Linda F. and Thomas D. Donley. 1997. "Retail Stores in Poor Urban Neighborhoods." *Journal of Consumer Affairs* 31, no. 1: 139–164.

Andreasen, Alan R. 1993. "Revisiting the Disadvantaged: Old Lessons and New Problems." *Journal of Public Policy & Marketing* 12, no. 2: 270–275.

Ayres, Ian. 1991. "Fair Driving: Gender and Race Discrimination in Retail Car Negotiations." *Harvard Law Review*, 817–872.

Ayres, Ian and Peter Siegelman. 1995. "Race and Gender Discrimination in Bargaining for a New Car." *American Economic Review* 85, no. 3: 304–321.

Baker, Stacey Menzel, Carol M. Motley, and Geraldine Rosa Henderson. 2004. "From Despicable to Collectible: The Evolution of Collective Memories for and the Value of Black Advertising Memorabilia." *Journal of Advertising* 33, no. 3 (Fall): 37–50.

Bean, Linda. 2001. "Retail Racial Profiling: Retrain Staff to Focus on Customer Service." *Diversity Inc.* April 18, 2001. Available at: http://diversityinc.com.

Bellware, Kim. 2015. "NBA Player Alleges Racial Profiling at Jewelry Store." *The Huffington Post,* October 19 (5:49 p.m.).

Consumer Ethics Inc. 2013. "Dillard's." Ethical Shopping: Consumer Ethics, Inc.

D'Rozario, Denver and Jerome D. Williams. 2005. "Retail Redlining: Definition, Theory, Typology and Measurement." *Journal of Macromarketing* 25, no. 2: 175–186.

Edelman, Benjamin, Michael Luca, and Dan Svirsky. 2016. *Racial Discrimination in the Sharing Economy: Evidence from a Field Experiment*. Boston, MA: Harvard Business School.

Ekpo, Akon E. 2012. "Transcending Habitus with IT: Understanding How Marginalized Consumers Use Information Technology." Dissertation, University of Illinois at Chicago.

Ekpo, Akon E., Geraldine Rosa Henderson, and Benet DeBerry Spence. 2013. "Subtle Faces of Discrimination: An Exploratory Study of Microaggressions in the Marketplace." In *Chicago Consumer Culture Community*, ed. Kent Grayson and Albert M. Muniz Jr. Chicago, IL: DePaul University.

Elliott, Stuart. 1996. "A New Campaign for Hanes Hosiery Features the Singer Tina Turner and Her Famous Legs." *The New York Times*, The Media Business: Advertising, September 17. Available at: http://www.nytimes.com/1996/09/17/business/new-campaign-for-hanes-hosiery-features-singer-tina-turner-her-famous-legs.html. Accessed March 7, 2016.

Filloon, Whitney. 2016. "Thandie Newton Puts Starbucks on Blast for Offensive Store Display." *Yahoo!*

Gibson, D. Parke. 1978. *$70 Billion in the Black: America's Black Consumers*. New York, NY: Macmillan Publishing Company.

Glinton, Sonari. 2015. "How an African-American Ad Man Changed the Face of Advertising." National Public Radio, June 15, Morning Edition. Available at: http://www.npr.org/2015/06/15/414561593/how-an-african-american-ad-man-changed-the-face-of-advertisinghttp://www.npr.org/2015/06/15/414561593/how-an-african-american-ad-man-changed-the-face-of-advertising.

Henderson, Geraldine and Jerome D. Williams. 2013. "From Exclusion to Inclusion: An Introduction to the Special Issue on Marketplace Diversity and Inclusion." *Journal of Public Policy & Marketing* 32, no. Special Issue (May): 1–5.

Henderson, Geraldine Rosa, Francisco Guzmán, Lenard Huff, and Carol M. Motley. 2013. "The Ian's Pizza Tribe: Reconceptualizing Cross-Cultural Research in the Digital Age." *Journal of Business Research* 66, no. 3: 283–287.

Henderson, Timothy P. 2004. "Another Potential Solution." February. Available at: http://www.stores.org/archives/chief.asp.

Hood, Ray. 2004. "Perspectives from the Boardroom." In *Symposium on Consumer Racial Profiling*, ed. Jerome D. Williams and Minette Drumwright. Austin, TX.

Humphreys, Jeffrey M. 2014. "The Multicultural Economy 2014." Selig Center for Economic Growth, Terry College of Business, The University of Georgia.

Jackson, Derrick Z. 1995. "Making Money by Any Means Necessary." *Baltimore Sun*, Feb. 7, at 15A.

Kong, Deborah. 2003. "New Lawsuits Draw Attention to Racial Profiling." *The Item*, Monday June 9.

Lindridge, Andrew, Geraldine Rosa Henderson, and Akon E Ekpo. 2015. "(Virtual) Ethnicity, the Internet, and Well-Being." *Marketing Theory* 15, no. 2: 279–285.

Lwin, May O. and Jerome D. Williams. 2004. "A Model Integrating the Multidimensional Developmental Theory of Privacy and Theory of Planned Behavior to Examine Fabrication of Information Online." *Marketing Letters* 14, no. 4: 257–272.

Matthews, Cate. 2014. "He Dropped One Letter in His Name while Applying for Jobs, and the Responses Rolled In." *Huffington Post,* September, 2. Available at: http://www.huffingtonpost.com/2014/09/02/jose-joe-job-discrimination_n_ 5753880.html.

McPhate, Mike. 2015. "Discrimination by Airbnb Hosts Is Widespread, Report Says." *The New York Times. Technology.* December 11.

Motley, Carol and Geraldine Rosa Henderson. 2008. "The Global Hip-Hop Diaspora: Understanding the Culture." *Journal of Business Research* 61, no. 3: 243–253.

Motley, Carol M., Geraldine Rosa Henderson, and Stacey Menzel Baker. 2003. "Exploring Collective Memories Associated With African-American Advertising Memorabilia: The Good, the Bad, and the Ugly." *Journal of Advertising* 32, no. 1 (Spring): 47–57.

Mulhern, Francis J. and Jerome D. Williams. 1994. "A Comparative Analysis of Shopping Behavior in Hispanic and Non-Hispanic Areas." *Journal of Retailing* 70, no. 3: 231–251.

Mulhern, Francis J., Jerome D. Williams, and Robert P. Leone. 1998. "Variability of Brand Price Elasticities Across retail Stores: Ethnic, Income, and Brand Determinants." *Journal of Retailing* 74, no. 3: 427–446.

Osorio, Arturo E., Maria G. Corradini, and Jerome D. Williams. 2013. "Remediating Food Deserts, Food Swamps, and Food Brownfields: Helping the Poor Access Nutritious, Safe, and Affordable Food." *AMS Review* 3, no. 4: 217–231.

Petty, Ross, Anne-Marie Harris, Toni Broaddus, and William Boyd. 2003. "Regulating Target Marketing and other Race-Based Advertising Practices." Lead Article. *University of Michigan Journal of Race and Law* 8: 335–394.

Schiffman, James R. 1990. "After Uptown, Are Some Niches Out?" *Wall Street Journal,* January 22.

Specter, Michael. 1990. "Reynolds Cancels Plans to Market New Cigarette: Uptown Brand Attacked as Aimed at Blacks." *Washington Post,* January 21.

Stoute, Steve. 2011. *Tanning of America: How Hip-Hop Created a Culture That Rewrote the Rules of the New Economy.* New York: Gotham Books.

Williams, Christine L. 2006. *Inside Toyland: Working, Shopping, and Social Inequality.* Berkeley, CA: University of California Press.

Williams, Jerome D. 2014. "A Message to Ponder on for Barney's, Macy's and the NYPD: Shoplifting Comes in All Sizes, Shapes, and Colors." *The Huffington Post,* January 25 (4:01 p.m.). Available at: http://www.huffingtonpost.com/ jerome-d-williams/barneys-shoplifting-racial-profiling_b_4318452.html.

Williams, Jerome D., Geraldine Rosa Henderson, Anne-Marie Hakstian, and Sophia R. Evett. 2015. "Racial and Other Types of Discrimination in Retail Settings: A Liberation Psychology Perspective." In *Race and Retail: Consumer Culture, Economic Citizenship, and Power,* ed. Mia Bay and Anne Fabian. New Brunswick, NJ: Rutgers University Press.

Williams, Jerome D., Wei-Na Lee, and Curtis P. Haugtvedt, eds. 2004. *Diversity in Advertising: Broadening the Scope of Research Directions*. Hillsdale, NJ: Lawrence Erlbaum Associates, Inc.

Williams, Jerome D., Yuvay Jeanine Meyers, and D. A. Parker. 2007. "Consumer Racial Profiling & Skin-Tone." Paper presented at the 12th Cross-Cultural Research Conference, Honolulu, Hawaii, December 14.

World Bank Social Capital Initiative. 1998. "The Initiative on Defining, Monitoring and Measuring Social Capital: Text of Proposals Approved for Funding." Washington, DC: The World Bank, Social Development Family, Environmentally and Socially Sustainable Development Network, June.

Zax, David. 2014. "Forget Five-Blade Razors: Bevel is a Better Shave for Black Men." *Fast Company*, February 14. Available at: http://www.fastcompany.com/ 3026432/most-creative-people/forget-five-blade-razors-bevel-is-a-better-shave-for-black-men. Accessed July 6, 2015.

Zonyee, Dominique. 2014. "This Day in Black History: March 9, 1996: Tina Turner Debuted as Model and Inspiration for Hanes Silk Reflections Hosiery." Bet.com March 9. Available at: http://www.bet.com/news/national/2014/03/09/ this-day-in-black-history-march-9-1996.html. Accessed March 7, 2016.

# Chapter 5

# Legal Protection

*Negro citizens, North and South, who saw in the Thirteenth Amendment a promise of freedom—freedom to go and come at pleasure and to buy and sell when they please—would be left with a mere paper guarantee if Congress were powerless to assure that a dollar in the hands of a Negro will purchase the same thing as a dollar in the hands of a white man.*
                                        —U.S. Supreme Court Justice Potter Stewart[1]

*I am a White man. I was born and raised in the suburbs and I have never experienced anything like the plaintiffs described. In fact, no one on the jury had been in a similar situation as those gentlemen . . . If there had been one or two Black men on the jury, they might have been able to relate to the plaintiffs' perception of what happened. No one on the jury was a peer of those plaintiffs.*[2]

On July 20, 1998, Whitney Joseph, her two sons, and her friend, Nancy Daddato, went to Yankee Stadium to see a Yankees game. Before the game, they decided to have dinner at the Stadium Club. Ms. Joseph, who is African American, was stopped at the entrance of the restaurant and told that the tank top she was wearing violated the Stadium Club's dress code. She was refused entry until she returned to her car and changed into a T-shirt. Ms. Daddato, who is white and also wore a "tank top" that day, was admitted to the Stadium Club without incident. Although the club's dress code expressly prohibits "tank tops," Ms. Joseph and her friend noticed that nonminority women inside the club were wearing tank tops and clothing "skimpier" than hers, including a "spaghetti strap top," a "midriff, no sleeve top," and a "backless, no sleeve top."[3]

   In general, to prove racial discrimination in court, a plaintiff must present evidence that she was treated differently than other "similarly situated" individuals who are not of her race or ethnicity. In other words, the judge or jury must conduct a comparison. In discrimination cases that arise in the employment context, an employee of color can compare herself to coworkers who perform the same type of work and are supervised by the same individual, for example. In the marketplace setting, finding a "comparator" is challenging. Therefore, it is often impossible to prove that a store clerk or security guard would have treated a white person differently than they treated the plaintiff. However, in her lawsuit against the Stadium Club, Ms. Joseph had a "comparator" so she was able to prove that she was treated differently than her white friend who was "similarly situated": both were wearing tank tops, both attempted to enter the club, but only Ms. Joseph was refused entry. Ms. Joseph's case is an unusual one because she could show that someone who was identical to her in every way except for her race was allowed to enter the establishment.

In the first part of this chapter, the laws that provide protection to consumers of color are explained in greater detail.

## Civil Rights Act of 1866

The Civil Rights Act of 1866 prohibits race discrimination in "making and enforcing contracts" including commercial transactions. Specifically, Section 1981 of the Act defines "the right to make and enforce contracts" as "the right to the enjoyment of all benefits, privileges, terms, and conditions of the contractual relationship."[4] The U.S. Supreme Court has described the purpose of Section 1981 as follows: "to remove the impediment of discrimination from a minority citizen's ability to participate fully and equally in the marketplace."[5] The law's language was clearly designed to ensure that all consumers should receive the same level of transaction experience.

To date, courts have narrowly interpreted the scope of Section 1981 by focusing on conduct that prevented the formation of the contract as opposed to conduct affecting the nature or quality of the contractual relationship. Many federal courts insist that Section 1981 plaintiffs must produce evidence that the company's employees completely denied—rather than merely degrading—the goods or services the plaintiff sought to purchase. Therefore, if the plaintiff was ultimately able to purchase the goods or services s/he sought, his/her claim is likely to be dismissed during a pretrial motion prior to the presentation of evidence to a jury. When they dismiss these cases prematurely, courts fail to acknowledge the subtle nature of modern discrimination.

As described in Chapter 3, black and brown consumers often receive substandard service. Examples abound where customers are told "If you want to be served, you will go to the section where we take you" or yelled at and told to go back to the end of the line. Sales clerks and store security officers harass customers of color by stopping them shortly after they enter the store or after they pay, treating them rudely and confronting them with racial epithets. Despite the poor treatment, in most cases, the customers are not prevented from completing their purchases. Because of that, most courts conclude that these customers' rights have not been violated. A typical finding is that "mere delay, even coupled with discourteous treatment, poor service, or racial animus, is insufficient to sustain a Section 1981 claim."[6] In other words, the courts often reject the notion that consumers of all races have the right to a harassment-free shopping experience. Perhaps most judges are unable to recognize the legal harms articulated in a consumer discrimination lawsuit because, as white individuals, they have not experienced this type of treatment.

Nevertheless, some courts have made exceptions to the general "rule" that a Section 1981 claim must fail if the plaintiff ultimately managed to complete his or her purchase. One such exception arises in cases where retailers imposed additional conditions on plaintiffs that were not imposed on white customers. For example, in some cases, the defendants required African-American customers to prepay for their purchases, whereas white customers were not required to do so. In the example presented at the beginning of this chapter, the court that heard Ms. Joseph's case against the Stadium Club found that her rights were violated when the Stadium Club placed additional conditions on Ms. Joseph that it did not place on Ms. Daddato.

In addition, some courts have developed a different standard for proving consumer discrimination. For example, in Minnesota, the case law has evolved so that probable cause that discrimination occurred can be established when the evidence shows "treatment so at variance with what would reasonably be anticipated absent discrimination that discrimination is the probable explanation."[7] In the federal courts, some appeals courts have adopted a standard similar to Minnesota's "so at variance" standard that is more appropriate for evaluating whether customers' rights were violated because of the unique nature of marketplace exchanges between customers and store personnel. Under that standard, plaintiffs have the option of proving that they "received services in a markedly hostile manner and in a manner that a reasonable person would find objectively discriminatory."[8]

## Federal Public Accommodations Law

Title II of the Civil Rights Act of 1964 prohibits discrimination in places of public accommodation. It protects consumers of color by providing a guarantee that all persons are "entitled to the full and equal enjoyment of the goods, services, facilities, privileges, advantages, and accommodations of any place of public accommodation . . . on the ground of race, color, religion, or national origin."[9] It promises to "eliminate the unfairness, humiliation, and insult of racial discrimination in facilities which purport to serve the general public."[10]

Although Title II does not require a plaintiff to prove intentional discrimination which is often extremely difficult, there are some limits to the protection that Title II provides. First, it covers only those people who were discriminated against in certain "places of public accommodation." Lodging establishments, restaurants, and places of entertainment are specifically listed in the statute. Most consumers and their lawyers are surprised to discover that retail stores are not considered places of public accommodation under Title II. In a 1968 decision, the Supreme Court explained its belief that: "Retail stores, food markets, and the like were excluded from [Title II] for the policy reason [that] there was little, if any, discrimination in the operation of them."[11] Some legal commentators argue that Title II should be amended to include all retail establishments among the list of covered entities especially because of their coverage in the Americans with Disabilities Act as well as many state public accommodations laws.

Title II also requires a plaintiff to notify the appropriate state or local civil rights agency of his/her complaint before filing suit. In many states, consumers must bring a complaint to the attention of the state agency no later than 180 days after the discriminatory incident occurred. Because many plaintiffs are not aware of this notification requirement, they fail to meet the deadline which results in the dismissal of their claims. The statute's usefulness to consumer discrimination plaintiffs is further limited because it prevents plaintiffs from seeking monetary damages. Plaintiffs may only obtain equitable or declaratory relief. Equitable relief includes the issuance of a court order prohibiting a defendant from engaging in discriminatory conduct. Declaratory relief is an official declaration of a court that determines the rights of the parties without ordering anything be done or awarding damages.

## State Public Accommodations Laws

Most states have enacted their own public accommodation laws, and most include retail stores among the businesses that are required to follow the law. Only Alabama, Georgia, Mississippi, North Carolina, and Texas do not have state laws that protect residents of color when they are treated unfairly in businesses and other places of public accommodation. Specific state agencies are charged with enforcing the public accommodations law. These agencies typically have the authority to process complaints of discrimination by investigating them and attempting to resolve them through a negotiated settlement. A 2004 study of state public accommodations laws revealed that approximately 50 percent of the complaints are dismissed based on a finding that there is no probable cause to believe that the individual was discriminated against and 25 percent of the complaints are settled.[12] Generally, settlement agreements require the company to provide the complainant with access to the establishment and compensate the complainant with monetary damages.

Complainants may appeal agency decisions in state court to enforce the agency's orders. However, very few public accommodations cases reach the courts in part because of the common perception that plaintiffs do not fare well in state courts. For those cases that are brought to court, civil and criminal remedies are available. Civil remedies consist of compensatory damages, injunctive relief, punitive damages, and attorney's fees. In some states, compensatory damages include damages for loss of dignity, humiliation, and embarrassment. Many states set minimum and maximum damage limitations and the amount plaintiffs may recover is often negligible. Civil penalties range from $25 to $100 in Connecticut, and from $10,000 to $50,000 in Illinois. Criminal penalties include fines ranging from $10 to $50,000 and imprisonment from 30 days to one year, but state prosecutors rarely bring criminal suits in public accommodations cases.

In theory, the state public accommodations statutes provide relief for consumers by facilitating the negotiation of settlements with business establishments. In practice, very few complaints are filed with state agencies, even fewer cases are litigated, and it is unclear whether the emphasis on conciliation effectively reduces discrimination in places of public accommodation. Some legal commentators have characterized state statutes as ineffective in terms of addressing systemic problems. Although settlements may efficiently resolve individual claims to the parties' satisfaction in some cases, they also allow defendants to shield themselves from greater scrutiny and bad publicity. In addition, potentially valid claims are not decided by a court which prevents the establishment of case precedent having the force of law.

Although legal protections exist, enforcing the rights of consumers of color can be challenging. Beyond the hurdles they must clear in order to present their cases in court, perhaps the greatest difficulty for plaintiffs is in demonstrating the harm that they experience. Because judges often prevent cases from moving forward, plaintiffs do not often have the opportunity to describe the damage that is associated with consumer discrimination. It is when juries are allowed to hear cases that people of color can publicly expose the harassment they endure in the marketplace. How jurors perceive plaintiffs' experiences with consumer discrimination is not well understood.

## Juror Perceptions of Cases of Retail Discrimination

We know that evidence presented during a trial is evaluated differently by jurors of different races. Many studies of criminal cases (e.g., Bowers et al., 2001) have demonstrated that white jurors are more likely to judge black defendants than white defendants guilty and to impose more severe punishment on black than white defendants.[13] Only one study has examined people's perceptions of a case of consumer discrimination.[14] The researchers conducted a large online survey of more than 1,000 participants from a broad range of geographic, age, racial, and socioeconomic backgrounds. The goal was to test two theoretical perspectives: first, Robinson's theory of perceptual segregation that states that different life experiences of white Americans and people of color lead to differential perceptions of racial situations; second, Martin-Baro's theory of liberation psychology, which includes the idea of conscientization, which is that a person's awareness of oppression increases his or her empathy for members of the oppressed group.[15]

The participants in the study read a retail discrimination scenario based on actual events that involved a shopper who was identified as either African American, Latina, or Asian American and who was attempting to purchase an expensive watch locked in a display case. In the scenario, the shopper received poor customer service: the sales associate treated her with disrespect, required her to wait a long time, and suspected her of theft and inability to pay. In addition, the shopper in the scenario was treated differently than a white customer. First, the results showed that participants of color had higher levels of perceived societal discrimination compared with white participants which means that they perceived more societal discrimination and suggests that participants of color and white participants had different perspectives of societal reality. Consistent with this different perception, white participants were more likely than participants of color to suggest that the customer should respond to the incident by simply leaving the store and come back and shop at another time. This customer response was offered as an alternative to complaining to the store manager about the unfair treatment and reporting the incident to outside agencies.

The more interesting findings related to the responses of participants— of all races—who had higher levels of perceived societal discrimination.

These participants were angrier about the unfair treatment in the scenario and more likely to believe that racial discrimination was its cause than the participants with lower levels of perceived societal discrimination. In addition, they were more likely to agree that the customer should take both internal and external action rather than leave the store and return later. Taking internal action includes complaining to the manager or to other store employees. A customer who takes external action might talk to friends about the incident, report it to the Better Business Bureau, or seek compensation with the assistance of a lawyer.

This work suggests that it is important to understand that customers have different perceptions of the social reality of discrimination which is only partly due to their own race. These different perceptions are associated with different ideas about what are appropriate remedies for an individual who has been treated unfairly. Although some customers believe that consumer discrimination is "not a big deal" and that victims should simply come back to the store later, others clearly feel that such incidents are serious enough to warrant taking action.

Other preliminary research about perceptions of consumer discrimination has begun to explore what factors jurors consider most important in deciding these cases. In the context of criminal cases, studies have explored whether the racial composition of juries affects the way in which they evaluate evidence presented during a trial. In fact, results of these studies suggest that the evidence may be evaluated differently by racially heterogeneous and racially homogeneous juries. Samuel Sommers (2006) demonstrated that, compared with all-white juries, racially mixed juries considered more evidence, deliberated longer, and were more likely to consider racism in evaluating a criminal case in which an African-American defendant was being prosecuted for having committed a sexual assault.[16] One question, among many, that needs to be studied is whether juries behave similarly when they are evaluating the evidence presented in a civil case rather than a criminal one.

In one mock jury study, the researchers attempted to answer that question by examining whether the racial composition of the juries and/or the type of legal claim they analyzed influenced the jury deliberations in a case of retail discrimination. For another study, the researcher interviewed people who were involved in actual consumer discrimination trials. Her analysis of the interviews allowed her to gain insight into jurors' perceptions of this type of discrimination. Both of these studies are described later. It is important to note that this research must be followed up by additional studies to confirm or disprove these early findings.

## Jury Research on Marketplace Discrimination

The first study required participants to serve as "mock jurors" on one of 20 juries, half of which had black participants and half that did not. All participants read about a case involving an incident that took place in a department store. The case summary was based on an actual lawsuit filed by an African-American woman who won $1.2 million against Dillard's Department Store. That case was described earlier in Chapter 3 (*Hampton v. Dillard Dept. Stores, Inc.*).[17] After reading the case materials, the participants were given jury instructions in which the plaintiff's claim against the department store was identified as either a race discrimination claim or an unlawful detention claim. The elements of the legal claim were provided to help the participants analyze the case. Prior to deliberating with their fellow mock jurors, the participants completed a brief survey indicating their individual verdicts in favor of the plaintiff, or the defendant. They were also asked to indicate which facts they found most important in making their decision. Then, in groups of six or eight, the mock jurors deliberated until they reached a decision. Juries that found in favor of the plaintiff were asked to determine the amount of damages to be awarded.

Racially mixed juries decided in favor of the plaintiff much more often (at least 50% of the time) than juries without black jurors. They also awarded more money to the plaintiff than those without black jurors (see Figures 5.2 and 5.3). Based on anecdotal evidence that juries may be more willing to find in favor of a plaintiff who alleges that she was wrongfully detained rather than one who claims race discrimination, the researchers examined whether the type of claim would influence jury outcomes. In fact, juries with black jurors were more favorable toward the plaintiff when her case was based on racial discrimination whereas those without black jurors were more favorable toward the plaintiff when she made a claim based on unlawful detention (see Figure 5.1). The nature of the claim also influenced the number of facts discussed by each jury. Participants discussed many more facts when they analyzed her claim of unlawful detention rather than her claim of racial discrimination. The racially mixed juries in which the plaintiff made a racial discrimination claim discussed the smallest number of facts, which is inconsistent with the findings of Sommers (2006).[18] Nevertheless, these juries were most likely to find for the plaintiff. It is possible that they reached a verdict easily because they were in agreement with each other and did not need to persuade dissenting jurors to change their position.

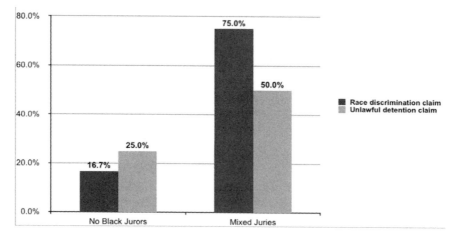

**FIGURE 5.1  Jury Decision in Favor of the Plaintiff**

(*Source:* Evett, S. R., L. Burk, and A.-M. Hakstian. 2012. "Making the Case for Retail Discrimination: A Mock Jury Investigation." Eastern Psychological Association, Annual Conference, Pittsburgh, PA, March 2–4, 2012.)

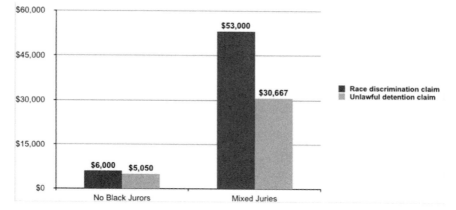

**FIGURE 5.2  Jury Award for the Plaintiff—Compensatory Damages**

(*Source:* Evett, S. R., L. Burk, and A.-M. Hakstian. 2012. "Making the Case for Retail Discrimination: A Mock Jury Investigation." Eastern Psychological Association, Annual Conference, Pittsburgh, PA, March 2–4, 2012.)

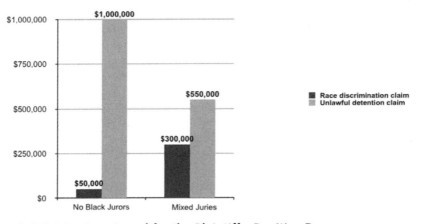

**FIGURE 5.3    Jury Award for the Plaintiff—Punitive Damages**

(*Source:* Evett, S. R., L. Burk, and A.-M. Hakstian. 2012. "Making the Case for Retail Discrimination: A Mock Jury Investigation." Eastern Psychological Association, Annual Conference, Pittsburgh, PA, March 2–4, 2012.)

Lastly, the participants' pre- and post-deliberation decisions were compared to determine whether their initial opinion, in favor of the plaintiff or the defendant, changed after jury deliberation. In fact, 65 percent of all participants did not change their decisions regardless of the racial composition of the jury. Of those participants who changed their decision, the direction of change depended on the racial composition of the jury. That is, participants who served on racially mixed juries were about as likely to amend their decisions to favor the plaintiff (15.9%) as in favor of the defendant (19.0%). In contrast, on juries without black jurors, the participants were much more likely to alter their decisions in favor of the defendant (27.4%) than the plaintiff (6.5%) (see Figure 5.4).

These preliminary results indicate that the concern of plaintiffs' lawyers about "playing the race card" may be legitimate when blacks are not represented on the jury. That is, these juries were more likely to decide against the black plaintiff and were successful at changing the minds of those jurors who initially supported her. The implications are serious because blacks are disproportionately absent from the nation's juries. Those individuals who bring suit against businesses must persuade judges and juries that consumer discrimination causes real harm to its victims. The difficulty of conveying that harm and the fear that their experiences will not be taken seriously may explain why potential plaintiffs avoid pursuing offending stores.

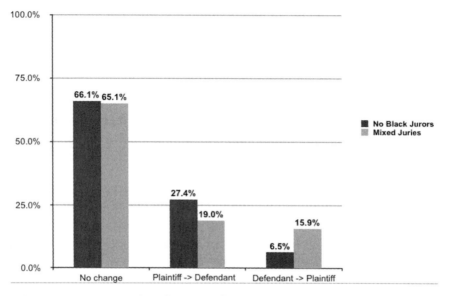

**FIGURE 5.4   Jurors Who Changed After Deliberation**

(*Source:* Evett, S. R., L. Burk, and A.-M. Hakstian. 2012. "Making the Case for Retail Discrimination: A Mock Jury Investigation." Eastern Psychological Association, Annual Conference, Pittsburgh, PA, March 2–4, 2012.)

The second study was conducted to try to answer that very question: are the experiences of African-American customers taken seriously by jurors? Using an exploratory research design, nine individuals were interviewed regarding three different consumer discrimination cases that were actually tried in court in 2007. Four of the interviewees had served as jurors in one of the trials (two white men and two white women), two had been the plaintiffs (two black men), and three were lawyers who represented the plaintiffs in marketplace discrimination cases (three white men). The defendants were a national pharmacy chain (two lawsuits) and a national restaurant chain (one lawsuit) located in different parts of the country.

The jurors were asked what they saw and heard at trial, how they assessed the appearance and demeanor of the plaintiffs, the defendants, and the other witnesses, what testimony they considered most salient and influential in their decision-making process, and what were their reasons for believing—or not—the plaintiffs' version of the facts. They were also asked whether they discussed the racial aspect of the plaintiffs' claims during deliberations and whether they believed that the absence of black jurors made a difference in terms of the nature, the content, and the outcome of the deliberations.

Three main themes emerged from these interviews. First, in assessing the credibility of the witnesses, the jurors focused on the plaintiff's motive in filing suit and whether the plaintiff appeared to be opportunistic. For example, one juror stated: "We believed the plaintiffs because they weren't just doing this [the lawsuit] for the money. They were doing it for the principle . . . They weren't trying to make a buck because they were all pretty comfortable and stable. Some of them owned businesses. Most had college educations." The jurors also discussed the fact that they did not believe that the plaintiffs suffered any damages as a result of the incident of consumer discrimination. For example, one juror summarized his thoughts this way: "Saying that they would be affected by this for the rest of their life—we didn't believe that. Some of [the plaintiffs] talked about loss of sleep and loss of appetite. I really don't think that happened."[19] The third theme was that the plaintiffs should take responsibility for their actions. Even in the case where the jury found in favor of the plaintiffs, the jurors believed the plaintiff bore some responsibility. One of the jurors described their deliberation as follows:

> So, our verdict was not for the plaintiffs' pain and suffering. We had to give two amounts: one for pain and suffering and the other to punish the defendant. We gave the plaintiffs $5,000 each for their pain and suffering. This was way less than we gave them as the restaurant's punishment [which was $35,000 each]. Our verdict reflected what we kind of thought about the plaintiffs. We thought they were entitled to something. This is because their dinner was ruined. Some of them didn't even get to eat. The birthday party was ruined, I suppose. We thought there were some things the restaurant had done wrong. But, we also thought that some of the plaintiffs were blowing some things out of proportion. None of the plaintiffs went and complained while dinner was going on. That was the only thing we [the jurors] thought: 'If they were hurt so bad by this, why didn't they leave?' Most people will get up and walk out. . . . Well, I guess when you have a party with that many people, where are you going to go if you walk out?[20]

One conclusion that can be drawn from this study is that the jurors were pro-business. This is consistent with other research findings that jurors serving on civil juries are more pro-business than expected. Valerie Hans (1998) found that more than 80 percent of jurors believed there are too many frivolous lawsuits and fewer than 30 percent believe that plaintiffs have legitimate grievances. In addition, based on her findings, Hans concluded that Americans see lawsuits against corporations as "attacks on authority and threats to the integrity and the strength of the business community."[21]

The study's findings raise questions about whether the jurors' references to money-hungry plaintiffs and their lawyers are merely smokescreens. Were the discussions about the plaintiffs' lack of harm and their need to take personal responsibility for their actions providing "cover" for jurors to avoid addressing the allegations of racial discrimination? Interestingly, the only jury that found in favor of the plaintiffs did so because the white manager on duty corroborated the plaintiffs' story. It is possible that white jurors—and possibly white judges—lack the necessary experience with which to judge the veracity of a black witness' assertions. In fact, several jurors conveyed the difficulty of relating to the plaintiffs' experiences since it was so different from their own.

Although these two studies provide a glimpse of insight into jurors' impressions about marketplace discrimination, more research must be conducted to understand differences in perceptions across racial and ethnic lines. Despite the challenges of conveying their experiences as consumers, more and more individuals have the courage to voice their complaints and file suit. In many cases, the challenge is compounded by the fact that plaintiffs are accused of shoplifting and treated as criminal suspects. Many shoppers of color believe they are profiled by sales associates and store security personnel in the same way they are targeted by police. As such, the phrase "shopping while black" has been used to describe the practice of following, stopping, questioning, investigating, detaining, and/or arresting customers of color based on their race or ethnicity rather than their behavior. In the next chapter, the issue of "consumer racial profiling" and criminal suspicion is further discussed.

## Notes

1. *Jones v. Alfred H. Mayer Co.*, 392 U.S. 409 (1968).
2. Hakstian, 2007.
3. *Joseph v. New York Yankees Partnership*, 2000 U.S.Dist. LEXIS 15417.
4. 42 U.S.C. §1981.
5. *Patterson v. McLean Credit Union*, 491 U.S. 164 (1989).
6. Harris, 2003.
7. *City of Minneapolis v. Richardson*, 239 N.W.2d 197, 202 (Minn. 1976).
8. *Christian v. Wal-Mart Stores*, 252 F.3d 862, 871 (2001).

9. Civil Rights Act of 1964, Pub.L. 88–352, 78 Stat. 241, enacted July 2, 1964.

10. *Daniel v. Paul*, 395 U.S. 298, 307–08, 89 S.Ct. 1697, 1702, 23 L.Ed.2d 318 (1969).

11. *Newman v. Piggie Park Enterprises, Inc.*, 377 F.2d 433 (4th Cir. 1967), 390 U.S. 400 (1968).

12. Harris, 2006.

13. Bowers, Steiner, Sandys, 2001.

14. Evett et al., 2013.

15. Martin-Baro, 1994.

16. Sommers, 2006.

17. *Hampton v. Dillard Dept. Stores, Inc.*, 247 F.3d 1091 (Court of Appeals, 10th Circuit, 2001).

18. Sommers, 2006.

19. Hakstian, 2007.

20. Ibid.

21. Hans, 2000.

## References

Bowers, W. J., B. D. Steiner, and M. Sandys. 2001. "Death Sentencing in Black and White: An Empirical Analysis of the Role of Jurors' Race and Jury Racial Composition." *Journal of Criminal Justice Constitutional Law* 3, no. 1: 171–274.

*Christian v. Wal-Mart Stores, Inc.*, 252 F.3d 862, Court of Appeals, 6th Circuit (2001).

*City of Minneapolis v. Richardson*, 239 N.W. 2d 197, Minn. Supreme Court (1976).

Civil Rights Act of 1964, Pub.L. 88352, 78 Stat. 241 (1964).

*Daniel v. Paul*, 395 U.S. 298, U.S. Supreme Court (1969).

Evett, Sophia R., Anne-Marie Hakstian, Jerome D. Williams, and Geraldine R. Henderson. 2013. "What's Race Got to Do with It? Responses to Consumer Discrimination." *Analyses of Social Issues and Public Policy* 13, no. 1: 165–185.

Hakstian, Anne-Marie. 2007. "*Trading Places? Juror Perceptions of Consumer Discrimination Cases, Final paper, Qualitative Analysis (CJ G260).*" Boston, MA: Northeastern University.

*Hampton v. Dillard Dept. Stores, Inc.*, 247 F.3d 1091 (Court of Appeals, 10th Circuit (2001).

Hans, Valerie P. 1998. "Illusions and Realities in Jurors' Treatment of Corporate Defendants." DePaul Law Review 48: 327–353.

Hans, Valerie P. 2000. *Business on Trial: The Civil Jury and Corporate Responsibility*. New Haven, CT: Yale University Press.

Harris, Anne-Marie G. 2003. "Shopping While Black: Applying 42 U.S.C. § 1981 to Cases of Consumer Racial Profiling." *Boston College Third World Law Journal* 23, no. 1: 1–57.

Harris, Anne-Marie G. 2006. "A Survey of Federal and State Public Accommodations Statutes: Evaluating Their Effectiveness in Cases of Retail Discrimination." *Virginia Journal of Social Policy and the Law* 13, no. 2: 331–395.

*Jones v. Alfred H. Mayer Co.*, 392 U.S. 409, U.S. Supreme Court (1968).

*Joseph v. New York Yankees Partnership*, No. 00 Civ. 2275(SHS), 2000 WL 1559019 (S.D.N.Y. Oct. 19, 2000).

Martin-Baro, I. 1994. *Writings for a Liberation Psychology*. Cambridge, MA: Harvard University Press.

*Newman v. Piggie Park Enterprises, Inc.*, 377 F.2d 433 (4th Cir. 1967), 390 U.S. 400, U.S. Supreme Court (1968).

*Patterson v. McLean Credit Union*, 491 U.S. 164 (1989).

Sommers, Samuel R. 2006. "On Racial Diversity and Group Decision Making: Identifying Multiple Effects of Racial Composition on jury Deliberations." *Journal of Personality and Social Psychology* 90, no. 4: 597–612.

# Chapter 6

# Consumer Racial Profiling and Shoplifting

*In a society in which shoplifting and vandalism are rife, merchants have a legitimate interest in observing customers' movements. So long as watchfulness neither crosses the line into harassment nor impairs a shopper's ability to make and complete purchases, it is not a violation of [the law].*
— Judge Bruce M. Selya, U.S. Court of Appeals for the First Circuit[1]

Lloyd Morrison, a financial analyst, and his six-year-old son were shopping for children's clothes at a Bloomingdale's department store in Hackensack, New Jersey, on February 10, 1996. Although Mr. Morrison did not exhibit any suspicious behavior, he and his son were suddenly surrounded by security guards who accused them of stealing children's pants. Mr. Morrison was threatened with arrest when he refused to follow the guards to a back room so he reluctantly did so. His son was crying and was very upset.

Mr. Morrison was frisked but the guards found nothing. They demanded that he pull down his pants. Again, they found nothing. Next, they demanded that Mr. Morrison pull down his son's pants. He initially refused but eventually complied after again being threatened with arrest. Once again, the guards found no evidence of stealing. When Mr. Morrison filed suit against Bloomingdale's,[2] his lawyer explained: "He feels frustrated that as a father he couldn't protect his son. Now, when they go shopping, his son is very concerned that they don't touch any clothes. The child tells his father they could get in trouble if they do."[3]

Why did the store security officers believe that Mr. Morrison and his son had stolen merchandise? Did they really think they were protecting the store from criminals? Because racial profiling is the symptom of broader societal ills, it appears in many different contexts including retail stores. As was explained in Chapter 2, the term "consumer racial profiling" describes the type of discrimination that typically occurs when security officers or other store personnel target shoppers of color for additional surveillance based on the race or ethnicity of those individuals rather than their behavior.

Racial profiling is thought to occur in part because of the unconscious biases of those who are empowered to enforce store policies. Like their counterparts who serve on a police force, private security officers are charged with the responsibility of deciding which individuals to stop and search. Due to the nature of their work, they make important decisions without a great deal of direct supervision. Therefore, in addition to other factors that influence their decision-making, the biases of store personnel may play a role in determining what actions they take. As was discussed in Chapters 2 and 3, those biases are influenced by the prevalence of stereotypes in our society that depict black and brown Americans as criminals. Much of the research suggests that there is a bias toward people of color that associates them with lawbreaking and specifically shoplifting.[4] Store employees may not even be aware that they view shoppers of color as thieves even while treating them as such. Because the phenomenon of consumer racial profiling intersects with the perception of people of color as criminals in general and thieves in particular, the focus of this chapter is on shoplifting.

Shoplifting generally refers to the theft of merchandise from a store or place of business. From a legal perspective, it is a type of larceny, which simply means taking the property of someone else without their permission and with the intent to permanently deprive the owner of the property taken. The crime of shoplifting has been officially recognized since 1965 when the FBI reported that it was the fastest-growing form of larceny in the previous five-year period. In the following decade, advances in technology began to make their way into the marketplace. Specifically, the invention of security tags meant that the subjective observations of sales associates and security personnel were replaced with an objective means of establishing probable cause that could be used to search and arrest shoplifters. Of course, these security measures drove shoplifters to invent new ways to steal. For example, since many of the security tags utilized magnets or radio frequencies to alert employees of impending theft, "booster bags" were lined with metal to deflect electronic technology and circumvent the new security measures.[5]

Each year, thousands of retail customers and employees are caught stealing from stores. Both shoplifting and employee theft account for approximately 30 to 40% of retail losses.[6] According to the 2015 National Retail Security Survey conducted by the National Retail Federation and Dr. Richard

Hollinger of the University of Florida, inventory "shrink" amounted to $44 billion in losses for retailers in 2014. Inventory shrink that year included shoplifting (38%), employee theft (34.5%), administrative and paperwork errors (16.5%), and vendor fraud or error (6.8%).[7] Among the costs associated with theft are the time and effort made by loss prevention employees in dealing with a shoplifter from the apprehension itself, contacting the police, and completing paperwork; the legal fees for civil demands and prosecution of shoplifters; as well as losses that result from stolen goods that are not recovered and those that are recovered but can no longer be sold due to their poor condition or other reasons.[8]

Because the protection of property is a legitimate concern, deterring theft is an important activity for all business owners. Various measures can be taken to reduce the incidence of theft crimes. In addition to hiring licensed loss prevention officers, businesses use surveillance and security systems such as hidden cameras (CCTV), video recording devices such as DVRs (Digital Video Recorders), sensor tags, and barcode sensors and other security equipment, as well as random bag checks and environmental design. Merchants also have legal tools at their disposal.

Merchant detention statutes allow store-owners to detain and search customers who they have probable cause to believe have shoplifted. However, shoppers who are suspected of shoplifting may be detained only if the detention is conducted in a reasonable manner and for a reasonable length of time. In most states, merchants have the right to seek payment from an individual who shoplifted. Civil recovery statutes prescribe the way in which merchants must proceed to obtain civil restitution of items that were stolen by customers. For example, merchants have the right to send letters demanding civil damages from shoplifters. The amount demanded varies based on state law and the amount of the goods stolen. Merchants also may refer individuals to the police for prosecution since shoplifting is a misdemeanor crime (larceny).

While merchants may legitimately pursue shoplifters, problems arise when store employees target customers of color as a strategy for apprehending shoplifters. It is an individual's behavior that should raise suspicion and trigger surveillance by store security. Although some have argued that profiling customers helps merchants to reduce losses from shoplifting, the practice of consumer racial profiling is ineffective in that regard. This argument is based on the assumption that apprehension statistics are representative of who shoplifts. However, as Dean Dabney, Richard Hollinger, and Laura Dugan explain: "It may be that black individuals are disproportionately represented in the apprehension statistics not because they shoplift more often than whites, but because they draw more attention from security personnel."

Unfortunately, besides arrest and conviction rates, there is not a great deal of information about the rates of criminal activity across race and ethnicity. Official data only tell part of the story because a very small proportion of shoplifters are referred to law enforcement and even fewer are formally charged. Hollinger and Davis (2002) report that "retailers participating in a national survey indicated that they prosecute a paltry 24% of all shoplifters that they apprehend."[9] This is partly due to the availability of civil recovery as a means of handling shoplifting cases.

One observational study conducted in a retail drugstore examined who shoplifts and how. The researchers used closed circuit, high-resolution, color television cameras to monitor the 7,500 square feet of retail space for a 12-month period. They observed 1,243 shoppers from entry into the store to their exit from the store and determined that 105 (8.5%) were clearly seen committing an act of merchandise theft and concealment while shopping in the drug store. The researchers found that nonwhites were no more likely to shoplift than were whites. To the contrary, two behavioral variables were important in predicting shoplifting. Specifically, those shoppers who exhibited "cues of shoplifting" ("scanning" the store, tampering with products, displaying awareness of security countermeasures, or sampling products) were 6.25 times more likely to shoplift than those who did not. Also, those who exited the store without having made a purchase were almost six times more likely to have stolen merchandise than those who purchased something. These results show that the stereotypical assumption that blacks and Latinos steal more than whites is incorrect.

In terms of public opinion, a study conducted by Shaun L. Gabbidon and George E. Higgins (2011) revealed that respondents did not believe that racial profiling is an effective method for identifying shoplifters. The practice of profiling customers based on their race or ethnicity undermines customer loyalty to the establishment and hurts a retailer's bottom line. Like police administrators and other public policy officials who have taken steps to address the perception of disparate traffic enforcement, it is critical for business leaders to acknowledge the likelihood that customers of color are sometimes treated differently than their white counterparts. Best practices for addressing consumer racial profiling as well as other forms of marketplace discrimination are discussed in greater detail in Chapters 10 and 11.

Most retail establishments have developed protocols for determining when a customer should be watched or searched and to guide security personnel in their interactions with potential shoplifters. Security guidelines may describe the behaviors that help to identify shoplifters. A store security officer who has followed the guidelines would be able to report what the customer did to trigger suspicion. Similarly, a police officer who decides to stop and frisk an individual by conducting a "pat-down" may do so only if there is a "reasonable suspicion" that a crime was in progress or imminent.[10] Given the nature of modern racism, it is virtually impossible to ascertain to what extent police and security officers make these decisions based on an individual's race or ethnicity.

While researchers have examined police practices that result in racial and/or ethnic disparities in stops and searches of individuals, very little research has investigated the behavior of private security officers. To date, only Shaun L. Gabbidon and Ojmarrh Mitchell have studied ways to measure security practices in retail stores.[11] One of the reasons for which little is known about the outcomes of the decisions made by private security officers is that commercial establishments are under no obligation to maintain and/or publicly share information about the treatment of customers. While police reports are considered public information and can be obtained and studied by social scientists, there are few official records that allow us to evaluate the policies and practices of private commercial enterprises. Since police do not have jurisdiction to patrol private property, no official records are generated about shoplifting incidents unless the police are called. Therefore, we do not know whether racial and ethnic disparities exist in store security practices and, if so, whether any disparities are caused by retailers' policies or practices.

One way to begin to study the prevalence of racial disparity in security practices is to examine official government data, in particular, arrest data. Because the work of private security officers parallels that of police officers, they are likely to mirror the way in which police interact with citizens of color. Therefore, utilizing arrest data can help us to understand the effects of security practices used in the marketplace. In this analysis, we examined the rates of arrest for larceny theft and for shoplifting in the nine states with the highest proportion of black residents and Washington, DC. We compared the percentages of black and white arrestees as reported by two data sources: The Uniform Crime Report and the National Incident Based Reporting System.

The United States' Federal Bureau of Investigation (FBI) compiles data on arrests for its annual Uniform Crime Report (UCR).[12] It is a nationwide, cooperative statistical effort by nearly 18,000 city, county, state, tribal, university and college, and federal law enforcement agencies to report on crimes they encounter. Crimes are broken into two major categories known as Part I and Part II in an attempt to examine the most serious crimes and gauge the fluctuation and rate of crimes throughout the nation. Part I crimes include the violent crimes of murder and nonnegligent manslaughter, forcible rape, robbery, and aggravated assault, and the property crimes of burglary, larceny-theft, and motor vehicle theft. To complement the UCR data, we used information from the Bureau of Justice Statistics' National Incident Based Reporting System (NIBRS).[13] Although fewer departments report to NIBRS (approximately one-third of all law enforcement agencies), specific data regarding shoplifting arrests are included: each incident and arrest, the victim, the nature of the property, as well as the characteristics of the arrested suspect.

The data from both sources are limited in a number of ways. Most obviously, the UCR and NIBRS only report crimes that are known to police. Clearly, many crimes go unreported for a variety of reasons. In the case of shoplifting, retail establishments may want to handle these situations privately for fear of negative publicity and litigation. Secondly, individual officers and police departments may falsify or under-report their crime statistics due to the pressure they experience to prove they are lowering crime and doing proper police work.

However, the main concern with studying arrest data is that, rather than showing who shoplifts with more frequency or prevalence, it tells us who got caught. Who got caught is a function of who was watched and who was watched is a function of who was doing the watching.[14] If we assume that the people behind the camera are affected by implicit biases—as we have seen, research shows that all of us are—then it seems safe to assume that racial/ethnic disparities between who's doing the watching and who's being watched can have some impact on who ends up in the "caught" category by race/ethnicity. This assumption is supported by the study described earlier in this chapter involving live unobtrusive observations of both the offender and nonoffender populations simultaneously that allowed for the collection of unbiased data and did not depend on the subjective judgments of store loss prevention personnel.[15] In sum, there remains a big question as to whether those who are apprehended for crimes are representative of those who actually violate the law.

Despite these limitations, arrest data still provide a starting point for achieving a broad understanding of who is arrested for shoplifting and/or larceny-theft. The most striking result of this preliminary analysis is that, in states with relatively larger black populations, the rates of arrests are higher for blacks. According to the 2010 decennial census, the District of Columbia, Mississippi, and Louisiana have the highest percentage of black citizens with 52.2 percent, 37.6 percent, 32.8 percent, of their total populations, respectively. These three states also have the highest percentage of blacks who were arrested for larceny-theft, 97 percent (District of Columbia), 58.7 percent (Mississippi), 56.6 percent (Louisiana) according to the Uniform Crime Report (see Table 6.1). Mississippi and Louisiana are also among the three states with the highest recorded shoplifting rates as reported by the National Incident Based Reporting System. The rates of arrests of black individuals are higher than their corresponding population rates whether we rely on data about the broader larceny-theft category reported in the UCR or the shoplifting specific data from the NIBRS.

For example, as shown in Table 6.1, in Mississippi, where 37 percent of the population is black, 60 percent of those arrested for larceny, and 38 percent of those arrested for shoplifting are black. Louisiana's black population represents 32 percent of its total population but it represents 57 percent of larceny arrests and 33 percent of shoplifting specific arrests. In Delaware, 21 percent of the population is black but 41 percent of arrests are for larceny-theft and 35 percent of arrests for shoplifting are of black individuals. In contrast, close to 70 percent of the population in the state of Delaware is white, while only 58.2 percent of those arrested for larceny are white and only 42 percent for shoplifting.

The most important finding is that, for whites, the arrest rate for larceny-theft at the national level from the UCR is 68 percent, compared to a national white population of 72 percent, for a ratio of 94 percent. Also, the arrest rate for shoplifting from the NIBRS database for whites ranges from 27 percent to 42 percent, representing ratios ranging from 42 percent to 70 percent compared to the respective percentage of the white population in each of the five states in Table 6.1. For blacks, the numbers tell a different story. The arrest rate for larceny-theft at the national level for blacks is 29 percent, compared to a national black population of 13 percent, for a ratio of 230 percent. Also, for the five states in Table 6.1, the arrest rate for shoplifting (from the NIBRS database) for blacks ranges from 32 percent to 38 percent, representing ratios ranging from 102 percent to 164 percent compared to the respective percentage of the black population in each of

**TABLE 6.1 Shoplifting**

| States | Population U.S. (2010 U.S Census) | % White | | | | | % Black | | | | |
|---|---|---|---|---|---|---|---|---|---|---|---|
| | | Population (2010 U.S Census) | Larceny-Theft Arrests (UCR, 2012) | Larceny-Theft Compared to % White Population | Shoplifting Arrests (NIBRS, 2012) | Shoplifting Arrests (NIBRS) Compared to % White Population | Population (2010 Census) | Larceny-Theft Arrests (UCR, 2012) | Larceny-Theft Compared to % Black Population | Shoplifting Arrests (NIBRS, 2012) | Shoplifting Arrests (NIBRS) Compared to % Black Population |
| United States | 308,745,538 | 72.4 | 68.2 | 94% | n/a | n/a | 12.6 | 29.0 | 230% | n/a | n/a |
| DC | 601,723 | 43.4 | 6.4 | 15% | n/a | n/a | 49.5 | 93.5 | 189% | n/a | n/a |
| MS | 2,967,297 | 59.1 | 39.4 | 67% | 41.5 | 70% | 37.0 | 60.1 | 162% | 38.0 | 103% |
| LA | 4,533,372 | 62.6 | 42.3 | 68% | 26.5 | 42% | 32.0 | 57.1 | 178% | 32.5 | 102% |
| GA | 9,687,653 | 59.7 | 44.9 | 75% | n/a | n/a | 30.5 | 54.2 | 178% | n/a | n/a |
| MD | 5,773,552 | 58.2 | 49.6 | 85% | n/a | n/a | 29.4 | 49.6 | 169% | n/a | n/a |
| SC | 4,625,364 | 66.2 | 54.3 | 82% | 35.6 | 54% | 27.9 | 45.2 | 162% | 31.9 | 114% |
| AL | 4,779,736 | 68.5 | 51.8 | 76% | 41.0 | 60% | 26.2 | 46.9 | 179% | 34.4 | 131% |
| DE | 897,934 | 68.9 | 58.2 | 84% | 41.9 | 61% | 21.4 | 41.4 | 193% | 35.2 | 164% |
| NC | 9,535,483 | 68.5 | 54.1 | 79% | n/a | n/a | 19.4 | 43.5 | 224% | n/a | n/a |
| VA | 8,001,024 | 68.6 | 56.2 | 82% | n/a | n/a | 19.4 | 42.6 | 219% | n/a | n/a |

*Source:* Compiled from Federal Bureau of Investigation. 2015. "Uniform Crime Reports." Available at: https://www.fbi.gov/about-us/cjis/ucr; Federal Bureau of Investigation. 2014. "National Incident-Based Reporting System." Available at: https://www.fbi.gov/about-us/cjis/ucr/nibrs/2014.

those five states. Basically, the data indicate that whites have been arrested for larceny-theft and shoplifting at rates lower than their population rates, while blacks have been arrested for larceny-theft and shoplifting at rates higher than their population rates.

These results showing racial disparities in arrest rates are consistent with other research examining racial and ethnic disparities. Gelman, Fagan, and Kiss (2007) suggest that "police . . . may substitute racial characteristics of communities for racial characteristics of individuals in their cognitive schema of suspicion, resulting in elevated stop rates in neighborhoods with high concentrations of minorities."[16] Although Gelman, Fagan, and Kiss studied the decisions of police officers to stop, question, and frisk citizens on the streets, their explanation may apply to the decisions made by private security officers as well because stop and frisk tactics are similar to the practice targeting of individuals who are perceived as potential shoplifters in stores.[17]

"Stop and frisk" or "stop, question, and frisk" is an aggressive tactic used by police searching for drugs and guns. Its goal is to identify suspicious behavior and preemptively interrupt a crime that is either underway or imminent. During the past decade, many claims have been made that the ways in which the New York Police Department (NYPD) enforced its stop and frisk policy was racially biased, unjustly targeted innocent citizens, and produced dubious results when attempting to reduce crime.[18] During the 1990s, a boom in this aggressive policing tactic was mirrored by increased concerns over retail security in the private sector and consequently, increased use of similar security tactics in the retail sector.[19] More recently, the Reverend Al Sharpton used the term "shop and frisk" to describe the practice whereby retailers involve the police to stop customers they view as suspicious. Major retailers in Manhattan were under the spotlight in the fall of 2013 when several black shoppers alleged that they were detained by NYPD officers and accused of fraud after making expensive purchases in stores.[20]

Given the similarity between these practices, studies that have analyzed stop and frisk data can provide valuable insight into the discretionary decision-making of the people charged with preventing losses in stores. In 2010, Jones-Brown, Gill, and Trone studied stop and frisk tactics in New York City and revealed that the majority of stops were concentrated in only a few police precincts that serve minority communities and that the vast majority of people who were stopped were black or Hispanic. "[T]he data also show that during stops, Blacks and Hispanics are more likely than Whites to be subject to frisks and physical force beyond the pat-down itself."[21] Analyzing the same data from New York City, Ferrandino (2013) found that stop and frisk stops tended to be inefficient in producing their desired outcome which is for police to confiscate weapons and contraband. Interestingly, as the frequency of stops increased, the rate of returns actually diminished.[22] In other words, the more stops were performed, the less effective they became. This shows that officers became progressively indiscriminate in making stops and their targeting was producing the opposite of the desired results.

Beyond simply recovering contraband, the broader issue is whether these types of aggressive policing tactics actually accomplish their overarching goal of reducing crime. Rosenfeld and Fornango (2014) studied the effect of the NYPD's stop and frisk tactics on robbery and burglary rates.[23] Upon initial examination, the aggressive policing tactics appeared to contribute to lowering of the crime rate for burglary and robbery. However, once the findings were viewed through a lens of lagged time to account for a cause-and-effect type of relationship, the effect sizes dwindled and the tactics lost significance. Therefore, the results of the study raise doubts that the heavy-handed stop and frisk tactics produce lasting results and it is questionable that these types of policies are worth the cost in liberty and freedom of the citizenry.

Similarly, our analysis shows there are noteworthy differences in shoplifting arrests between black and white residents of states with high minority populations. This initial analysis reveals that blacks are no more likely to commit either larceny or shoplifting than members of any other group, a result that is consistent with the findings of Dabney, Hollinger, and Dugan. In addition, in many of the states with the largest black population, the majority of these crimes are committed by white citizens. Though the results indicate that there is a correlation between race and arrest rates, other factors may explain that relationship and provide evidence to help understand its causal direction. Therefore, additional research is needed. Clearly, a more accurate description of the effects of security practices on people of color could emerge if more reliable and complete data were made available by the businesses that employ them. Perhaps a thorough analysis of the currently available public data could encourage corporations to share information about their security policies and practices. At this time, it is primarily when they have been sued that retailers have supplied data about the individuals they detain.

Because the police play a key role in ensuring the primacy of the rule of law, the practice of racial profiling can undermine the legitimacy of the law in American communities. Indeed, the use of factors such as race and ethnicity in police decision-making impacts the public's overall trust and confidence in the law and in the police as enforcers of the law. Similarly, customers who are subjected to additional surveillance based on their race may lose faith in the business sector and seek alternatives for meeting their wants and needs. This problem is beginning to gain recognition among business leaders who can take a proactive approach to addressing it. As we know, increasing numbers of people of color are turning to the courts to seek redress when they are profiled or otherwise treated unfairly in retail stores and other commercial establishments.

In the next three chapters, we share summaries of legal decisions involving consumers who claimed they were discriminated against by sales associates or store security personnel. The cases are among those that have been compiled into an extensive database for analyzing marketplace discrimination. Although it would be tempting to provide an exhaustive list of the cases and incidents, our focus is on providing more details on a subset of these cases. This approach allows for more insightful understanding about the nuances of marketplace discrimination, consumer and company responses, and the challenges that researchers face in understanding this phenomenon.

## Notes

1. *Garrett v. Tandy Corp.*, 295 F.3d 94 (1st Cir. 2002).
2. See 20/20, 1998.
3. Sutton, 1997.
4. For example, Liska, Lawrence, and Sanchirico, 1982.
5. Shteir, 2011.
6. 27th Annual Retail Theft Survey, Jack L. Hayes International, Inc. www.hayes international.com and National Retail Security Survey, https://nrf.com/resources/retail-library/national-retail-security-survey-2015
7. https://nrf.com/resources/retail-library/national-retail-security-survey-2015
8. http://www.thelaw.com/law/civil-demand-letters-retail-theft-and-recovery .415/
9. Dabney, Hollinger, and Dugan, 2004.
10. *Terry v. Ohio*, 392 U.S. 1, 1968.
11. Gabbidon and Mitchell, 2015.
12. Federal Bureau of Investigation, 2015.
13. Federal Bureau of Investigation, 2014.
14. McCoy, 2015.
15. Dabney, Hollinger, and Dugan, 2004.

16. Gelman, Fagan, and Kiss, 2007.
17. Caputo and King, 2015.
18. Gelman, Fagan, and Kiss, 2007.
19. Carmel-Gilfilen, 2013.
20. O'Donnell, Francescani, and Dobuzinskis, 2013; Bhasin, 2014; Farrington, 2014.
21. Jones-Brown, Gill, and Trone, 2010, p. 36.
22. Ferrandino, 2013.
23. Rosenfeld and Fornango, 2014.

# References

ABC Television, 20/20. 1998. "Under Suspicion: Security Guards Unfairly Target Black Shoppers." *ABC Television*, June 8.

Bhasin, Kim. 2014. "Barneys Pays $525,000 to Settle Allegations of Racial Profiling." *The Huffington Post*, August 11.

Brunson, R. K. 2007. "'Police Don't Like Black People': African-American Young Men's Accumulated Police Experiences." *Criminology & Public Policy* 6, no. 1: 71–101.

Caputo, G. A. and A. King. 2015. "Shoplifting by Male and Female Drug Users Gender, Agency, and Work." *Criminal Justice Review* 40, no. 1: 47–66.

Carmel-Gilfilen, C. 2013. "Bridging Security and Good Design: Understanding Perceptions of Expert and Novice Shoplifters." *Security Journal* 26, no. 1, 80–105.

Carr, P. J., L. Napolitano, and J. Keating. 2007. "We Never Call the Cops and Here Is Why: A Qualitative Examination of Legal Cynicism in Three Philadelphia Neighborhoods." *Criminology* 45, no. 2: 445–480.

Carvalho, I. and D. A Lewis. 2003. "Beyond Community: Reactions to Crime and Disorder among Inner-City Residents." *Criminology* 41, no. 3: 779–812.

Cronk, C. E. and P. D. Sarvela. 1997. "Alcohol, Tobacco, and Other Drug Use among Rural/Small Town and Urban Youth: A Secondary Analysis of the Monitoring the Future Data Set." *American Journal of Public Health* 87, no. 5: 760–764.

Dabney, Dean A., Richard C. Hollinger, and Laura Dugan. 2004. "Who Actually Steals? A Study of Covertly Observed Shoplifters." *Justice Quarterly* 21, no. 4: 693–728.

Dertke, M. C., L. A. Penner, and K. Ulrich. 1974. "Observer's Reporting of Shoplifting as a Function of Thief's Race and Sex." *The Journal of Social Psychology* 94, no. 2: 213–221.

Doyle, Mark R. 2015 "27th Annual Retail Theft Survey."

Fagan, J. October 15, 2010. "Report of Jeffrey Fagan." Available at: https://ccrjustice.org/files/Expert_Report_JeffreyFagan.pdf. Accessed May 13, 2015.

Fagan, J. and G. Davies. 2000. "Street Stops and Broken Windows: Terry, Race and Disorder in New York City." *Fordham Urban Law Journal* 28: 457.

Farrington, Dana. 2014. "Macy's to Pay $650,000 in Settlement over Alleged Racial Profiling." *NPR*, August 20.

Federal Bureau of Investigation. 2014. "National Incident-Based Reporting System." Available at: https://www.fbi.gov/about-us/cjis/ucr/nibrs/2014.

Federal Bureau of Investigation. 2015. "Uniform Crime Reports." Available at: https://www.fbi.gov/about-us/cjis/ucr.

Gabbidon, Shaun L. and George E. Higgins. 2011. "Public Opinion on the Use of Consumer Racial Profiling to Identify Shoplifters: An Exploratory Study." *Criminal Justice Review* 36: 201–212.

Gabbidon, Shaun L. and Mitchell, Ojmarrh. 2015. "Toward the Development of a New Approach to Determine the Prevalence of Racial Profiling in Retail Settings: The Population Benchmark vs. the Violator Benchmark." *Security Management.*

*Garrett v. Tandy Corp.*, 295 F.3d 94 (1st Cir. 2002).

Gau, J. M. 2012. "Consent Searches as a Threat to Procedural Justice and Police Legitimacy: An Analysis of Consent Requests during Traffic Stops." *Criminal Justice Policy Review.*

Geller, A., J. Fagan, T. Tyler, and B. G. Link. 2014. "Aggressive Policing and the Mental Health of Young Urban Men." *American Journal of Public Health*, 104, no. 12: 2321–2327.

Gelman, A., J. Fagan, and A. Kiss. 2007. "An Analysis of the New York City Police Department's "Stop-and-Frisk" Policy in the Context of Claims of Racial Bias." *Journal of the American Statistical Association*, 102, no. 479.

Hakstian, A.-M. G. 2013. *Racial and Ethnic Profiling in Massachusetts: An Examination of Police Policy and Practice.* Boston: Northeastern University.

Ingram, J. R. 2007. "The Effect of Neighborhood Characteristics on Traffic Citation Practices of the Police." *Police Quarterly* 10, no. 4: 371–393.

Jones-Brown, Delores D., Jaspreet Gill, and Jennifer Trone. 2010. *Stop, Question & Frisk Policing Practices in New York City: A Primer.* New York: Center on Race, Crime and Justice, John Jay College of Criminal Justice.

Kane, R. J. 2002. "The Social Ecology of Police Misconduct." *Criminology* 40, no. 4: 867–896.

Klinger, David A. 1997. "Negotiating Order in Patrol Work: An Ecological Theory of Police Response to Deviance." *Criminology* 35: 277.

Liska, A. E., J. J. Lawrence, and A. Sanchirico. 1982. "Fear of Crime as a Social Fact." *Social Forces* 60, no. 3: 760–770.

McCoy, T. 2015. "The Black Man Arrested in Georgetown Because He Looked Like a Shoplifter." *Washington Post*, p. 5, October 16.

Miller, J. 2010. "Stop and Search in England: A Reformed Tactic or Business as Usual?" *British Journal of Criminology* 50, no. 5: 954–974.

O'Donnell, Noreen, Chris Francescani, and Alex Dobuzinskis. 2013. "Macy's Joins Barneys in NYC 'Shop-and-Frisk' Scandal." *Reuters*, October 26.

Paoline III, E. A. and W. Terrill. 2005. "The Impact of Police Culture on Traffic Stop Searches: An Analysis of Attitudes and Behavior." *Policing: An International Journal of Police Strategies & Management* 28, no. 3: 455–472.

Ridgeway, G. 2007. *Analysis of Racial Disparities in the New York Police Department's Stop, Question, and Frisk Practices.* Santa Monica, CA: Rand Corporation.

Rosenfeld, Richard and Robert Fornango. 2014. "The Impact of Police Stops on Precinct Robbery and Burglary Rates in New York City, 2003–2010." *Justice Quarterly* 31: 96–122.

Sahin, N. M. 2014. "Legitimacy, Procedural Justice, and Police-Citizen Encounters: A Randomized Controlled Trial of the Impact of Procedural Justice on Citizen Perceptions of the Police during Traffic Stops in Turkey." Doctoral dissertation, Rutgers University-Graduate School, Newark.

Shearing, C. D. and P. C. Stenning. 1981. "Modern Private Security: Its Growth and Implications." *Crime and Justice*, 193–245.

Shteir, R. 2011. *The Steal: A Cultural History of Shoplifting.* New York: Penguin Group.

Sutton, Larry. 1997. "Bloomie's Slapped with Bias Suit." *New York Daily News*, September 25.

*Terry v. Ohio*, 392 U.S. 1, 1968.

# Chapter 7

# Criminal Suspicion Cases

*The fact is, in too many parts of this country, a deep distrust exists between law enforcement and communities of color. Some of this is the result of the legacy of racial discrimination in this country.*

—President Barack Obama[1]

On February 20, 1997, Lynette Chapman, an African-American woman, was shopping at Dillard's Department Store in Cleveland, Ohio. After choosing some clothing, she entered a fitting room from which a white woman had just exited. She noticed that a sensor tag called a "kno-go" was on the floor. After trying on the clothing, she decided not to purchase anything. She left the fitting room to return the clothing to the racks. When a Dillard's sales assistant noticed the sensor on the floor of the fitting room, she suspected Ms. Chapman of shoplifting and notified a Dillard's security officer who stopped Ms. Chapman and directed her back to the fitting room. The officer, an off-duty sheriff's deputy, was wearing his official sheriff's department uniform and badge. He also carried a side arm.

The officer and a female manager first searched Ms. Chapman's purse. After determining that it contained no Dillard's merchandise, the officer informed Ms. Chapman that it would be necessary to check her clothes. In doing so, the security officer failed to obey Dillard's Rules and Procedures for Security Personnel which clearly state: "Strip searches are prohibited. If you suspect that stolen objects are hidden on [the shopper's] person, call the police." Nevertheless, he asked Ms. Chapman to accompany the manager into the fitting room in order to be searched. The manager asked Ms. Chapman to remove her coat and suit jacket and lift up her shirt. Finding nothing, she apologized and Ms. Chapman left the store.

As a result of this incident, Ms. Chapman brought suit against Dillard's alleging that her rights under Section 1981 of the Civil Rights Act of 1866 were violated among other claims. Specifically, she argued that the security officer's decision to stop and search her on suspicion of shoplifting was racially motivated. Although the trial court judge granted Dillard's motion for summary judgment, the Court of Appeals for the Sixth Circuit reversed that decision and sent the case back to the trial court.[2] The practical outcome of the Appeals Court's decision was to give Ms. Chapman the opportunity to present her case in court. However, following the issuance of the Appeals Court's decision, the parties arrived at a confidential settlement agreement. We can presume that Dillard's was not willing to risk losing the lawsuit at trial and/or face the publicity that could potentially accompany such a trial.

Like Lynette Chapman, many people of color have the experience of being viewed and treated as potential criminals in the marketplace. The cases described in this chapter involve these types of situations. Before exploring some examples of cases, two points need to be emphasized. First, in reading the cases presented in this chapter and the next two (Chapters 7 through 9), the reader is cautioned about jumping to conclusions regarding the culpability of the parties. In each case, there could be many reasons, procedural and otherwise, that could account for the outcome. Randy Oyler, partner in the law firm of Barack Ferrazzano Kirschbaum & Nagelberg in Chicago explains that the "adjudication of a case in favor of a defendant does not necessarily imply that the court did not believe the plaintiff's claims" or that the court did not understand the experiences of consumers of color. A decision in favor of a defendant could be based on grounds that have nothing to do with believability, and similarly, a ruling in favor of a defendant may be an indication that the judge must interpret the law as it currently exists and that changes in the law must be pursued through the legislative process.[3]

Unfortunately, following a presentation at a national conference during which we described the facts alleged in a complaint filed against Cracker Barrel Old Country Store restaurants (discussed in Chapter 8), we received a stern letter from the company (see Exhibits 7.1 and 7.2). In that situation, a company representative who was in the audience assumed that we were ascribing guilt to Cracker Barrel merely by presenting the complaint as an example of what happens when the discrimination experienced by consumers rises to the level of filing a lawsuit.

The purpose for presenting the cases here is to illustrate the types of situations that law-abiding people of color encounter when attempting to spend their money. Therefore, another word of caution: much of the language was modified only slightly from court decisions. To provide the reader with a sense of the judge's perspectives on the issue of consumer discrimination, very little editorializing has been done. Next, here are some of those incidents that found their way into court.

The following case provides many examples of the ways in which shoppers of color are subjected to more surveillance than white shoppers. It involves 17 African-American plaintiffs who had different experiences at the Dillard's Department Store in Columbia, Missouri, between 1998 and 2002. The plaintiffs alleged that Dillard's discriminated against them by harassing them in various ways. In particular, they presented evidence that they were each subjected to race-based surveillance and denial of service that deprived them of their equal right to make and enforce contracts under Section 1981 of the Civil Rights Act of 1866.

For example, plaintiff Crystal Gregory was a 31-year-old full-time student and the wife of a police officer when she visited the Columbia Dillard's in February 2001 intending to purchase a "dressy outfit." As she examined the merchandise and made her selections, a sales associate asked if she could help. Despite Gregory's assurances that she did not require assistance, the associate followed her closely as she shopped. Gregory chose a pair of pants and carried them to a fitting room to try on. When she emerged with the pants, she found the sales associate guarding the fitting room door with her arms crossed and a smirk across her face. Two police officers were also waiting just outside the entrance to the fitting rooms. Gregory described the atmosphere as "very hostile."

Offended and humiliated by the sales associate's conduct and her suspicions, Gregory asked to speak to a manager. The manager on duty seemed not to take Gregory's complaint seriously. Gregory testified that the manager "was not of much help, almost as if she did not care, and so I left very upset." Gregory did not complete her purchase.

Another plaintiff in the same case, Alberta Turner, was a 52-year-old daycare provider. She and her adult daughter Carla, an insurance agency employee, patronized Dillard's Columbia store on Memorial Day, 2002. Alberta and Carla were regular customers who, despite having previously purchased hundreds of dollars' worth of merchandise from the store, had both been routinely subjected to overbearing behavior on the part of store personnel. On Memorial Day, the two women were accompanied by Alberta's two granddaughters, one of whom was Carla's daughter. Alberta and Carla purchased several pairs of shoes for the children before splitting up to continue shopping. Carla selected several outfits for her daughter who tried them on in a fitting room. As mother and daughter exited the fitting room, they were confronted by a sales associate and a security guard.

The sales associate stared at Carla's Dillard's bag which held the previously purchased shoes. She did not ask to examine the bag's contents, but the security guard began trailing Carla closely as she walked back to the department where her mother was shopping. When Carla asked the guard why he was following, he did not respond. Alberta became upset to see her daughter treated in this manner and decided against making her purchase. Alberta started to challenge the security guard about his behavior, but quickly changed her mind when she realized how upset her granddaughters had become by what was occurring. Before leaving the store, Alberta told a sales associate that the store had just lost a large sale. The employee asked with a "weird grin," "So? So what?"

Yet another plaintiff in this case, Jefferson McKinney, was in his early 50s and was a United Parcel Service employee when he visited the cologne counter at the Columbia Dillard's. He testified that he made eye contact with a sales associate in an attempt to gain her attention, but the associate ignored him in favor of later arriving white customers. While waiting to be served, McKinney and his two cousins tested various cologne samples displayed on the counter. After having ignored McKinney and his cousins for 15 minutes, the sales associate finally approached their counter. But instead of speaking to them or offering assistance, she simply swept the counter samples away. One of McKinney's cousins asked the associate why they were being ignored and asked to speak to a store manager. Upset at the associate's "rude . . . tone" in response, McKinney left the store without completing a purchase.

Complaints from other plaintiffs included close and continuous trailing, even up to the bathroom, discriminatory practices in returns and exchanges, delays in being waited on, and discriminatory enforcement of the policy on suspected shoplifters. In addition to the testimony of the plaintiffs that they were greeted with hostility and suspicion at Dillard's, there is also testimony from former Dillard's employees indicating that the company had a custom and practice of singling out African-American shoppers for inferior treatment and intimidation. In particular, former men's fragrance saleswoman, Tammy Benskin, testified that the security code "44" was customarily announced over the store's intercom system whenever an African-American person entered the store. She also reported that the store manager and his assistants routinely subjected black customers to intense scrutiny and surveillance while allowing white patrons to browse the store undisturbed.

Former men's department salesman, Rick Beasley, testified that black customers faced higher burdens than white customers when attempting to return purchases without a receipt. Former employee, Theresa Cain, testified that "other Dillard's employees often stereotyped African-American customers as likely shoplifters," that she "regularly observed security officers and sales clerks watching and/or following African-American customers for no reason except that the customers were African American," and that "Dillard's security officers so focused their surveillance on African-American customers to the exclusion of white customers that on numerous occasions [she] observed white customers openly shoplift items without being noticed by store security."

Police sergeant Kenneth Gregory, husband of plaintiff Crystal Gregory, worked as a security guard at the Columbia Dillard's during the 1990s. At trial, he testified that black customers were subjected to more searching scrutiny and surveillance than white customers. In addition, suspected white shoplifters were allowed to surrender their stolen merchandise and leave the store whereas suspected black shoplifters were detained and arrested. For instance, Gregory testified that he once followed a white man in the store on suspicion that he intended to shoplift a hat, but the store manager stopped and questioned the man before he exited the store, and the man left without the hat. Gregory concluded that the manager would not have stopped a similarly situated black person, but would have allowed him to leave the store and face arrest.[4]

Maren Snell who had worked in the women's fragrance department of Dillard's Columbia store also testified on behalf of the plaintiffs. She testified that she observed store employees refuse a black customer's attempts to return merchandise despite providing proof of purchase labels while accepting the returns of white customers who lacked receipts. She stated that she was instructed by supervisors to "watch those Black kids" and not to give fragrance samples to black girls because "they're not going to buy anything anyway."

Dillard's defense to these allegations was that each of the plaintiffs left the store without attempting to make purchases, so they did not suffer the loss of an actual contract interest with Dillard's. The trial court granted Dillard's motion for dismissal or summary judgment concluding that "mere" discriminatory surveillance of customers does not amount to an interference with the plaintiffs' ability to complete a transaction with the store therefore the plaintiffs' rights were not violated. This means that the trial judge decided that, even if the plaintiffs' version of the facts was true, there was no need for a trial because they still would not be able to prove that Dillard's discriminated against them. On appeal, the court affirmed the district court's decision to dismiss the plaintiffs' Section 1981 claims.

The Court of Appeals reasoned that the plaintiffs must prove that Dillard's conduct, policies, or practices interfered with their attempt to complete a contract with the store. According to the court, the plaintiffs failed to present that kind of evidence. The court identified other cases where it felt the plaintiffs had shown an attempt to complete a purchase. Some of those individual cases, were when the plaintiff (a) selected a specific item in the display case and communicated to a sales clerk the desire to purchase that item; (b) purchased and received a gift package entitling the recipient to a variety of salon services; (c) offered to pay for items by check; and (d) placed merchandise in a cart and had the means to purchase it before being asked to leave the store. The court explained that a customer who lifts an item from a shelf or rack to determine its price has not demonstrated a contractual relationship with the seller.

Second, the Appeals Court found that Section 1981 of the Civil Rights Act of 1866 does not prohibit the discriminatory surveillance of patrons and rude behavior by sales associates. It interpreted the statute to require plaintiffs to prove that the retailer "thwarted" the shopper's attempt to make a contract. In other words, the merchant must "block" the creation of a contract. According to the court, examples of such "blocking" behavior by a merchant include a retailer asking a customer to leave a retail establishment to prevent the customer from making a purchase or explicitly refusing service to a shopper based on race. The court reasoned that racially biased watchfulness, however, reprehensible, does not "block" a shopper's attempt to contract. And, in Ms. Gregory's situation, the Appeals Court found that she was not blocked from making a purchase. Instead, she herself declared that she would not make a purchase.

The Appeals Court concluded its opinion in this case with some interesting—and arguably political—comments explaining its belief that other branches of government must step in to address the problem of consumer discrimination.

We recognize that the plaintiffs were offended by the alleged conduct of Dillard's employees. . . . We do not express the view . . . that a certain level of race discrimination in retail establishments is "acceptable." Private parties engage in a variety of behavior that individual federal judges may deem unacceptable, but not all of it is unlawful. Whether and how federal law should regulate particular activity that is considered morally or socially unacceptable is a policy judgment made by Congress and the President. That judgment presumably involves inquiry into such matters as the scope and severity of the problem, the potential that private industry or decentralized regulators will address the problem, the likely effectiveness of federal legislation in solving the problem, and the collateral costs to the national economy of additional federal regulation. In a significant economic sector such as retail shopping, the potential benefits of sanctioning and deterring offensive and undesirable conduct through federal legislation likely must be weighed against the costs of litigation (including nonmeritorious claims) that may be generated by expanded regulation, the potential costs of different retail security measures that may be necessitated by such legislation, and the potential increase in shoplifting (presently estimated to be a $13 billion annual drain on retailers) if merchants are discouraged from conducting legitimate security activity for fear of triggering additional lawsuits. We make no judgment about the wisdom of any policy option.

The U.S. Supreme Court declined to hear the case.[5]

In another case involving an incident at a different Dillard's Department Store, the same Court of Appeals arrived at the opposite conclusion. The situation that gave rise to the lawsuit occurred on August 11, 2002, when Rodney and Charlan Green went to the Dillard's store in the Metro North Mall in Kansas City, Missouri, to buy a purse, and watch for Charlan. They went directly to the watch counter in the accessories section where the watches were displayed in a locked display case. Although there were two clerks in the section, neither approached the Greens who looked at the watches in the glass case for about 10 minutes while waiting to be helped. One of the clerks was leaning against a wall with her arms folded. Charlan went up to her and asked, "Ma'am, can you help us?" The clerk, Linda McCrary, said "no" and continued to stand in the same position. The Greens testified that they were stunned by her response and immediately turned to leave the store, but the other clerk in the section, Veronica Aguero, yelled, "Ma'am, I'll help you when I'm finished here." Aguero was helping other customers at the time, so the Greens waited at the purse counter. Although McCrary was still in the accessories department, she made no move to help the Greens while they waited.

When Aguero came over to the purse counter to assist the Greens, McCrary followed. She stood by the register with her arms crossed and glared at the Greens while they looked at the merchandise. With Aguero's help, Charlan selected a purse, a matching wallet, and a keychain to buy. When she saw this, McCrary loudly asked Aguero, "Are they getting all that? How are they paying for it?" Aguero said nothing in response, and Rodney wrote a check to Dillard's in the amount of $555.62 to pay for the items. Aguero asked for identification, then accepted the check, and rang up the sale.

Throughout the transaction, McCrary kept staring at the Greens and muttering under her breath. After the check was accepted, Rodney asked McCrary, "Ma'am, there's other people, can you help somebody else?" McCrary answered, "I can, but I'm not." Mr. Green was offended and asked Aguero to call a manager, which she did. Aguero asked the Greens if there was anything else they were interested in buying, and Charlan said she would like to purchase a wristwatch. Aguero and Charlan then went to the nearby watch counter.

Meanwhile, Rodney stayed behind at the register waiting for the manager. McCrary remained there with a hostile expression on her face. During an uncomfortable silence, Mr. Green pulled out his identification and credit cards and laid four credit cards on the counter to show McCrary that he was a bona fide customer. He told her, "Ma'am, I don't have to steal anything. I can buy anything in the store I like. I have four platinum cards here." He added that he was a police officer. McCrary approached the counter, looked at the cards, and said, "Platinum, huh." Then she stepped back and said, "Fucking niggers" and stalked off.

By then, Charlan and Aguero had returned from the watch counter to get keys for the watch case. They both heard McCrary's epithet. Charlan and Rodney Green both testified that, in addition to feeling humiliated, they felt as if they had been physically assaulted. Aguero apologized and told the Greens that McCrary had been disciplined for this before.

At this point, a Dillard's sales manager, Amanda Andreasen, arrived. When she was informed of what had happened, she apologized several times and said that Dillard's had "had problem with McCrary with this before." Another customer told Ms. Andreasen that she had overheard what was said. The Greens testified that they were so upset by the incidents with McCrary that they were unable to complete their intended purchase of the watch. They also returned the items they had already purchased. The next day, the store manager called the Greens and indicated that McCrary "had been disciplined for this before" and had now been terminated. He offered them a 20-percent discount on their next purchase, but they declined it. He later sent a letter of apology with the same discount offer. Although the plaintiffs also presented evidence that Dillard's lacked procedures to remedy discrimination toward customers, did not consistently keep records of complaints, and employed managers who did not take prompt corrective action against discrimination, the trial court granted Dillard's motion for summary judgment. The Greens appealed that decision.

In this case, the Court of Appeals found that the Greens presented sufficient evidence to show that Dillard's kept McCrary on its sales floor and authorized her to interact with customers although it had reason to know that her hostile propensities could lead to incidents such as the Greens experienced. The court stated that the plaintiffs "produced evidence that goes beyond bad manners, isolated rudeness, or neglect of a customer," and instead, included evidence of "a most egregious racial slur" as well as "a series of actions" that could lead a judge or jury to find that the Greens were prevented from completing their purchase of the wristwatch. The series of actions included McCrary's refusing service to the Greens, actively discouraged her coworker from assisting them by questioning their ability to pay, and treated them with hostility. Furthermore, the court highlighted the fact that no other employee reproached McCrary or tried to stop her behavior "[a]lthough other Dillard's employees were more civil to the Greens." The Court of Appeals reversed the District Court's decision. Perhaps the overt nature of the discrimination in this case made a difference in the judges' perception of the incident. Dillard's petitioned the U.S. Supreme Court to accept the case for review but the petition was denied.[6]

The next two cases involve a pair of friends, one white and one black, shopping together. In both cases, the plaintiffs alleged that the store personnel treated the two friends differently. As has been discussed, to prove discrimination, an individual must show that she was treated differently than someone who is of a different race. In most cases, individuals are shopping alone and cannot necessarily compare themselves to someone of another race who is behaving in the same way. When no comparison is possible, it is difficult to determine whether bad service is due to employee incompetence or to illegal discrimination. In the cases that follow, there is a white "comparator" who was in the store at the same time, interacted with the same store personnel, and yet, was treated differently than her black counterpart.

Ms. Lewis, a black woman, was shopping at a J.C. Penney store with a white female friend. The two were accompanied by three children. Ms. Lewis and her friend both made purchases at the store, although the friend bought considerably more than Ms. Lewis. The two women were followed by store security because, in the guards' opinions, they displayed nervous behavior, avoided sales help, and were shopping in darkened, deserted areas of the store. In his report that was written after the fact, one guard commented that he noticed several black males waiting outside the exit door, apparently a reference to Ms. Lewis's son and his friend.

The two women shopped until the store closed. They made their purchases and left the store. In the store's parking lot, the store's security guards approached Ms. Lewis' car and asked the women to return to the store so they could inspect their bags. The women complied and the guards conducted the search in the loss-prevention office. Ms. Lewis claimed that the search of her bags was completely different from the cursory search of her friend's bag. Despite the fact that she had purchased far more merchandise than Ms. Lewis, the guards gave her receipt a quick glance. In contrast, after determining that Ms. Lewis' bags contained no stolen merchandise, the guard requested her identification and questioned her about a discrepancy between the name on her charge card and the name on her work identification card. The incident lasted between 10 and 20 minutes after which one of the guards apologized to both of the women. Ms. Lewis brought suit against J.C. Penney and the store's employees alleging that she was wrongfully stopped and interrogated on suspicion of shoplifting but the district court granted J.C. Penney's motion to dismiss all claims.[7]

A similar case occurred on December 15, 1997, in Jackson Township, Ohio. Lois Christian and Amber Edens, who are close friends, entered a Walmart store at 1:45 a.m. to shop for Christmas presents for their children. Ms. Christian is black and Ms. Edens is white. Both women stayed in the toy department, but they shopped separately. They were the only two shoppers in the toy department. Christian walked around with a shopping cart; Edens occasionally placed items in Christian's cart because she did not have her own cart. According to Christian, Rose Monnot, a Walmart employee, watched her as she shopped and repeatedly offered her assistance. Edens, however, was never offered assistance.

Sometime close to 3:00 a.m., Christian put her purse on a shelf, unzipped it, and reached into her purse for a jar of Vaseline. At that moment, Christian noticed Monnot "jogging down" the aisle toward her. Monnot, upon reaching Christian, again asked if she could be of assistance, but Christian declined her help. Monnot testified that she then paged the manager, Richard Clark, and informed him that a woman had placed an item in her purse. Clark told Monnot to call the police and to keep an eye on the woman. Monnot then returned to the toy department. Christian testified that she approached Monnot and said, "Excuse me, ma'am. Do you believe I'm stealing? Because I'm not. I went into my purse for something for me."

At approximately 3:33 a.m., the police arrived. Monnot directed the police officers to Christian and Edens. According to Christian, the officers then approached her and Edens and asked them to leave the store. Christian testified that the officers stated, "They do not like your business. They would like you to leave." The officers did not accuse Christian of shoplifting nor did they search her bag. They escorted Christian and Edens out of the store. Christian was forced to leave behind her shopping cart of merchandise.

At trial, Police Officer Todd Macaluso testified that, when he arrived at the store, Monnot explained that she did not see the customer place an item in her purse, but that an item was missing. Monnot testified that she informed first the police that one woman was white and the other was black when he arrived at the store. The district court determined that Christian did not prove that Monnot had the intent to discriminate against her on the basis of her race because Clark, the store manager, made the decision to ask the plaintiffs to leave the store and the evidence showed that Clark never knew either woman's race.

The Appeals Court acknowledged the near impossibility of proving differential treatment in a retail environment. Therefore, the court determined that plaintiffs in consumer discrimination cases should have the option of proving that "they received services in a markedly hostile manner and in a manner that a reasonable person would find objectively discriminatory." It identified factors for deciding whether conduct is "markedly hostile" including whether the behavior is (a) so profoundly contrary to the manifest financial interests of the merchant and/or her employees; (b) so far outside of widely accepted business norms; and (c) so arbitrary on its face, that the conduct supports a rational inference of discrimination. The Appeals Court concluded that a jury should decide whether Christian was removed from the store, and thus denied the right to contract with store for the sale of goods, because of race discrimination. Therefore, the court reversed the district court's decision and sent the case back for further proceedings.[8]

Another way in which customers of color are treated with criminal suspicion involves the use of different payment policies for people of different races. The next case provides an example of this type of differential treatment. The plaintiff is an African-American man who was a graduate student at Shenandoah University in Winchester, Virginia. He attempted to purchase a printer cartridge at Staples using his out-of-state check, which was imprinted with his permanent address in Clinton, Maryland. At the time, Staples had a nationwide policy of accepting all checks (as long as they met certain criteria not material to this case). Clerks were supposed to insert all checks into a device on the cash register, which would electronically verify the checks through a neutral, third-party check guarantee system. Contrary to Staples' policy, the sales clerk informed Mr. Williams that Staples did not accept out-of-state checks. Williams offered to show various forms of identification, but was still refused. Because he assumed the clerk was applying store policy, he left the store and purchased the cartridge elsewhere.

Several weeks later, during a conversation with another graduate student who is white, Williams learned that his friend had used an out-of-state check to purchase goods at the same Staples store without incident. He reported the incident to the Equal Rights Center, a civil rights advocacy agency. The Equal Rights Center hired two testers to conduct a matched-pair test. During the test, the white man's check was initially refused but later accepted after inspection by a manager. The African-American man's check was refused. Mr. Williams filed suit alleging that Staples applied a different check-cashing policy for blacks and whites. The trial court dismissed Mr. Williams' case. The U.S. Court of Appeals reversed the lower court's decision finding that Williams was denied the opportunity to enter into a contract with Staples although Staples afforded such an opportunity a White customer. On November 18, 2004, Williams accepted a $50,000 out-of-court settlement from Staples.[9]

The next case involves Avis, the car rental company. In May 1995, Linda Pugh, an African-American businesswoman, reserved two minivans from an Avis franchise in Wilmington, North Carolina, for a family trip to Florida. When she arrived to pick up the vans, she was treated rudely and not permitted to rent the vans. Calling an Avis toll-free number to complain, Ms. Pugh was told that the company had received other complaints about the Wilmington franchise. In the fall of 1996, she filed a complaint against Avis, along with two other black women who had been refused rentals at other locations owned by the same Avis franchise in North and South Carolina.

In sworn statements, a former manager and many former employees at these locations said they were instructed to find reasons to refuse rentals to black customers. Statements from other ex-employees made it clear that top Avis officials at its reservation center in Tulsa and its world headquarters in New York were aware of the discrimination but took no action to stop it. In 1997, the plaintiffs amended their complaint to add class action allegations, including declarations from more than 100 African Americans who said they had experienced discrimination at the Carolina locations.

Specifically, the class of customers alleged that African-American customers were questioned more vigorously than similarly situated white customers, required to have more credit available on their credit cards than whites, quoted higher car rental rates than white customers, and falsely told that no rentals were available. In addition, African Americans were denied car rentals if the address on their driver's license was not current, if they were unable to provide proof of employment, and if they expressed an intention to drive a long distance. The plaintiffs reached a class action settlement agreement with Avis and the franchise owner for $5.4 million in April 1998. The settlement included a consent decree that covered the operations of the franchise owner for three years.[10]

In a lawsuit against Toys R Us, plaintiffs alleged that the company discriminated against them on the basis of their race by asking to inspect their sales receipts after they made purchases at Toy R Us stores, yet not inspecting the sales receipts of white shoppers.[11] A similar case involved Samaad Bishop, an African-American man who purchased a Kodak camera and a bottle of water at the Best Buy store located at 1280 Lexington Avenue in Manhattan, New York, on August 20, 2005. As he exited the store, Best Buy employees Ricardo Quiles, Brian Placek, Brian Legister, and Carl Larsen asked to see his sales receipt. Mr. Bishop asked the employees whether he was being accused of shoplifting. When they told him that he was not, Bishop responded, "Then there is no legal basis for you to demand inspection of my sales receipt and impede my forward progress." He attempted to leave the store without showing his receipt and was allegedly attacked by Quiles, Placek, Legister, Larsen, and others. Mr. Bishop alleged that as he "struggle[d] to get free from being pummeled by fist," defendant Peter Troupas yelled, "Drag his black ass back in the store!" Bishop alleges that "while being punched," he "managed to free himself and dial 9-1-1."

Soon after, Police Officers Green and Morales arrived. After discussing the situation with the Best Buy employees, Officer Green asked to see Mr. Bishop's sales receipt. He initially refused, but then handed his receipt to Officer Green "under threat of incarceration." Officer Green showed the receipt to the Best Buy employees and Bishop was then permitted to leave the store. The next day, Bishop received medical treatment at Barnabas Hospital. He sued various defendants, including Best Buy, the Best Buy employees, and the responding New York Police Department officers, alleging various claims.

The district court denied Best Buy's motion to dismiss Mr. Bishop's Section 1981 claim. The court held that Bishop adequately stated a claim under Section 1981 of the Civil Rights Act of 1866 by alleging that he was assaulted as a result of racial discrimination when security employees at the store pummeled him after he refused to show them his sales receipt. In support of its decision, the district court noted that Bishop alleged that one of the employees shouted "drag his black ass back in the store!" Such a statement was enough to state a claim that racial animus was a motivating factor in the alleged assault. Bishop and Best Buy subsequently reached a settlement on these claims. As in the Green case against Dillard's Department Store, this case involved an overt expression of hostility based on Mr. Bishop's race. It is possible that this fact influenced the judge's perception of the severity of Mr. Bishop's case.[12]

In contrast, Office Max employees did not explicitly refer to the race of two shoppers they believed were acting suspiciously. Within minutes of entering an Office Max store to purchase office supplies, Darryl Morris and Leggitt Nailor were approached by police officers who had been summoned by the store's assistant manager to investigate two black males. The only two black men in the store at the time, Morris and Nailor showed identification and answered questions posed by the officers, who then apologized and left. Morris and Nailor filed suit alleging that the only reason Office Max called the police was that they are African American. They alleged that they would have purchased timestamps if they had not been detained by the police. Therefore, the men claimed that the store's actions interfered with their right to make and enforce a contract in violation of Section 1981 of the Civil Rights Act of 1866. The district court granted summary judgment to Office Max and the Court of Appeals affirmed that decision reasoning that the plaintiffs were never denied access to the store and their claim that they would have made a purchase was speculative.[13]

The next case is an unusual situation that arose after an African-American man made a purchase at Radio Shack. The plaintiff, John Garrett, is a disabled black Vietnam veteran who was shopping for a police scanner at Radio Shack in Brunswick, Maine, on December 21, 1998. For the duration of his stay, he was the only African American on the premises. Three employees—all of whom were white—monitored his movements, and at least one of them accompanied him throughout his visit. Upon inquiry, a clerk told Garrett that the scanner he wished to buy was not in stock. Mr. Garrett found a book, a telephone, and some batteries that he purchased. At the checkout counter, he asked whether the scanner might be available at another branch. After calling around, the store manager, Steven

Richard, responded in the negative. Richard requested Mr. Garrett's name and address and Garrett obliged. Then, Garrett left the store.

Afterwards, Richard and two employees noticed that a $2000 computer was missing. Richard told the police that he suspected Mr. Garrett of stealing it. Police went to Mr. Garrett's house and asked whether they could search his house and car. He agreed. They did not find the computer. When Mr. Garrett called the store to complain about having been singled out due to his race, the manager told him he had reported white shoppers as well. In fact, the manager had not done so. Radio Shack made no other efforts to locate the missing computer. The court found that Radio Shack did not interfere with Mr. Garrett's right to contract since the transaction between them was already complete when the Radio Shack manager singled out Mr. Garrett as the thief. Therefore, Radio Shack's motion for summary judgment was granted. The Court of Appeals affirmed that decision reasoning that the alleged harassment—the appearance of the police on his doorstep—did not occur until long after he had left the Radio Shack outlet. Therefore, the court concluded the police visit was not connected to the contractual relationship between Garrett and Radio Shack. The court did not consider this intrusion as amounting to harassment. Stating that "the challenged surveillance must have some negative effect on the shopper's ability to contract with the store," it found that the events that took place did not violate the statute.[14]

Regardless of the outcomes of lawsuits against commercial establishments, many consumers of color believe that the additional surveillance they experience is discriminatory whether it deters them from completing their transaction or not. As discussed in Chapter 2, every individual copes with the discriminatory treatment differently and even the same person might handle a situation differently from one day to the next or one shopping encounter to the next. A host of factors can influence a person's decision to walk out of the store without making an intended purchase or to go through with the transaction despite being treated like a thief. For example, a shopper might be tired, in a hurry, with or without children or other companions. But a distinctive feature of racial profiling that occurs in the marketplace is that customers of color have choices. Black and brown customers have the option of spending their money elsewhere when they feel that they have been treated unfairly. In other words, unlike motorists who cannot avoid driving on public roadways, consumers can stop patronizing—or boycott—business establishments where they believe they are discriminated against. As a result, consumers have the power and agency to effectuate change.

Unfortunately, while being suspected as a thief is a common experience, it is not the only story that people of color tell. In addition to being viewed with suspicion, they are treated differently than whites in other respects. Among the many ways in which people of color are made to feel that they do not belong in the marketplace are prepay requirements, differential enforcement of dress codes, and refusals to style black hair. The next two chapters explore these types of discriminatory treatments that occur in all sorts of commercial establishments.

## Notes

1. President Barack Obama, Washington, DC, November 24, 2014. Remarks presented at the White House after the announcement of the decision by the grand jury in Ferguson, Missouri, not to indict police officer Darren Wilson who fatally shot Michael Brown.

2. *Chapman v. The Higbee Company d/b/a Dillard Department Stores, Inc.,* 319 F.3d 825 (6th Cir. 2003).

3. Oyler, 2005.

4. See *Gregory v. Dillard's,* 565 F.3d 464 (8th Cir., 2009).

5. *Gregory v. Dillard's,* 494 F.3d 694 (8th Cir., 2007).

6. *Green v. Dillard's,* 483 F.3d 533 (8th Cir., 2007).

7. *Lewis v. J.C. Penney Co., Inc.,* 948 F.Supp. 367 (D. De., 1996).

8. *Christian v. Wal-Mart Stores, Inc.,* 252 F.3d 862 (6th Cir. 2001).

9. *Williams v. Staples, Inc.,* 2003 WL 1873937 (W.D.Va., 2003).

10. *Pugh v. Avis Rent-A-Car Systems Inc.,* Case No. 96-CV-9-F (E.D.N.C., 1997).

11. *Drayton v. Toys "R" Us Inc.,* 645 F.Supp.2d 149 (S.D.N.Y., 2009).

12. *Bishop v. Best Buy, Co. Inc.,* 2010 WL 4159566 (S.D.N.Y., 2010).

13. *Morris v. Office Max, Inc.,* 89 F.3d 411 (7th Cir., 1996).

14. *Garrett v. Tandy Corp.,* 295 F.3d 94 (1st Cir., 2002).

## References

*Bishop v. Best Buy Co., Inc.,* 2010 WL 4159566, U.S. District Court for the Southern District of New York, October 13, 2010.

*Chapman v. The Higbee Company d/b/a Dillard Department Stores, Inc.,* 319 F.3d 825, U.S. Court of Appeals for the 6th Circuit, 2003.

*Christian v. Wal-Mart Stores, Inc.,* 252 F.3d 862, U.S. Court of Appeals for the 6th Circuit, 2001.

*Drayton v. Toys "R" Us Inc.*, 645 F.Supp.2d 149, U.S. District Court for the Southern District of New York, July 17, 2009.

*Garrett v. Tandy Corp.*, 295 F.3d 94, U.S. Court of Appeals for the 1st Circuit, 2002.

*Green v. Dillard's, Inc.*, 483 F.3d 533, U.S. Court of Appeals for the 8th Circuit, 2007.

*Gregory v. Dillard's, Inc.*, 494 F.3d 694, U.S. Court of Appeals for the 8th Circuit, 2007.

*Gregory v. Dillard's, Inc.*, 565 F. 3d 464, U.S. Court of Appeals, 8th Circuit, 2009.

*Lewis v. JC Penney Co., Inc.*, 948 F.Supp. 367, U.S. District Court for the District of Delaware, 1996.

*Morris v. Office Max, Inc.*, 89 F.3d 411, U.S. Court of Appeals for the 7th Circuit, 1996.

Obama, President Barack. 2014. "Remarks Made by the President after Announcement of the Decision by the Grand Jury in Ferguson, Missouri." White House, Washington, DC.

Oyler, Randall L. 2005. "Discrimination in the Consumer Marketplace: A Response to Harris, Henderson, and Williams." *Journal of Public Policy & Marketing* 24, no. 1: 172–173.

*Pugh v. Avis Rent-A-Car Systems Inc.*, Case No. 96-CV-9-F, U.S. District Court for the Eastern District of North Carolina, 1997.

*Williams v. Staples*, 2003 WL 1873937, U.S. District Court for the Western District of Virginia, 2003).

# Chapter 8

# Mundane Consumption

*Consumption has to be recognized as an integral part of the social need to relate to other people, and to have mediating materials for relating to them. Mediating materials are food, drink, and hospitality of home to offer, flowers and clothes to signal shared rejoicing, or mourning dress to share sorrow. Goods, work, and consumption have been artificially abstracted out of the whole social scheme. The way the excision has been made damages the possibility of understanding these aspects of life.*

—Mary Douglas and Baron Isherwood[1]

What is more "mundane" than stopping at a gas station to fill up? Daron Hill and three other African Americans observed a similar pattern in the way they were treated at Shell-branded stations when they purchased gasoline. They noticed that they were required to prepay for cash purchases of gasoline but white customers could pump the gas first and then pay for it. Based on this differential treatment, which they documented on videotape, they filed a complaint against Shell-branded facilities alleging that Shell engaged in a pattern or practice of discriminating against African-American customers. Most Shell-brand gas stations are equipped with gas pumps that can be turned on or off from a console inside the service station. Therefore, customers can be viewed by the operator of the station through a window or video camera. The plaintiffs' claim was based on the fact that they were required to pay in advance for gasoline before the operator of the station would turn on the pump (prepay) while white customers arriving within minutes of such marketplace encounters were allowed to pump their gas first and then pay (postpay).

In this particular case, a settlement was negotiated between the parties but countless others experience indecencies such as these every day. In other words, what should be every day, mundane activities for consumers of color, become negative, hurtful experiences which prey on their psyches. In this chapter, we discuss other cases of mundane consumption which impact persons of color on a regular basis.

## Classification Scheme: From the Mundane to Special Occasion

When looking at the range of cases analyzed over the years of conducting research on marketplace discrimination, it seems that many cases fall into the mundane consumption category. According to Kleine and his colleagues, "'mundane and everyday' refers to those activities which constitute the bulk of daily life—preparing meals, relaxing, or getting to work, for example. Mundane, everyday consumption occurs during and as an integral part of negotiating these daily life-tasks."[2] After exploring several classification schemes for all these cases, it was concluded that although no one classification scheme fully captured all the nuances, Rob Kleine and his colleagues came closest to providing a workable framework for presenting a logical flow for the analysis of selected cases. As noted by the opening quote to this chapter, understanding consumer behavior should be studied as part-and-parcel of mundane, everyday consumption.

Kleine and his colleagues argue that many consumption tasks are carried out in social settings and that consumption is undertaken to help us get along with others.[3] Thus, mundane consumption facilitates and mediates social interaction.[4] Kleine, Schultz-Kleine, and Kernan also explain that mundane consumption is self-relevant which means that it involves goods and services that people feel they need. Because of this, mundane consumption (1) involves the patterned use of product clusters (such as buying the same items at the grocery store each week); (2) occurs within an activity stream within the daily routine; and (3) frequently involves social interaction.

As has been discussed, people perceive incidents differently and there can be a great deal of subjectivity in attributing negative interactions to discrimination. Those attributions may differ based on whether a situation takes place in a mundane consumption context versus a special occasion one. In this chapter, the focus is on the former, whereas the next chapter is dedicated to more special occasion occurrences. Because of the variability among consumers from different racial, ethnic, and cultural backgrounds in terms of what equals mundane or special occasion consumption or even criminal treatment, there may be some ambiguity as to whether a particular case belongs in one category rather than another.

For example, research by Bone, Christensen, and Williams investigates what they call the experience of "systemic restricted choice" and its impact on individuals' self-concept among white versus racial and ethnic minority consumers seeking financing at a bank. Their research showed that minority consumers framed themselves as striving in a world of limited resources, fighting and often losing battles (i.e., requiring a special effort, a special occasion). These experiences are juxtaposed against those of educationally and economically similar white consumers who viewed the bank encounters as welcoming and easy to navigate. In other words, for white customers, securing a bank loan was a routine, mundane journey.[5] On the other hand, for black customers, obtaining a loan is anything but routine and mundane. This difference in the perception of a marketplace encounter as being "mundane" versus "special occasion" was typified when the African American on the multiracial Bone, Christensen, and Williams research team was not at all amazed by the stories told to them during the qualitative data collection phase of interviewing a number of minority entrepreneurs who had struggled to obtain bank loans to support their business enterprises. However, one of his white colleagues on this same research team was somewhat astounded by the responses of the minority entrepreneurs. As he expressed it, "These folks live a completely different experience than I do, You go to the Bronx and you see how they have to go beyond typical creativity to survive, both as a business and as a family . . . It's an uphill battle for minority entrepreneurs."

When interviewed about their work for a business magazine, the two white coauthors of this multiracial research team made the following observations as they reflected on what each of them faced in applying for a loan:

> I grew up White, in upper middle-class America. . . . I had no idea. I was completely oblivious. When I was eighteen, my dad co-signed on a loan to help me build some houses. . . . I went through the whole process completely oblivious to my race. I never thought once, "Oh, I'm White."
>
> There is a belief among White people that things like this *used to happen.* . . . They think it is no longer real. Unfortunately, this still remains a reality for a significant portion of the U.S. population.
>
> There is a general belief among Americans that we're the land of opportunity and that anyone can pull themselves up by their bootstraps. . . . It is a land of opportunity, but that opportunity is not always equally accessible.[6]

The distinction made by these researchers about the same marketplace encounter, that is, applying for a bank loan, that is perceived as mundane by whites but as challenging and nonmundane by African Americans reflects a similar distinction between mundane and special occasion incidents utilized to categorize the cases described in this book. By capturing the whole spectrum of marketplace experiences, this typology addresses an issue raised by some skeptics who downplay the importance of everyday discrimination in the marketplace, whether they are nonminority consumers, marketers, juries, or even judges.

## Mundane Consumption

In a case involving another gasoline station venue, Willie Bentley Jr., the plaintiff, an African-American man, on the way home from work, stopped at Red Apple Kwik Fill. Mr. Bentley pumped $5.00 worth of gas into his vehicle, and then went inside to pay for the gas and purchase lottery tickets. As he waited his turn in line, he noticed that other customers who were ahead of him purchased items, including lottery tickets, in addition to gas. When he arrived at the counter, he told the sales clerk that he wanted to pay for gas and $3.00 worth of lottery tickets. She told the plaintiff to go back to the end of the line. Mr. Bentley refused, and explained that he simply wanted to pay for the gas, purchase lottery tickets, and leave. The sales clerk argued with him about the fact that the store did not make money off the lottery machine. The sales clerk started yelling at the plaintiff. Eventually, she allowed the plaintiff to pay for his gas and to purchase the lottery tickets. The sales clerk did not use any racial epithets during the argument. At the time of the incident, Mr. Bentley was the only black person in the store. However, it was noted that five years earlier, this same sales clerk after waiting on an African-American customer stated, "I hate niggers." Bentley argued that his Section 1981 right to contract was violated when the sales clerk denied him service. The court found that he was not denied service and that the six- to seven-minute delay he experienced did not alter a fundamental characteristic of the service to which he was entitled. Despite this delay, Bentley maintained his position in line and completed his intended purchases. Although the jury awarded Mr. Bentley $5,000 in compensatory damages and $100,000 in punitive damages, the district court granted the defendant's motion for judgment as a matter of law, and a final judgment was entered in favor of Red Apple Kwik Fill.

Rathea Williams, an African-American woman, also experienced hostility at a convenience store in Reisterstown, Maryland, on her way to work on December 13, 1996. As she approached the counter with her purchase, she made a passing comment about some confusion behind the check-out counter. The store clerk and a customer, both white, who had been talking and laughing, began to make racially derogatory comments toward Ms. Williams and didn't let up. The customer took change from his pocket and hurled it at the plaintiff. The clerk laughed and continued talking to the customer. Eventually, another cashier came over to help Ms. Williams, who paid for her purchases, gave her a receipt and her change. The customer spit in Ms. Williams' face, ran out of the store, and threatened to kill her. Ms. Williams noted his license plate number and attempted to call the police. When the police came, she told her story. The sales clerk was terminated from her job for use of profanity and improper handling of the dispute.

Finding that the defendant, Cloverland Farms Dairy, could be vicariously liable for the actions of its employee, the court found that Ms. Williams attempted to make a purchase from the clerk but was deterred by the racial attack. Although she was able to complete her transaction with another clerk, Ms. Williams experienced a delay that could be viewed by a jury as a violation of her civil rights. The court denied the defendant's motion for summary judgment stating: "Although the length . . . of the violation may affect the plaintiff's award, the fact that an act of contractual discrimination was short . . . does not make it any less a violation."[7] This means that the trial judge believed there were factual issues that a judge or jury must decide at trial. In other words, Ms. Williams must be given the opportunity to present evidence to support her claim in court.

In another case arising from an interaction in a convenience store, the court similarly refused to grant the defendant's motion for summary judgment. Michael Leach, an African-American man, was a conductor for the Norfolk Southern Railroad. Because he and his coworkers routinely traveled between Toledo and Bellevue, Ohio, to meet trains to which they had been assigned, they sometimes stopped at the Speedway SuperAmerica store in Clyde, Ohio. The altercation began when Leach was purchasing some items, including cigarettes. The sales clerk, Jenny Heyman, was talking on the telephone as she waited on Leach. When he asked her about the price of cigarettes, she seemed annoyed but gave him the information. The transaction was completed, and Leach told Heyman that she might handle her customers better if she got off the phone. She looked at him "blankly" and made a dismissive gesture with her hand. He muttered "cunt" which Heyman may or may not have heard. She became upset, asked Leach what he had said, stated that she was not a whore, and called him a "nigger." Heyman jumped over the counter and assaulted Leach, slapping him on the side of his face. The police was called and Heyman was charged with assault. She eventually pleaded guilty to a lesser offense.

With respect to Mr. Leach's race discrimination claim, the court found that, "although he had completed his purchase before the discriminatory conduct occurred, a jury could find that Heyman's treatment of plaintiff was continuous . . . during the entire period that he was in the store." Furthermore, the fact that Heyman called Michael Leach a name that any African American would find deeply offensive is clear and direct proof of bias. "It also indicates that the 'service' she provided was less than that which she might have provided, had plaintiff been Caucasian."[8]

On June 24, 1985, Charles Lewis and five friends stopped at a 7-Eleven to purchase Slurpees. As he entered the store, the store clerk yelled at Mr. Lewis to get out. Mr. Lewis looked around to see who the clerk was yelling at, and the clerk responded "Yes, you. Out!" Mr. Lewis proceeded to the counter to purchase the Slurpees, he was informed that the store did not serve blacks. The clerk stated the store had a problem with black shoplifting. After discussing the policy with the clerk, Mr. Lewis left the store, and called the police from a nearby payphone. An officer arrived, spoke first to Mr. Lewis, and then the clerk. After the officer left the store, he told Mr. Lewis he would be served if he and his friends entered two at a time. The clerk had informed the officer that the store had a problem with blacks shoplifting. The clerk did not identify Mr. Lewis or anyone in his party as suspected shoplifters. At the same time, a group of white males entered the store and were served. Mr. Lewis filed a complaint with the Washington Human Rights Commission. He later hired an attorney, but withdrew the complaint and filed a civil action. At trial, the jury found in favor of the store owner. Mr. Lewis appealed the lower court decision. The appeals court reversed the jury verdict and remanded the case for a determination of damages, costs, and attorney's fees.[9]

Hair styling services are typically viewed as mundane consumption experiences that are part of everyday life. In the next case, being a good husband, Mr. Perry made an appointment for his wife's hair to be washed and set at the Command Performance hair salon in King of Prussia, Pennsylvania. However, when she arrived, the hair stylist, a white woman, informed Mrs. Perry that she had a bad cold and felt sick and would like to go home. Mrs. Perry agreed to allow another hair stylist to do Mrs. Perry's hair. That stylist allegedly refused to do so saying "I don't do black hair!" Mrs. Perry was very upset, began to cry, and her husband took her home. Although the salon sent Mrs. Perry a gift certificate, she filed suit. The court determined that the salon had not refused to enter into a contract with Mrs. Perry, and therefore made a finding in favor of Command Performance.[10]

Another case involving the denial of hair styling services arose in University Heights, Ohio, when several black women seeking out reasonably priced services, attempted to be seen at Great Clips, the defendant's hair salon. Although Great Clips offered "fades" and "relaxers" to its white customers, it did not offer those services to African-American customers. Great Clips also did not offer styling products for black hair. In addition, the price of services used primarily by African-American customers was higher than those used by white customers. The parties arrived at a confidential out-of-court settlement in 2000.[11]

Arranging for daycare services for one's child is another everyday activity that involves consumption in the marketplace. On or about June 11, 2001, Annie Gainey, an African-American female, called Plainfield Daycare Center to inquire about services for her son. Ms. Gainey had been referred to the Center by a coworker whose child attended the center. Ms. Gainey was told that the Center had no openings. Suspecting she was denied services due to her race, Ms. Gainey asked a friend to call and inquire about openings. This friend was told there were openings and was invited to visit the school. Ms. Gainey called the school a second time, and during this conversation she advised the clerk she had been told there were openings by a current parent. Subsequently, she was provided services. Ms. Gainey filed a complaint with the Connecticut Commission on Human Rights and Opportunities. The complaint was dismissed. The commission investigated the daycare center's admission policies and found they were being applied without racial bias because eight of the 14 children being served were children of color.

The following incidents are classified as discrimination involving daily consumption experiences because they arose in eating establishments. Of course, we must all eat, whether we purchase groceries and cook our own meals or dine in a restaurant. In the next few cases, African Americans were prevented from eating out or treated differently than whites when they attempted to be served in restaurants. During an annual Memorial Day Bike rally that attracts a predominantly African-American clientele, four local restaurants actually closed down for the week. The rally, known as "Black Bike Week," has been held every Memorial Day weekend since 1980 in the predominantly black town of Atlantic Beach, South Carolina close to Myrtle Beach. The festival had become so popular that Atlantic Beach hotels were incapable of accommodating all the bikers. In May of 2004, the National Association of the Advancement of Colored People (NAACP) filed a federal lawsuit against the four restaurants. The restaurants named in the suit alleged that the closings were due to traffic congestion and poor business; however, they were open for business during the Harley-Davidson rally the previous week. That rally attracts a predominantly white clientele.[12]

One year earlier, the NAACP had filed suit against 28 restaurants, hotels, and city officials, alleging that the establishments and the city's officials established policies to make the location inhospitable to African-American visitors. In addition, 12 African-American motorcycle enthusiasts filed a lawsuit in federal court against the Yachtsman Resort Hotel. According to their complaint, African-American bikers who participated in the annual rally between 2000 and 2002 encountered markedly different conditions than their white counterparts attending the Harley Rally. The bikers, the NAACP, and its Conway, South Carolina branch, accused the Yachtsman Hotel of engaging in discriminatory practices when it charged significantly more for rooms and adopted special rules in effect only one week each year: during Black Bike Week. For example, the hotel required guests to sign a 34-rule guest contract and to prepay for their entire stay. In contrast, guests staying at the Yachtsman during Harley Week were neither required to sign a guest contract or pay in advance. Also, individuals attempting to reserve a room during Black Bike Week were required to submit photo identification before their stay and were asked to present a photo ID every time they entered the hotel. During Harley Week, there were no photo ID requirements. Among other efforts to discourage African-American guests from patronizing the hotel, the Yachtsman is said to have limited guest parking by barricading lots where bikes were allowed to park during Harley Week. In addition to implementing severe cancellation and eviction policies, the hotel increased security and police presence during Black Bike Week.[13]

The parties agreed to settle the case for $1.2 million. Under the terms of the settlement, the Yachtsman Hotel provided discounts to African-American customers for their next stay at the hotel, paid for the plaintiffs' costs and legal fees, applied consistent policies for all guests year-round, expanded its nondiscrimination policies and training for employees, designated an ombudsman to investigate future complaints of discrimination, and allowed monitoring by the NAACP's counsel.[14]

On July 25, 2001, at approximately 9:48 p.m., Chandra Harmon and her friend Renee Daniel, arrived at a Cracker Barrel Country Store in Chattanooga, Tennessee. Ms. Harmon, who is African American, and Ms. Daniel, who is multiracial, were accompanied by their children, all of whom are either African American or multiracial. The restaurant and parking lot were full. As they walked from the parking lot to the restaurant, they passed a white customer who told Harmon's party that the Cracker Barrel was still open, and that the restaurant seated customers until 10:00 p.m. When Harmon's party entered the restaurant, a server stopped them and informed Daniel that the restaurant was about to close. Harmon and Daniel asked if they could be seated because they were from out of town and had hungry children. The server responded that she would check with the manager to see if she could seat them. A few minutes later, a manager approached Harmon and informed her that the restaurant had stopped seating patrons for the evening and that Cracker Barrel would be unable to serve their party. Daniel asked the manager to make an exception because their children were hungry. The manager refused Daniel's request. At approximately 10:00 p.m., four white men walked into the restaurant behind Harmon and Daniel. To both parties, the manager stated that, "If I let one of you in, I have to serve you all." The Harmon party left the restaurant.

After placing the children in the car, Harmon and Daniel discussed the incident, noting that the four white customers had not left the restaurant. Harmon and Daniel returned to the restaurant. Through the window, they could see that the four white customers, who had arrived after them, were seated and drinking beverages. Harmon knocked on the restaurant door, now locked, and demanded to speak to the manager again. When the manager came outside, he initially denied that the four white customers were being served. When Harmon and Daniel pointed out that the four customers in question were visible from the front window, the manager went back into the restaurant and spoke with them. At approximately 10:15 p.m., while the manager was inside, Daniel and Harmon watched another white male enter the restaurant. He, too, was seated and served. This was witnessed by a young man, Sam Tisdale, who was waiting outside of the restaurant. When the manager returned, he stated, "I just looked at our tapes and I don't have anything rung up after 10:00." The manager also said that the four white customers, who entered the restaurant after Harmon, were seated before 10:00 p.m.[15]

These facts reflect the experience of just one of many plaintiffs in a lawsuit against Cracker Barrel. The company was investigated by the U.S. Justice Department and at least 42 plaintiffs, including the NAACP, sued Cracker Barrel, which at that time owned and operated 450 restaurants in 41 states. The plaintiffs claimed that Cracker Barrel segregated black customers in the smoking section and denied them service. Also, African-American customers from 16 states alleged that they were subjected to racial slurs and served food taken from the trash, according to the plaintiffs and some 400 witnesses, including Cracker Barrel employees and customers. In addition to settling the lawsuits for $8.7 million, Cracker Barrel entered into a consent decree with the U.S. Department of Justice. The settlement required the restaurant to change its practices and it enforced these changes with undercover investigations. In addition, Cracker Barrel restaurants agreed to expand sensitivity training for employees as part of the settlement agreement. However, the restaurant did not admit any wrongdoing and did not pay any fines.[16]

## Key Takeaway from Examining Mundane Consumption Cases

We all need to shop for everyday, mundane items to live. As consumers, we must still interface in the public sphere and cannot protect ourselves behind the anonymity of a computer screen although online shopping is presenting a new frontier, as Chapter 10 further explores. Gas for the car, groceries, and salon services cannot be purchased through online delivery. And despite the growing number of people known as "voluntary simplifiers" who strive for independence off the grid supplying their own needs, most households are not self-reliant when it comes to everyday items. So each and every time a person of color steps outside his or her home to engage in retail commerce, even if it's for something as simple as Skittles and a Brisk Ice Tea, as in Trayvon Martin's case, there is the possibility of encountering a problem in the marketplace. And whether one is obtaining a bank loan for a luxury item or simply stopping at the corner store to buy a sandwich, the potential for marketplace inequality is present at both ends of this spectrum. Now moving beyond mundane consumption, cases of consumer discrimination in the realm of special occasions are presented in Chapter 9.

## Notes

1. Douglas and Isherwood, 1979, p. 4.
2. Kenneally, 2016.
3. Kleine, Kleine, and Kernan, 1993.
4. Douglas and Isherwood, 1979.
5. Bone, Christensen, and Williams, 2014.
6. Hollingshead, 2016, p. 24.
7. *Williams v. Cloverland Farms Dairy Inc.*, 78 F. Supp. 2d 479, at 486 (D. Md. 1999).
8. *Leach v. Heyman*, 233 F.Supp.2d 906, at 911 (N.D. Ohio, 2002).
9. *Charles Lewis et al. v. Jill Doll, John Doll and the Southland Corporation*, d/b/a Seven-Eleven, 53 Wash. App.203, 765 P2d 1341.

10. *Perry v. Command Performance*, 1991 WL 46475 (E.D. Pa. 1991); aff'd, 945 F.2d 395 (3d Cir. 1991); cert. denied, 112 S.Ct. 1166 (U.S.Sup.Ct. 1992).

11. *Halton v. Great Clips*, 94 F.Supp.2d 856 (N.D.Ohio 2000).

12. Harris, 2004.

13. *NAACP et al. v. Shawnee Development, Inc. et al.,* Civ.No.4-03-1733-12, D.C.S.C., 2003.

14. Harris, 2004.

15. This scenario reflects a situation encountered by two of the named plaintiffs in a lawsuit filed against Cracker Barrel Old Country Stores, Inc. See Amended Complaint 121–128, *NAACP v. Cracker Barrel Old Country Store, Inc.*, No. 4:01-CV-325-HLM (N.D. Ga. filed Apr. 11, 2002).

16. "Cracker Barrel Settles Racial Discrimination Lawsuits for $8.7M," 2004.

## References

Barr, Johanna. 2011. "Danny Glover: Latest Taxi Crackdown Is Similar to Mine." *NBC New York*, New York.

Bone, Sterling A., Glenn L. Christensen, and Jerome D. Williams. 2014. "Rejected, Shackled, and Alone: The Impact of Systemic Restricted Choice on Minority Consumers' Construction of Self." *Journal of Consumer Research* 41, no. 2: 451–474.

*Charles Lewis et al. v. Jill Doll, John Doll and the Southland Corporation*, d/b/a Seven-Eleven, 53 Wash. App. 203, 765 P.2d 1341.

"Cracker Barrel Settles Racial Discrimination Lawsuits for $8.7M." 2004. Available at: http://www.foxnews.com/story/2004/09/09/cracker-barrel-settles-racial-discrimination-lawsuits-for-87m.html. Accessed September 9, 2004.

Douglas, Mary and Baron Isherwood. 1979. *The World of Goods: Towards an Anthropology of Consumption*. New York: Basic Books.

*Halton v. Great Clips*, 94 F.Supp.2d 856 (U.S. District Court for the Northern District of Ohio, 2000).

Harris, Anne-Marie. 2004. "South Carolina Hotel Settles Biker Lawsuit." *The New Crisis* 111, no. 6 (Nov/Dec): 54–55.

Hollingshead, Todd. 2016. "Broken Dream." *Marriott Alumni Magazine*, Brigham Young University.

Kenneally, Tim. 2016. "Al Roker's Revenge: Cabbie Who Passed Him Up for 'White Guy' Pleads Guilty." *The Wrap*.

Kleine, Robert E., Susan Schultz Kleine, and Jerome B. Kernan. 1993. "Mundane Consumption and the Self: A Social-Identity Perspective." *Journal of Consumer Psychology* 2, no. 3: 209–235.

LaRosa, Paul. 2014. "Almost No More White NYC Cab Drivers, but Blacks Still Can't Catch a Ride." *The Huffington Post*, November 6.

*Leach v. Heyman*, 233 F.Supp.2d 906, at 911 (U.S. District Court for the Northern District of Ohio, 2002).

*NAACP et al. v. Shawnee Development, Inc. et al.,* Civ.No.4-03-1733-12, D.C.S.C., 2003.

*NAACP v. Cracker Barrel Old Country Store, Inc.,* No. 4:01-CV-325-HLM (N.D. Ga. filed Apr. 11, 2002).

Oyler, Randall L. 2005. "Discrimination in the Consumer Marketplace: A Response to Harris, Henderson, and Williams." *Journal of Public Policy & Marketing* 24, no. 1: 172–173.

*Perry v. Command Performance,* 1991 WL 46475 (U.S. District Court for the Eastern District of Pennsylvania, 1991); aff'd, 945 F.2d 395 (3d Cir. 1991); cert. denied, 112 S.Ct. 1166 (U.S.Sup.Ct. 1992).

Rylah, Juliet Bennett. 2015. "Former Baseball Player Says LAX Cab Driver Demanded He Take the Bus." *LAist.* Los Angeles, CA.

West, Cornel. 1993. *Race Matters.* New York: Vintage Books.

Williams, Monte. 1999. "Danny Glover Says Cabbies Discriminated against Him." The New York Times, November 4.

*Williams v. Cloverland Farms Dairy Inc.,* 78 F. Supp. 2d 479, at 486 (U.S. District Court for the District of Maryland, 1999).

# Chapter 9

# Special Occasions of Marketplace Discrimination

*I'm in a store, and the person doesn't obviously know that I carry the black card, and so they make an assessment based upon the way I look and who I am. . . . You should be able to go in a store looking like whatever you look like and say, "I'd like to see this." That didn't happen.*

—Oprah Winfrey, August 2013[1]

Oprah Winfrey made this comment after an incident that occurred to her when she was in Switzerland for Tina Turner's wedding to her longtime partner, Erwin Bach. There was such a firestorm regarding Oprah's claims of being racially profiled over a $38,000 purse that she ended up apologizing for making such a big deal about it and suggested that it was an isolated incident. However, this was not the first time she has been racially profiled in a retail store. In a 2001 *Good Housekeeping* article, Oprah reported that she and her long-time hairstylist, Andre Walker, were denied entrance to a store on Madison Avenue in New York City. She even called from a pay phone across the street, and the store's employees assured her that they were open. However, despite knocking quite loudly on the store door and window, they were not allowed entry. Later when Ms. Winfrey returned to Chicago and called the manager to inquire about why they did not let her in, the manager told her that they thought she and her hairstylist were the transsexuals who had robbed their store the week before.

If Oprah Winfrey, one of the richest and most famous people in the world has been denied entry into a store, then it is reasonable to believe that countless numbers of less rich, less famous people have also had this experience. Consider the case of Rochelle DeRosa, an African-American female. On April 26, 1995, she and a male companion attempted to enter Quang Loi Jewelry located in the Chinatown section of Boston, Massachusetts. Although there was an open sign in the window, as she tried to open the door, she found it locked. She rang a bell and knocked. An Asian woman came to the door and told Ms. DeRosa that the store was closed. Ms. DeRosa could see store employees in the store. She walked a few feet away and observed the store. She could see Asians and whites entering and exiting the store. Ms DeRosa approached a white man on the street and asked him to try to enter the store. He was able to do so. Ms. DeRosa filed a complaint against the store alleging race-based discrimination. Neither the owners nor legal counsel for Quang Loi Jewelry appeared at the public hearing and a default judgment was entered. Quang Loi Jewelry was ordered to cease and desist from discriminating based on race and color, and Ms. DeRosa was awarded $5,000.00 in damages.

Without knowing the actual intended purchase that Ms. DeRosa had in mind, it is clear that jewelry stores and bridal shops do a brisk business with women and men who are preparing for one of the most important days of their life, their wedding day. Stacey Masters, an African-American female, was one of those hopeful brides on August 15, 2000 when she scheduled an appointment at a bridal shop. As she and her mother shopped at the Creative Bridals store, Ms. Masters chose a dress to try on and was shown to a dressing room by the owner, Peter Kujawa. Ms. Masters alleges he told her she would be assisted by a female employee. Ms. Masters waited in the dressing room for several minutes, but no employee came to assist her. Later, she saw a female employee and asked for assistance. The employee allegedly responded that she did not help customers try on gowns. As Ms. Masters was leaving, she noticed the employee assisting a white female customer. Ms. Masters filed a complaint with the Connecticut Commission on Human Rights and Opportunities.

The commission found it was unlikely Ms. Masters could show reasonable cause to support a claim of discrimination. On May 30, 2001, the commission released jurisdiction of the case so that a lawsuit could be brought in Superior Court. Records do not reflect whether Ms. Masters went on to file and win a suit in Superior Court against Creative Bridals, but they did not win her business that day in August 2000. Even a famous actress like Lorraine Toussaint (of "Orange Is the New Black" fame), has had occasion to return a dress that she bought for a friend's wedding to a store that accused her of being part of a shoplifting ring that had robbed the store the week before.[2]

As many have experienced, weddings are a great time to catch up with friends and family members who have not been seen in a long time. So too are high school and college reunions. The National Association for the

Advancement of Colored People (NAACP) filed suit on behalf of guests who attended the Black College Reunion in 1999 at an Adam's Mark Hotel in Florida. The guests alleged they were charged higher room rates and deposits, were required to wear identification wristbands, were provided substandard services, confined to a less desirable section of the hotel, subjected to hostile security measures, and required to pay in advance. The lawsuit initially filed by five guests was joined by the State of Florida and the U.S. Justice Department. The justice department found that the chain routinely charged African Americans higher room rates and engaged in other discriminatory practices to discourage their patronage. In March 2000, a settlement decree was entered into. It required Adam's Mark to pay $8 million including $1.5 million to traditional black colleges to provide scholarships and internships in hotel management.[3] The chain also agreed to provide diversity training to its employees and monitor the treatment of future guests. Reunion attendees were eligible to receive $1,000 each through the Florida-administered settlement fund. According to former Attorney General Janet Reno, this was the largest settlement in a hotel discrimination case. However, as of December 2001, the final settlement that had actually been paid was only $1.1 million.[4]

The NAACP is not the only civil rights organization to take up the fight of marketplace discrimination. The American Civil Liberties Union (ACLU) brought a class action lawsuit against Patrick and Ray Nardone, owners of the Le Terrace club. The Nardones operated Le Terrace allegedly as a private swim club and catering company; however, the only criteria for membership was payment of a membership fee and race. The Nardones denied membership and the use of the facilities to people of color. The complaint detailed three incidents of discrimination. On one occasion, a family, who were members in good standing, was not allowed to host a birthday party for their minor child unless the guest list was limited to whites only. On another occasion, a family had its membership revoked after family members tried to enter the pool with two guests, one of whom was African American. On the third occasion, a white woman and guest of a member in good standing, was denied entrance because her adoptive daughter had dark hair and dark skin. The case was settled out of court for $1 million.

In addition to civil rights organizations such as the NAACP and the ACLU, other organizations may also weigh-in on issues relating to marketplace discrimination, especially if they have some type of leverage over the company alleged of discriminating. Consider the case of *Hyatt Corporation v. The Honolulu Liquor Commission*. Hyatt Corporation received three notices from the Honolulu liquor commission alleging it had violated a commission rule prohibiting discrimination. The rules stated it was unlawful for a licensee with a business open to the public to refuse or deny any person the full use and enjoyment of the licensee accommodations, advantages, and facilities based on the person's race, religion, sex, or ancestry. Hyatt sought injunctive and declaratory relief. Hyatt alleges that the commission's rule was promulgated without authority; that the rule, if lawful, should apply only to the sale of liquor and not to admission, and that the commission lacked jurisdiction. The court held that state public policy disfavors discrimination, that the commission had broad powers to create rules consistent with its statutory authority, and that a rule relating to entrance of a licensed establishment was related to sale as one could not buy if one could not enter. The court properly dismissed the complaint.

Hyatt and Adam's Mark are not the only hotels that have discriminated against (potential) patrons. Another such case is the case of Gail Walker, an African-American female. Ms. Walker had a confirmed reservation for a room at the Sheraton Inn on June 10, 1987. Ms. Walker arrived at the hotel at approximately 5:50 p.m. She was refused a room and was told that her reservation had been cancelled at 4 p.m. Ms. Walker asked for assistance in locating another room; the clerk refused. When Ms. Walker learned that the hotel had provided a room to a white male coworker, she complained to the manager. The manager, Mr. Ciesler, told Ms. Walker that the hotel had a policy whereby management could determine who of the "walk-ins" would receive rooms. Ms. Walker told the manager that the policy "had a very bad flavor" and asked if he knew what she meant. He replied he did, stating "And if this gets out, it can be very bad for this hotel as well as the chain." Ms. Walker sued alleging a violation of the Illinois Human Rights Act. Complainant's motion for a default judgment was granted. At the damages hearing, Ms. Walker was awarded $622.72 in out-of-pocket expenses and $3,500.00 for emotional distress (damages totaled $4,122.72).

Even smaller lodging places such as inns and motels have been found to discriminate in such as the next two cases. Thomas and Nancy Clark, two black individuals, live within five or six miles of the Maryland Inn. On July 5, 1988, a desk clerk denied them a room, telling them that the motel did not rent to local residents. The Clarks filed a complaint with the Prince George's County Human Relations Commission alleging racial discrimination. The commission sent two testers to the motel, one black and the other white. The desk clerk asked the black tester for identification, then told him he could not stay in the motel because he was a local resident. Although the white tester used a local address when registering, the clerk on duty rented him a room without asking for identification or questioning his reasons for staying at the motel. The jury found in favor of the plaintiffs. In 1992, the 4th Circuit Court affirmed the district court's denial of the defendant's motion for judgment notwithstanding the verdict.

Also in the state of Maryland was Ocean's Mecca, which as we discussed in Chapter 3, was sued for discrimination by Marie Murrell, who is white. What made Ms. Murrell's decision both so interesting and yet compelling is the presence of a comparison case. Herself. That is, because she was with the party, it was easier to demonstrate that discrimination had occurred. Likewise consider the case of Ms. Joseph, an African-American woman, her sons, and her white friend, all of whom attempted to enter the "Stadium Club," a restaurant and bar located in Yankee Stadium that requires a separate pass for admission. Ms. Joseph and her friend were both wearing tank tops. The ticket-taker at the entrance admitted Ms. Joseph's sons and her friend but told Ms. Joseph that her tank top did not conform to the stadium's dress code. In fact, tank tops are expressly prohibited by the dress code. Ms. Joseph returned to her car, changed into a T-shirt, and returned to the club. She was admitted and served. Ms. Joseph claimed that nonminority women inside the club were wearing tank tops and clothing skimpier than hers. Defendant's motion for summary judgment was denied; and court-ordered mediation resulted in settlement.[5] This situation, like many others, highlights the issue of differential enforcement of the rules. As Nancy DiTomaso writes in her book, *The American Non-Dilemma: Racial Inequality without Racism*, it is not overt racism against people of color per se that is at work in society today. Instead, she suggests that it is the preferential treatment of whites that causes racial inequality to persist.[6]

However, despite DiTomaso's findings, still there are instances of overt racism in the marketplace, such as the race codes that Dillard's former security guards attested to during the *Hampton v. Dillard* case, the targeted practices toward black customers as told by Amanda Berube as a whistleblower about The Children's Place, and as alleged in the case of Baur's Opera House, a dance bar in Springfield, Illinois.[7] Mark Stearnes, a black patron at Baur's Opera House, alleged that he asked the manager to play rap music and that he refused to do so. Mr. Stearnes believed that the manager changed musical selections from those blacks enjoy to those whites enjoy to keep blacks out. As Mr. Stearnes was leaving, one of Baur's bouncers accused him of walking too slowly and shoved him from behind. The bouncers then held Mr. Stearnes to the floor despite the situation being under control and his requests to be released. The police arrived and arrested the plaintiff, charging him with assault. The charge was later dismissed because the plaintiffs failed to exhaust their administrative remedies (not first filing with the proper state agency in Illinois) prior to filing suit under Title II (1993). In other words, although Mr. Stearnes did not win his case, he might have if he had followed proper administrative procedure. However, as documented in the case decision:

> According to former Baur's disc jockey, Brad Schroeder, Baur's owner George Baur had become concerned that Baur's was becoming a "nigger bar." . . . George Baur apparently could tolerate up to ten percent Blacks, but no more. . . . Accordingly, when an unacceptably high number of Blacks came to Baur's, manager Kim Koratsky would tell disc jockeys that it was getting "too dark in here." . . . Koratsky used this phrase to instruct the disc jockeys to stop playing rap music and start playing hard rock. The music switch effectively emptied the dance floor, which Koratsky had nicknamed "Zimbabwe West." . . . The switch in music was intended to drive Blacks from the bar. . . . Apparently, rap music was considered "Black music." Correspondingly, hard rock music was considered "White music." This happened every weekend at Baur's "just like clockwork."

Although Stearnes was not successful in his suit against Baur's Opera House, the U.S. Department of Justice was successful with its suit on behalf of the government and a group of African Americans alleging the Glass Menagerie had engaged in discriminatory practices.[8] The Glass Menagerie is a nightclub located on the banks of the Ohio River. It attracts customers from both Kentucky and Ohio. The government sought a preliminary injunction to prevent the continuation of the discriminatory acts. The court heard testimony from African-American customers who had been denied access to the club by being forced to wait in long lines while White customers were allowed entrance through a separate door under the guise of VIP cards. Two former doormen also testified that they had been instructed to discourage African-American customers. The court found that the discrimination, although sporadic, was intentional. The court found the use of VIP cards or special VIP entrance an illegal discriminatory act in violation of the Civil Rights Act 42 USC 2000a et seq. The government's motion for preliminary injunction was granted.

The Glass Menagerie's usage of separate entrances is similar to "poor doors" which were built by developers who were able to obtain affordable housing subsidies under a loophole in the Inclusionary Housing Program in New York City, which went into effect in 2009. However, it was reported on June 29, 2015 that the loophole had been closed and that for future developments, poor doors have been outlawed.[9] Although New York City is one of the most diverse cities in the world, it is home to other issues of marketplace discrimination besides denying customers access to stores and the "poor door."

One of the most often-reported offenses is the inability to hail a taxicab and/or get the cab driver to drop off at the desired destination. Even the Mayor of San Juan, Puerto Rico, Carmen Yulin Cruz, who was in New York for the New Museum's "Ideas City" Conference, had difficulty getting a cab driver to take her from Manhattan to a hotel in the Bronx on May 27, 2015. Both the first cab driver who refused her altogether and the second cab driver who finally agreed, but complained about it the entire way, were fined by the New York City Taxi and Limousine Commission as of June 26, 2015.[10]

Professor Cornel West writes of his experiences in his book, Race Matters:

> After the ninth taxi refused me, my blood began to boil. The tenth taxi refused me and stopped for a kind, well-dressed smiling female fellow citizen of European descent. As she stepped in the cab, she said, "This is really ridiculous, is it not?"[11]

Danny Glover even filed a complaint with the New York Taxi and Limousine commission which helped to spark a crackdown on noncompliant taxicab drivers.[12] And even though most of the taxicab drivers in NYC were people of color, the bias against potential black riders persisted. A similar crackdown was initiated again in 2011.[13] Yet the effectiveness of these crackdowns is questionable since, as of November 2015, it was still happening. That time, it happened to Al Roker, the long-time chief meteorologist and co-host of the Today Show on NBC. Like Danny Glover, Al Roker took his case to the New York Taxi and Limousine Commission. When asked about his experience, he said:

> Filed a complaint today after getting passed up again by a NYC Yellow cab. Cabbie picked up a white guy a block away. . . . This happens to folks of color every day.[14]

Others who have had similar experiences include such notables as the late civil rights leader and union organizer, A. Phillip Randolph,[15] former

Major League baseball player Doug Glanville,[16] and former journalist Leon Collins.[17] New York City is not the only place where people of color have difficulty with cab drivers nor are celebrities the only victims. Joel Bolden, an African-American male and a white friend attempted to hail a cab in Washington, DC, on May 25, 1998. The cab driver stopped to take the friend, but when he learned Mr. Bolden would be a passenger, he refused the fare. Mr. Bolden sued J&R, the cab company. He won the suit, and a jury awarded him $6,000 in compensatory damages and $45,000 in punitive damages. When J&R appealed the award, the court affirmed it, finding that the award was proper.

In another situation involving a taxi, Richard Carpenter, an African-American man, left the Amtrak train station in Springfield, Massachusetts, on the evening of June 18, 1995, and approached the first cab at the station's taxi stand. The white driver told him that although he was the first cab in the row, he was not the first driver at the stand. Mr. Carpenter proceeded to the second cab. When he saw that cab already had a passenger, he returned to the first cab and entered it. He told a driver his destination. The driver asked if the destination was near a restaurant named the "China Sails." Mr. Carpenter responded affirmatively. The driver then stated he had to prepay for the fare, as he had had trouble in that area before. When Mr. Carpenter told the driver he had cash to pay the fare, but refused to prepay, the driver became upset. Mr. Carpenter asked for his taxi license number, but the driver refused to provide it and asked him to exit the cab. Mr. Carpenter left the cab, reentered the station, and called Yellow Cab's dispatcher to complain. The dispatcher said that some drivers requested prepayment at times, and that most of their customers are minorities. Mr. Carpenter filed a complaint with the Massachusetts Commission Against Discrimination. The defendant, Yellow Cab, did not appear at the hearing, and a default judgment was entered for Mr. Carpenter. The hearing officer ordered Yellow Cab to cease and desist from its discriminatory practices, to train its employees, and take other preventative measures in addition to awarding Mr. Carpenter $3,000 in damages.

Of course, taxis are not the only form of transportation in which people of color have had difficulty. Consider the case of Abdur-Rahman Kantamanto who filed a complaint with the Massachusetts Commission Against Discrimination alleging his family was victim of discrimination when he attempted to purchase bus tickets. Mr. Kantamanto and his family are practicing Muslims and wear traditional religious attire. On April 18, 2003, he attempted to buy bus tickets for himself, his wife, and three minor children. He was told that he could not purchase the tickets unless he showed proof of identity by producing a birth certificate. Mr. Kantamanto was told that the requirement was new since the September 11, 2001 attacks; however, he saw no other passengers being required to show proof of identity. The case was settled with Peter Pan Bus Lines providing Mr. Kantamanto an undisclosed monetary payment and also agreeing to a training program for its employees.[18]

Since 9/11, Muslims and other ethno-racial minorities are often racially profiled at airports and on airplanes. Southwest Airlines is known to be fun but sometimes that fun may be had at the expense of others. In the case of *Sawyer v. Southwest Airlines*, two African-American women contend that they were humiliated, angered, and alienated. According to them, it all started when they were denied access onto Flight 2441. It is uncontested that the two women arrived at the gate less than ten minutes before the flight, and that Southwest Airlines has a "ten-minute" policy. The women then flew standby on the later Flight 524. After boarding, but while the women were standing in the aisle looking for seats, a flight attendant asked that all passengers to take a seat by saying over the intercom: "eenie meenie minie moe, pick a seat, we gotta go." The women alleged that other passengers snickered and directed their attention to them. For these women, and many other African Americans, that rhyme is racially charged and as a result, they felt humiliated. It also caused one of the women to worry that she would suffer a seizure, which she typically experienced as a result of stress. She did, in fact, suffer one or more petit mal seizures on the flight, a grand mal seizure when she got home, and she was bedridden for three days after the incident. The women also alleged that Southwest Airlines had billboards in San Jose, California, with the "eenie, meenie, minie, moe" phrase. Despite these claims, however, the women were not successful with their lawsuit. However, when Dr. Charles Whitcomb saw the billboards, he called and wrote to the company to complain. In response to his complaint, Southwest took down 30 billboards in the San Jose area. It did not instruct its employees to stop using the phrase, however.

These cases as presented in this chapter are but just a small subset the vast number of cases that have been filed and adjudicated through the various court systems and commissions throughout the United States. In the chapter that follows, we focus on just those cases in which there has been some aspect of criminal suspicion.

## Notes

1. Monde, 2013.
2. Fitfield and O'Shaughnessy, 2001.
3. *United States of America v. HBE Corporation, d/b/a Adam's Mark Hotels*, U.S. District Court for the Middle District of Florida, filed November 6, 2000.
4. Jonsson, 2001.
5. *Joseph v. New York Yankees Partnership*, 2000 WL 1559019, U.S. District Court for the Southern District of New York, 2000.
6. DiTomaso, 2013.
7. *Stearnes v. Baur's Opera House, Inc.* 3 F.3d 1142, U.S. Court of Appeals for the 7th Circuit, 1993.
8. *US v. Glass Menagerie, Inc.* 702 F. Supp. 139, U.S. District Court for the Eastern District of Kentucky, 1988.
9. Kasperkevic, 2015.
10. Jamerson, 2015.
11. West, 1993, p. xxv.
12. Barr, 2011; Williams, 1999.
13. LaRosa, 2014.
14. Kenneally, 2016.
15. Barr, 2011.
16. Rylah, 2015.
17. LaRosa, 2014.
18. American Civil Liberties Union of Massachusetts. "Legal Docket (July 2004–July 2006)." 2006.

## References

American Civil Liberties Union of Massachusetts. 2006. "Legal Docket (July 2004–July 2006)."

DiTomaso, Nancy. 2013. *The American Non-Dilemma: Racial Inequality without Racism.* New York, NY: Russell Sage Foundation.

Fitfield, Adam and Elise O'Shaughnessy. 2001. "Shopping While Black." *Good Housekeeping* (November): 129–136.

Jamerson, Joshua. 2015. "2 Cabdrivers Are Disciplined for Refusing to Take Puerto Rican Mayor to the Bronx." *New York Times*, June 26.

Jonsson, Greg. 2011. "NAACP, Adam's Mark Are Settling Bias Suit After Two-Year Fight." *St. Louis Post-Dispatch*, December 4, Five Star Lift Edition.

*Joseph v. New York Yankees Partnership*, 2000 WL 1559019, 2000.

Kasperkevic, Jana. 2015. "New York Bans 'Poor Doors' in Win for Low Income Tenants." *The Guardian*, June 29.

Monde, Chiderah. 2013. "Oprah Winfrey Apologizes for Naming Switzerland in Store Racism Incident: I'm Sorry 'It Got Blown Up'," Speaking to reporters at the premier of "The Butler, *New York Daily News*, August 13, 10:37 a.m.

*Stearnes v. Baur's Opera House, Inc.* F. Supp., Dist. Court, CD Illinois. 788: 375, 1992.

*Stearnes v. Baur's Opera House, Inc.* F. 3d, Court of Appeals, 7th Circuit. 3: 1142, 1993.

*United States of America v. HBE Corporation, d/b/a Adam's Mark Hotels*, United States District Court for the Middle District of Florida, Orlando Division, Filed November 6, 2000.

*U.S. v. Glass Menagerie, Inc.* F. Supp., Dist. Court, ED Kentucky. 702: 139, 1988.

# Chapter 10

# Rx for Success: A Multicultural Plan That Strengthens the Marketplace

*We cannot solve our problems with the same level of thinking that created them.*
—Albert Einstein[1]

Jim Adamson knows the prescription for success with marketplace diversity because he actually wrote the book on how to turn a company besieged with marketplace discrimination lawsuits into one of America's 50 Best Companies for Minorities (as rated by *Fortune* in 2001) and one of the Best 40 Companies for Diversity (rated by *Black Enterprise* in 2006 and 2007).[2,3] In 1994, one year after he took over as chief executive officer (CEO) of Denny's, the company settled marketplace discrimination lawsuits for over $54 million.[4] The Denny's name had become synonymous with discrimination.[5] When she joined the company in 1995, Ray Hood-Phillips, then chief diversity officer (CDO) of Denny's:

> . . . the board of directors were all White males. There were no women. There were no minorities. . . . There were no African Americans or Hispanic Americans or Asian Americans or even women in senior management.

Only 12 percent of Denny's overall management team consisted of members of minority groups and the company had no minority supplier contracts. Just 10 years later, the board was comprised of 50 percent women and persons of color, senior management had 54 percent women and people of color, and overall management was 29 percent minority and 44 percent women. The total workforce at Denny's was 46 percent minority and 53 percent women and franchises (63% of all Denny's restaurants were franchises) were 46 percent minority-owned.[6] The company's supplier contracts amounted to approximately $100 million a year and between

12 and 18 percent of the suppliers were minority-owned. Denny's gave $10 million in philanthropic donations 90 percent of which went to organizations involved with minorities. Twenty years later, Denny's is still a very diverse firm:

> As of 2014, minorities make up sixty-three percent of Denny's total workforce and forty-four percent of our overall management. The board of Denny's Corporation consists of eleven directors of whom forty-five percent are minorities and women. Since the inauguration of Denny's Supplier Diversity Initiative in 1993, the company has spent over $1.6 billion with minority and women owned business enterprises.[7]

After writing the book, *The Denny's Story: How a Company in Crisis Resurrected Its Good Name*, Adamson became one of the most sought out speakers on what NOT to do to avoid marketplace discrimination and what to do to promote marketplace diversity and inclusion.[8] The Denny's story is a great example of learning and turnaround. According to Ray Hood-Phillips, the company identified 10 Drivers of Change (see Table 10.1)[9] each of which is discussed in detail later.

There is striking overlap between Denny's "Drivers of Change" and the 10 best practices for ensuring shopping equity described in 2015 by Kristen Clarke, then-chief of the Civil Rights Bureau in the Office of the New York State Attorney General. The list of best practices can be found in Table 10.2.[10]

**TABLE 10.1   Ten Drivers of Change at Denny's**

1. Committed leadership
2. Diversify the board
3. A chief diversity officer who reports to the CEO
4. Company-wide ownership of diversity
5. Clear, enforceable nondiscrimination policies
6. Educate and train the workforce
7. Eliminate structures that impede inclusion
8. Monitor, measure, and report the results
9. Reward and recognition system
10. Celebrate success and showcase it externally

*Source:* Hood, Ray. 2004. "Perspectives from the Boardroom." In *Symposium on Consumer Racial Profiling*, ed. Jerome D. Williams and Minette Drumwright. Austin, TX.

**TABLE 10.2    Ten Best Practices for Retail Equity**

1. Data-driven approach—analyzing data on stops and detentions
2. Chief executives must make clear messages frequently and persistently
3. Effective training with real-life examples
4. Antidiscrimination policies
5. Disciplinary action and/or incentives for employees (i.e., change the way employees are evaluated)
6. Ground rules for interactions with local law enforcement
7. Robust complaint procedures
8. Consumer Bill of Rights
9. Address language barriers
10. Policies concerning detentions must be clear

*Source:* New York State Attorney General. 2015. "Ten Best Practices for Retail Equity." Presented at the Retail Equity Symposium, New York.

## A Committed Leader

Denny's first step was having a committed leader such as Jim Adamson. When he first learned about the discrimination issues at Denny's, his initial reaction was that it all could have been avoided with an apology to those who were impacted.[11] Something so simple could have saved the company from alienating its customers, tarnishing its reputation, and losing tens of millions of dollars.

The leader of the organization sets the direction for everyone else and change starts at the top. The message from the leader cannot be ambivalent as it transfers down to the "troops," as part of the chain of command. In the case of Denny's, the pre-Adamson regime did not set clear standards and this resulted in a disarray of directions when they filtered down to the level of individual restaurants. However, when Adamson took over, he made marketplace diversity and inclusion one of his highest priorities.[12]

Ron Sargent, chairman and CEO of Staples, the office supplies company, also made it a high priority and published his Statement of Diversity on Staples' webpage:

> At Staples, we embrace and promote inclusion and diversity. We know how important it is for all associates to feel valued for who they are. We're continually evolving our inclusive company culture by celebrating associates' similarities and differences. We strive to create an environment in which the

diversity of our workforce allows for diversity of ideas, so that all associates have the opportunity to be unique and innovative in their contributions.

But our commitment to diversity does not end with our associates. As we aim to provide every product a business needs to succeed, we also strive to strengthen the relationships we have within the diverse markets we serve and with the global suppliers and vendors with whom we do business.

I am proud of the progress we've made over the years and look forward to continuing our journey toward becoming an even more inclusive and diverse organization.[13]

## A Diverse Board of Directors

Because of Adamson's commitment to diversity, one of his first decisions was to diversify the board of directors. Although a board can be filled with brilliant leaders, the diversity of vantage points on a newly configured board has the ability to focus on issues and problems of which the previous board was completely unaware. Organizations such as the Alliance for Board Diversity and the Director Diversity Initiative at the University of North Carolina at Chapel Hill School of Law "encourage boards of directors of public companies to increase their gender, racial, and ethnic diversity."[14] The Alliance for Board Diversity reported that as of 2012, "women and minorities remained underrepresented at the decision-making table of boardrooms, with White men comprising nearly seventy percent of the 1,214 seats."[15] *DiversityInc* magazine each year recognizes the top 50 companies with respect to all aspects of diversity. It is no surprise that during 2012, when the Fortune 500 companies had only 15.6 percent women directors and 12.7 percent either black, Latino, or Asian, the *DiversityInc* Top 50 had 23 and 30 percent, respectively. When just the *DiversityInc* Top 10 are considered, the number increases to 30 percent female directors. In response to the question posed in the title of an article about why a company should diversify its board, *DiversityInc* replied:

> It gives organizations new ideas and innovative solutions at the strategic level; it helps attain and retain the best talent; and it helps organizations market and protect the brand.[16]

Although the focus of this book is on race, research has demonstrated that greater social diversity, which can encompass race, ethnicity, gender, sexual orientation, etc., can improve the bottom line of companies and lead to greater innovative and creative thinking. For example, a study conducted by Credit Suisse found that:

> companies with women in senior management positions tend to outperform their peers in key financial metrics, resulting in higher returns to shareholders. . . . From January 2005 through December 2013, the ROE of companies with at least one female board member was 14.1% compared with 11.2% for those with zero representation. In line with this, the report finds that since 2005, companies with female representation on their boards have been valued higher, with an average P/B value over those nine years of 2.3 times versus 1.8 times for companies with all male boards. Not surprisingly, from January 2005 through June 2014, investors in such companies have profited: the stocks of those companies with more than one woman on the board returned a compound 3.7% a year over those that had none.[17]

Research indicates that racial diversity can deliver these same kinds of benefits.[18,19]

## A Chief Diversity Officer

Adamson appointed a chief diversity officer (CDO) to manage the change and to keep the issue in focus rather than simply allowing it to become an appendage to the corporation's other concerns.[20] The idea was to integrate diversity into operations rather than relegating it to the level of a task force or a committee. Because officers at the top of the management structure lead the various divisions of the company such as finance or human resources, Adamson felt the same should be true for diversity. Although it was unusual for a company to have a CDO in the late 1980s to early 1990s, Denny's wasn't the only one. For instance, IBM's vice president of Global Workforce Diversity, Ted Childs, was the company's long-standing CDO. His actual job was much broader than the title implied and included issues related to marketplace diversity. According to Lou Gerstner, IBM's former CEO, "We made diversity a market-based issue. . . . It's about understanding our markets, which are diverse and multicultural."[21]

Around that time, researchers sponsored by the U.S. Department of Labor observed cultural trends that directly affected the American labor force.[22] With the American economy growing at a relatively healthy pace, the researchers determined that the demographic composition of the labor force would "grow slowly, becoming older, more female, and more disadvantaged." Many companies that had previously primarily employed white men responded with anxiety about how to manage and prepare for the dynamic changes that were forecasted to result in workforce diversity.

After having developed an interest and expertise concerned with ethnic marketing, Geraldine Rosa Henderson speculated about the impact the changing workforce, also called Workplace 2000, would have on the marketplace.[23] In 1994, she and Marcus Alexis contended that if 85 percent of the new entrants to the workplace in 2000 were ethnic minorities and women, there would be a completely different Marketplace 2000 as well. The companies that really understood the business case for diversity, as discussed in Chapter 4, were also more likely to understand the connection between workplace diversity and marketplace diversity.

## Company-wide Ownership of Diversity/Inclusion

Lou Gerstner and Jim Adamson, as committed CEOs, and Ted Childs and Ray Hood-Phillips, as CDOs, took important steps in the diversity leadership of their respective firms. However, these leaders also understood that diversity is not accomplished solely by the CEO, the board of directors, or even the CDO. Diversity and inclusion must be a priority at every level of the organization. A commitment to diversity and inclusion needs to permeate the entire company at both corporate and franchise levels.

Consider Hilton Hotels Worldwide. Like Denny's, this hotel group has had problems with marketplace discrimination. For example, a lawsuit against the hotel chain was brought by motorcycle enthusiasts who attended Black Bike week in South Carolina alleging that they were treated differently than the white bikers who attended Harley Week (see the description of the case in Chapter 8). Because lodging facilities typically provide services to and interact with customers from diverse backgrounds, they need to have company-wide ownership of diversity. Today, Hilton Hotel's Diversity and Inclusion Policy is posted on its website:

> We are a company of diverse cultures serving diverse guests, with more than forty languages being spoken by our Team Members. Our diverse global workforce of more than 300,000 Team Members in more than 4,000 owned, managed and franchised hotels across ninety countries continues to remind us of the importance of celebrating diversity and inclusion throughout our company . . .

Our diversity and inclusion approach is aligned with our mission to become the preeminent global hospitality company. We seek to leverage the unique cultures of our global communities, and to develop culture, talent and marketplace strategies to create a work environment of inclusiveness. As such, we hold ourselves and all of our Team Members to the highest standards of integrity, ethics and service excellence. We will achieve and maintain this status by living our core values; attracting the best and brightest talent; and valuing and leveraging the diversity of our Team Members, Guests, Suppliers, Partners and Owners.[24]

## Clear, Enforceable Nondiscrimination Policies

As they sought to integrate a commitment to diversity throughout their companies, Hilton Hotels and Denny's learned that the lack of a policy is a policy in and of itself. Without a policy, people will defer to their own discretion, as it was with Denny's in 1993. Some managers throughout the company had problems with customers who "dined and dashed" who felt that African Americans were the most likely culprits to leave the restaurant without paying for their meals. Because the company did not have a strong policy in place, these managers insisted that African Americans prepay. When Adamson's new regime took over at Denny's, his team reminded the entire organization that a prepay requirement was not only immoral, but also illegal. Moreover, all employees were informed that the consequences for discriminating against someone was termination and that franchises would be pulled from any franchisees who were found discriminating. In fact, the company did cancel franchises from owners who were found to have discriminated against customers of color.[25] The no-tolerance policy was clearly articulated and it was enforced.

Randy Oyler agrees with Ray Hood of Denny's that the lack of a cogent policy on discrimination amounts to a policy.[26] As previously mentioned, Oyler is a partner in the Chicago-based law firm Barack, Ferrazzano, Kirschbaum, & Nagelberg. Because consumers are likely to view any incidents of consumer discrimination as an action of the corporation, it does not matter whether an independently owned entity that carries the corporate brand is legally at fault. During a symposium on Consumer Racial Profiling at the University of Texas, Oyler highlighted the corporate push-and-pull that occurs with franchises: at the corporate level, the leaders must be vigilant in eliminating discriminatory treatment by its franchisees while simultaneously balancing how much pressure they can exert on franchisees as independent business owners. According to Oyler, this can be a delicate balancing act. The prescription for success is to start with basic business issues that work in the retail sector nationwide and then focus on broader concerns. Leaders must determine whether a problem is systemic, and if so, they must address it to avoid widespread damage.

Just ask Honda's U.S. financing division, American Honda Finance that agreed to pay $24 million to blacks, Latinos, and Asians for the higher interest rates that dealers charged for loans.[27] This illustrates the tension between corporations and their franchisees, in this case, the dealers. Although Honda Finance denied any discrimination on their part, it allowed the dealers to use their own discretion in financing and interest rates. However, when (potential) customers learn about this practice, they do not distinguish the overall Honda brand from the locally owned and operated dealership that may be responsible for charging differential interest rates based on customers' race.

When a company is faced with allegations of marketplace discrimination, it is important to first assess at what level the mistreatment of customers is occurring. This is a key factor in developing the proper strategy to deal with the issue both internally with employees and externally with customers and other stakeholders. For example, in a retail setting, if a customer alleges that s/he has been racially profiled, an investigation must be conducted to determine whether the incident is an isolated one or whether it is part of a pattern in that particular store. The investigator must try to ascertain whether only one sales clerk is involved or whether complaints have been lodged against several employees. If the problem is confined to a particular location, an important question is whether local management has turned a deaf ear to customer complaints so that store employees feel that there are no consequences for treating people of color differently than whites. At the highest level, there might be a systemic problem across franchises owned by particular franchisees or across all corporate-owned locations.

The Shell case described in Chapter 8 involved complaints of discrimination submitted by customers at the franchise level that were ignored at the corporate level. Typically, in a lawsuit, identifying the appropriate level at which the consumer inequality treatment is occurring will have significant ramifications for the plaintiffs, defendants, judge, jury, and expert witnesses. Attorney Oyler suggests that a franchisor must also consider the legality of the situation in terms of the potential damage to the company. The question is how much will it cost to undo the damage of a consumer discrimination incident and prevent it from happening in the future? One answer is to litigate. But, if the franchisor does not believe that the franchisee is violating their agreement, and what the franchisee is being asked to do would jeopardize the franchise relationship, then discovering ways to resolve the problems without litigation is a viable option. Are there ways to be creative so the franchisee will do what the corporation would prefer? Furthermore, will this open the floodgates for more claims that are now shown to be lucrative? But is this the right thing to do? Does this reflect who the firm is as a company and a brand? How can the firm find a solution that balances its overarching concern about discrimination but is harmonious with the way the business operates? The core issue in a corporate setting is that people who run these companies want to resolve problems in good faith, but do not want to overstep the bounds of the relationship they have already agreed upon with franchise owners.

## Educate and Train Your Workforce

Ray Hood indicates that 85 percent of all companies begin and end diversity interventions with clear, enforceable nondiscrimination policies. Although a nondiscrimination policy drives the cultural change, it cannot stand alone. There is a structural element that cannot be ignored in order for firms to get everyone on board.[28] Rather than use a single format for all diversity training, they must tailor training for each level of the company from the board of directors, to senior managers, and all the way to security guards.

Carol Jackson agrees. When she was vice president of external affairs at Macy's West, a division of Federated Department Stores, she said:

> . . . we do this by looking at the initiatives that address the behaviors to improve the shopping experience. Of course behaviors that do not conform to the high standards of the store policy detract from the shopping experience and at their worst can cause customers to: leave and not come back, file a complaint, or word of mouth that can damage the store at a grass roots level. So the idea is to work very hard to train not only at the level of the board room from a policy perspective, but the message must be taken to the management and sales associate level.[29]

Education about implicit bias is becoming a popular approach for addressing race-based discrimination in organizations. Previously described in Chapter 2, implicit or unconscious biases can be measured using the Implicit Association Test (IAT) which measures reaction time to certain stimuli as the participant sorts categories of pictures and words.[30] After completing the test, the participant receives an implicit bias rating of "slight," "moderate," or "strong." The research indicates that implicit biases are held by everyone and that they predict a person's behavior especially in certain spontaneous situations. However, training can reduce the impact of bias on behavior simply by making a person aware of his/her unconscious biases. Therefore, companies should encourage employees to take the IAT to identify their own biases.[31] One example of this in practice is the case of Bob Golomb, the extremely successful car sales director whose winning strategy was described by Malcolm Gladwell in his book, *Blink*. Gladwell writes:

> What Golomb is saying is that most salespeople are prone to [implicit bias]. They see someone, and somehow they let the first impression they have about that person's appearance drown out every other piece of information they manage to gather in that first instant. [Golomb, by contrast follows] a very simple rule. . . . He assumes that everyone who walks in the door has the exact same chance of buying a car . . . "Prejudging is the kiss of death. You have to give everyone your best shot." . . . The secret of Golomb's success is that he has decided to fight [implicit bias].[32]

Important messages to convey to employees are (1) all people, even well-intentioned people, have implicit biases and (2) those biases can affect their decision making unless they are controlled. Supervisors should be trained to take appropriate action in response to a pattern or practice of inappropriate behavior by individual employees, including security officers. Although these conversations can be uncomfortable, understanding that all people have biases may reduce defensiveness of employees and motivate change.

## Eliminate Structures that Can Impede Inclusion

For Denny's, structures that could impede inclusion were the hiring, firing, promotion, and development of the people within the company.[33] For any firm, there is the possibility of both formal/official structures as well as informal/unofficial structures. However, even though the informal/unofficial structures may seem to be invisible, they are very real to anyone who may have been negatively impacted by them. In the domain of workplace diversity, such unofficial structures could include a glass ceiling, where certain people have meetings before the real meeting, or hold a meeting at a country club that is members only.[34] In the realm of marketplace diversity, these unofficial structures could include requiring additional identification from customers of color, seating customers of color in the back of the restaurant near the kitchen, making customers of color prepay for gasoline. Those people who believe they have been victims of these types of unofficial policies, practices, or processes can bring attention to these otherwise-invisible tactics. Thus, these unofficial structures should be replaced by policies and practices that foster inclusion. If a firm conducts training without addressing the structural issues, it will end up with a frustrated workforce that desires change and inclusion but does not have the structural stability to back it up. Both the conduct of the individuals and a company's systems must be addressed in tandem.

Dan Butler, vice president of retail operations for the National Retail Federation, the world's largest retail trade association, explains that the organization's purpose is for all of the separate business entities to move forward together. Each one is on its own journey. He says:

> Denny's took seven years to turn itself around, meaning that just because a company may not have a stellar reputation, if it dedicates resources and energy into changing the culture, they can become an example . . . Some retailers do not even have a loss prevention policy in place and do not stop shoplifters ever. They absorb the theft. Anyone who breaks this policy will literally be terminated on the spot. This is because the accusations happen when a customer believes they have been profiled. Loss prevention wants to look at people's behavior because anyone can be a shoplifter. Retailers are working to train their teams to look for behaviors, such as looking at security cameras. . . . The goal is to stop the stealing, not the type of person.[35]

Changing the culture of a company requires adapting to the changing marketplace and developing a competence to deal with the various subcultures within it. Research conducted by Redmond and Baveja (2002) suggests that one method for doing so involves matching the racial demographics of employees to the demographics of customers. The researchers developed a racial match factor that measures whether the ethnic composition of the police force matches that of the population of the community it serves. This is understood to be a key factor for garnering community help in community policing.

The same concept can be applied to retail settings in identifying the proportion of people of different races and ethnicities visiting a retail store and determining whether that proportion closely matches the proportion

**Resilience Building Actions:**

## Phases of Intercultural Competency Development

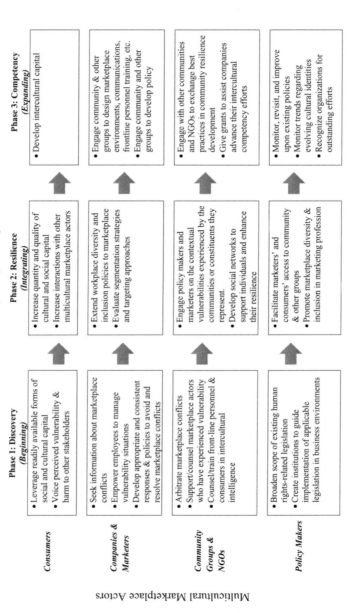

**Phase 1: Discovery** *(Beginning)*

**Phase 2: Resilience** *(Integrating)*

**Phase 3: Competency** *(Expanding)*

Multicultural Marketplace Actors

**Consumers**
- Leverage readily available forms of social and cultural capital
- Voice perceived vulnerability & harm to other stakeholders

- Increase quantity and quality of cultural and social capital
- Increase interactions with other multicultural marketplace actors

- Develop intercultural capital

**Companies & Marketers**
- Seek information about marketplace conflicts
- Empower employees to manage vulnerability situations
- Develop appropriate and consistent responses & policies to avoid and resolve marketplace conflicts

- Extend workplace diversity and inclusion policies to marketplace
- Evaluate segmentation strategies and targeting approaches

- Engage community & other groups to design marketplace environments, communications, frontline personnel training, etc.
- Engage community and other groups to develop policy

**Community Groups & NGOs**
- Arbitrate marketplace conflicts
- Support/counsel marketplace actors who have experienced vulnerability
- Counsel/train front-line personnel & consumers in intercultural intelligence

- Engage policy makers and marketers on the contextual vulnerabilities experienced by the communities or constituents they represent.
- Develop social networks to support individuals and enhance their resilience

- Engage with other communities and NGOs to exchange best practices in community resilience development
- Give grants to assist companies advance their intercultural competency efforts

**Policy Makers**
- Broaden scope of existing human rights-related legislation
- Create institutions to guide implementation of applicable legislation in business environments

- Facilitate marketers' and consumers' access to community & other groups
- Promote marketplace diversity & inclusion in marketing profession

- Monitor, revisit, and improve upon existing policies
- Monitor trends regarding evolving cultural identities
- Recognize organizations for outstanding efforts

**FIGURE 10.1  Demangeot et al.'s Framework for Intercultural Competency**

*(Source:* Demangeot, Catherine, Natalie Ross Adkins, Rene Dentiste Mueller, Geraldine Rosa Henderson, Nakeisha S. Ferguson, James M. Mandiberg, Abhijit Roy, Guillaume D. Johnson, Eva Kipnis, and Chris Pullig. 2013. "Toward Intercultural Competency in Multicultural Marketplaces." *Journal of Public Policy & Marketing* 32 (Special issue): 156–164.)

of surveillance/security staff employed by the retail establishment to monitor the shopper population. Racial matching also has been employed in the banking industry where some banks go to great lengths to match the racial/ethnic composition of people behind the counter with the racial/ethnic composition of the neighborhood in which the bank is located. It should be noted that race matching is only one way to combat marketplace discrimination and consumer racial profiling. As Catherine Demangeot and her colleagues note, with sufficient effort, training, and immersion, intercultural competency may be achieved by all marketplace actors, regardless of their ethno-racial background.

Demangeot and her colleagues write about intercultural competence that plays a pivotal role in creating a more equitable and just marketplace where situations of marketplace vulnerability are minimized.[36] They define intercultural competency as the ability to understand, adapt, and accommodate to another's culture and they provide a framework of intercultural competency development in multicultural marketplaces (see Figure 10.1). For marketers, it is important to develop marketing plans that show an understanding of the multicultural consumers they serve. At PepsiCo, they call this *cultural fluency*, according to Carlos Saveedra, director of multicultural marketing at Pepsi:

> Cultural Fluency means to market at the intersection of interests (e.g. Fashion, Sports etc), rather than to one group in particular . . . It is about being inclusive about the entire texture of multicultural consumers.[37]

## Monitor, Measure, and Report Results

As is the case with any business process, it is important to monitor, measure, and report the results of marketplace diversity and inclusion efforts, the mere act of which ensures that there will be results.[38] Evaluation is a crucial step in the process to show that there has been palpable and meaningful change: change that was envisioned, implemented both culturally and structurally, and achieved. Paul C. Lubin is president of Lubin Research and former owner of Barry Leeds & Associates, one of the leading financial services customer satisfaction and service quality market research firms in the country.[39] Leeds pioneered the use of market research and mystery shopping to detect and prevent discrimination in the marketplace. Many corporations, especially large financial institutions, have used Leeds's services to help ensure that they are treating customers fairly and equitably and adhering to consumer protection laws and regulations. Lubin indicates that mystery shopping is a prescription for monitoring and measuring success, which is used by many companies especially in the banking industry.[40]

Mystery shopping has become increasingly popular for addressing today's business issues. The early programs had, as their goal, to evaluate retail conditions: what products were available, whether a salesperson recommended one product over others, or how prominently a product was displayed and where. These early programs were deemed observational because the program objective was for the shopper to observe and record what they saw. Mystery shopping became much more useful when mystery shoppers posing as customers or potential customers, based their evaluations not only on observations, but also upon actual retail transactions (e.g., purchasing a product from a sales clerk at a department store, opening an account at a bank, or buying gas).

Unlike customer satisfaction research that measures the recollections and perceptions of customers, mystery shopping captures information at a moment in time when the employee is serving the consumer. It takes into account customers and potential customers and provides information about the nature and consistency of the customer-employee interaction. Today, mystery shopping is used by companies to improve relationships with customers. It is also a viable strategy for companies as a preemptive, prescriptive action to minimize the potential for a lawsuit. In some cases, mystery shopping is part of an agreement to settle a lawsuit. For example, a matched-pair testing program was implemented to settle the lawsuit against Shell Oil, discussed earlier, in which African-American plaintiffs alleged that they were required to pay in advance for gasoline although white customers were allowed to pump their gas first and pay afterward. Interestingly enough, the Shell lawsuit began with the plaintiff conducting his own research by videotaping customers at Shell stations. As Oscar Holmes writes for *Psychology Today*, if companies are not using their own mystery shoppers, they should worry that their customers might be doing it on their own![41]

## Rewards and Recognition

Denny's model included stimulating change through its bonus system. The "Chairman's Discretionary Portion" involved tying 25 percent of the senior management bonuses to the progress of women and persons of color in the company.[42] The company examined race and gender statistics for the

14 senior managers of the regions and if there was no positive progress, a bonus would be withheld. This reward system drove the change in the complexion of the Denny's corporation. The company continued this reward system, feeling it was necessary for three years until it became engrained within the values and culture of the company.

In her book on *Diversity in Organizations*, Professor Myrtle Bell published an Interactional Model of the Impact of Diversity on Individual and Organizational Outcomes, which was adapted from that of Taylor Cox and his colleagues. The model includes customer outcomes such as customer satisfaction and organizational loyalty.[43,44]

## Celebrate Success and Showcase It Externally

Denny's recognized employees who embraced the company's new diversity and inclusion ideals by asking every executive to identify one person who did the most to drive diversity progress in his or her area.[45] They were commended on their accomplishments and rewarded for them. It was a demonstration that was important to the company and an honor for the employees. For Denny's, it became the most highly celebrated event to correspond with how highly valued diversity became to them. Other firms celebrate diversity and inclusion in a myriad of ways. Allstate has posted the following statement on its website:

> U.S. Census Data shows that our communities are becoming more ethnically and culturally diverse. At Allstate, we believe diversity is critical to meeting the needs of the diverse customers that we serve . . . In fact, inclusive diversity is one of our core values . . . We define inclusive diversity as the collective mixture of *all* of our differences in our workforce, marketplace and community . . . It defines who we are and what we believe in, holding each other personally and professionally accountable to welcome *all* as we strive to win in a diverse, global marketplace.
>
> Allstate has made inclusive diversity a central part of our business strategy. The strategy is set and guided by an Executive Diversity Council and implemented by a Chief Diversity and Organization Effectiveness Officer . . . As a result of these efforts, Allstate is bringing diverse perspectives to our workforce, providing new opportunities for small and diverse businesses, and better serving more diverse customers.[46]

In addition to this bold statement, Allstate lists the multiple awards it has received to demonstrate its achievements.[47]

Denny's Ten Drivers of Change have had enduring success over a 20-year span. Although this model was established in 1995, it is still consistent with best practices in 2015. Still, many organizations today need to change and update their culture. In this chapter, the responsibility of marketers in furthering intercultural competency has been explored. Businesses/marketers, policy makers, academics, consumers and community groups and nongovernmental organizations (NGOs) are all critical actors in the development of intercultural competency (see Figure 10.1).[48] In Chapter 11, the focus shifts to the role that these other marketplace actors can play.

## Notes

1. Calaprice, 2005.
2. Adamson, 2000.
3. Esposito et al., 2001; Alleyne, 2006; Alleyne, 2007.
4. Labaton, 1994.
5. For example, in 1996 Denny's conducted a study to inform management of issues important to the company and found that 50 percent of African Americans in the United States said they associated Denny's with discrimination and they would never go to a Denny's restaurant. Within a few years, this number had dropped dramatically and was down to 13 percent, based largely on the aggressive efforts by Denny's to address marketplace inequality issues that had plagued the company.
6. Hood, 2004.
7. Denny's Corporation.
8. Brisseaux, 2013.
9. Hood, 2004.
10. New York State Attorney General, 2015.
11. Brown and White Staff, 2013.
12. Hood, 2004.
13. Sargent, 2013.
14. Broome, 2014.
15. Alliance for Board Diversity, 2013.
16. Diversity Inc., 2012.
17. The New Republic Staff, 2014.
18. Phillips, 2014.
19. Phillips, Liljenquist, and Neale, 2010.
20. Hood, 2004.
21. Thomas, 2004.
22. Johnston and Packer, 1987.
23. Boyett and Conn, 1992; Alexis and Henderson, 1994; Henderson, 2004.
24. Hilton Worldwide, 2015.
25. Hood, 2004.

26. Oyler, 2004.
27. McCoy, 2015.
28. Hood, 2004.
29. Jackson, 2004.
30. "ProjectImplicit.com." 2016; Greenwald, McGhee, and Schwartz, 1998.
31. Gove, 2011.
32. Gladwell, 2007, p. 90.
33. Hood, 2004.
34. Lawrence Otis Graham, a Harvard Law School graduate, wrote in his book *A Member of the Club* (2009) about his observations as a undercover staff member at a Country Club.
35. Butler, 2004.
36. Demangeot et al., 2013.
37. Portada Online Editorial Staff, 2013.
38. Hood, 2004.
39. Lubin, 2015.
40. Lubin, 2010.
41. Holmes, 2014.
42. Hood, 2004.
43. Bell, 2011, p. 27.
44. Cox, 1993.
45. Hood, 2004.
46. Allstate Insurance Company. "Diversity," 2015.
47. Allstate Insurance Company. "Awards and Recognition," 2015.
48. Demangeot et al., 2013.

## References

Adamson, Jim. 2000. *The Denny's Story: How a Company in Crisis Resurrected Its Good Name.* New York: Wiley.

Alexis, Marcus and Geraldine R. Henderson. 1994. "The Economic Base of African American Communities: A Study of Consumption Patterns." In *The State of Black America.* New York: National Urban League, 51–84.

Allstate Insurance Company. 2015. "Awards and Recognition." Available at: http://www.allstatenewsroom.com/channels/Awards-and-Recognition/pages/awards-recognition?_ga=1.5538295.594768259.1436815315. Accessed July 8, 2015.

Allstate Insurance Company. 2015. "Diversity." Available at: https://www.allstate.com/diversity.aspx. Accessed July 8, 2015.

Alleyne, Sonia. 2006. "The 40 Best Companies for Diversity." In *Black Enterprise.*

Alliance for Board Diversity. August 15, 2013. "Missing Pieces: Women and Minorities on Fortune 500 Boards—Fact Sheet." Alliance for Board Diversity Fact Sheet.

Bell, Myrtle. 2011. *Diversity in Organizations.* Boston, MA: Cengage Learning.

Boyett, Joseph H. and Henry P Conn. 1992. *Workplace 2000: The Revolution Reshaping American Business*. New York: Plume Books.

Brisseaux, Karl. 2013. "Former Denny's CEO Discusses Importance of Diversity Training." *Lehigh University News*. Published electronically Friday September 27. Available at: http://www4.lehigh.edu/news/newsarticle.aspx?Channel=/Channels/News%202013&WorkflowItemID=522e2736-ab6b-403a-8380-da6f69606f12. Accessed July 8, 2015.

Broome, Lissa. 2014. "Director Diversity Initiative." TheCorporateCounsel.net—Inside Track with Broc, January 6. Available at: https://ddi.law.unc.edu/. Accessed January 17, 2015.

Brown and White Staff. 2013. "Author James B. Adamson Tells Story of Denny's Turnaround to Lehigh Community." Lehighvalleylive.com. Published electronically September 23.

Butler, Dan. 2004. "Perspectives from the Boardroom." In *Symposium on Consumer Racial Profiling*, ed. Jerome D. Williams and Minette Drumwright. Austin: University of Texas at Austin.

Calaprice, Alice. 2005. *The New Quotable Einstein*. Princeton, NJ: Princeton University Press.

Cox, Taylor, Jr. 1993. *Cultural Diversity in Organizations*. San Francisco, CA: Berrett-Koehler Publishers.

Demangeot, Catherine, Natalie Ross Adkins, Rene Dentiste Mueller, Geraldine Rosa Henderson, Nakeisha S. Ferguson, James M. Mandiberg, and Abhijit Roy. 2013. "Toward Intercultural Competency in Multicultural Marketplaces." *Journal of Public Policy & Marketing* 32 (Special Issue): 156–164.

Denny's Corporation. "Dennysdiversity.Com." Available at: http://dennysdiversity.com/about.asp. Accessed July 8, 2015.

DiversityInc. August 14, 2012. "Why Should My Company Care if Our Board Is Diverse?" *DiversityInc*.

Esposito, Fabiana, Sarah Garman, Jonathan Hickman, Noshua Watson, and Alynda Wheat. 2001. "America's 50 Best Companies for Minorities." *Fortune*, July 9.

Gladwell, Malcolm. 2007. *Blink: The Power of Thinking without Thinking*. New York, NY: Little, Brown and Company.

Gove, Tracey G. October 2011. "Implicit Bias and Law Enforcement." *The Police Chief* 78: 44–56.

Graham, Lawrence Otis. 2009. *A Member of the Club*. New York, NY: HarperCollins.

Greenwald, Anthony G., Debbie E. McGhee, and Jordan L. Schwartz. 1998. "Measuring Individual Differences in Implicit Cognition: The Implicit Association Test." *Journal of Personality and Social Psychology* 74, no. 6: 1464.

Henderson, Geraldine Rosa. 2004. "Perspectives from the Classroom." In *Symposium on Consumer Racial Profiling*, ed. Jerome D. Williams and Minette Drumwright. Austin: University of Texas at Austin.

Hilton Worldwide. 2015. "Diversity and Inclusion." In *Hilton WorldWide*. Available at: http://hiltonworldwide.com/assets/pdfs/diversity-one-pager.pdf. Accessed January 16, 2016.

Holmes IV, Oscar. 2014. "What Happened to the Customer is Always Right? Brand Management in the Age of Social Media." *Psychology Today.*

Hood, Ray. 2004. "Perspectives from the Boardroom." In *Symposium on Consumer Racial Profiling,* ed. Jerome D. Williams and Minette Drumwright. Austin: University of Texas at Austin.

Jackson, Carol. 2004. "Perspectives from the Boardroom." Paper Presented at the Symposium on Consumer Racial Profiling, Austin, Texas, March 30.

Johnston, William B. and Arnold E. Packer. 1987. *Workforce 2000: Work and Workers for the Twenty-First Century.* Darby, PA: Diane Publishing.

Labaton, Stephen. 1994. "Denny's Restaurants to Pay $54 Million in Race Bias Suits." *The New York Times,* May 25.

Lubin, Paul C. 2015. paullubin.com. Accessed July 13, 2015.

Lubin, Paul C. 2010. *Protecting Main Street: Measuring the Customer Experience in Financial Services for Business and Public Policy.* New York: Routledge.

McCoy, Kevin. 2015. "Honda's U.S. Auto Financing Arm Agrees to $25M Settlement." *USA Today.*

The New Republic Staff. 2014. "Study: Putting Women in Charge Makes Companies More Successful." *New Republic.*

New York State Attorney General. 2015. "Ten Best Practices for Retail Equity." Presented at the Retail Equity Symposium, New York.

Oscar, Holmes IV. 2014. "What Happened to the Customer Is Always Right? Brand Management in the Age of Social Media." *Psychology Today,* October 9.

Oyler, Randall L. 2004. "Perspectives from the Courtroom." In *Symposium on Consumer Racial Profiling,* ed. Jerome D. Williams and Minette Drumwright. Austin, TX.

Phillips, Katherine W. 2014. "How Diversity Makes Us Smarter," *Scientific American,* September 16.

Phillips, Katherine W., Katie A. Liljenquist, and Margaret A. Neale. 2010. "Better Decisions through Diversity: Heterogeneity Can Boost Group Performance." *Kellogg Insight,* October 1.

Portada Online Editorial Staff. 2013. "Content Marketing: How Pepsi's 'Cultural Fluency' Concept Translates into Content Marketing Executions." *Portada Online.* Published electronically November 6. Available at: http://www.portada-online.com/2013/11/06/content-marketing-pepsi/. Accessed January 16, 2016.

"ProjectImplicit.com." Available at: https://implicit.harvard.edu/implicit/education.html. Accessed January 15, 2016.

Sargent, Ron. 2013. "Staples CEO Diversity Statement." Published electronically March 27. Accessed January 16, 2016.

Thomas, David A. 2004. "Diversity as Strategy." *Harvard Business Review,* September.

Chapter 11

# How to Help

*You're either part of the solution or you're part of the problem.*
—Eldridge Cleaver[1]

## Legal, Regulatory, and Public Policy Makers Community

Given the evidence presented in this book about the lingering prevalence of marketplace discrimination in contemporary society, why is there such a low number of lawsuits filed? Are existing laws adequate for addressing the type of harm that occurs on a daily basis in today's consumer environment? A century and a half ago, Congress designed the Civil Rights Act of 1866 to ensure "that a dollar in the hands of a Negro will purchase the same thing as a dollar in the hands of a white man. . . ." However, as has been explained, there are serious limitations in the current laws. For example, although the law is very specific about outlawing discrimination in a "place of public accommodation," it does not include shopping malls or retail stores among those places.

Already members of this community are speaking out in support of amending the law. For example, at a 2014 American Marketing Association Marketing & Public Policy annual conference, held in Boston, Massachusetts, a special session addressed many of the issues surrounding consumer discrimination. Dariely Rodriguez, New York State Assistant Attorney General, commented that Title II's failure to cover the discrimination that takes place in retail stores is a glaring omission.[2] The prevalent thought in the 1960s when the law was enacted was that with the passing of Title II, consumer discrimination would be eradicated. Unfortunately, as the evidence in this book supports, that has not occurred. Despite the gaps, Ms. Rodriguez acknowledged that Title II has been a huge enforcement tool, and pointed to the evidence of several cases that received national attention. She also noted that given the gap with federal law, state civil rights laws can be used to cover retail establishments, such as in New York State.

Ms. Rodriguez also urged the legal and regulatory community to be more vigilant as marketplace interactions between providers and consumers are taking different shapes and forms. For example, because many companies now conduct business online, they are engaging more in delivery services. People living in certain communities may be negatively affected by "retail redlining" policies, which result in the exclusion of goods and services to neighborhoods of color. As we described in an earlier chapter, a pizza delivery store engages in redlining when it refuses to deliver to certain minority neighborhoods that are perceived as more dangerous.

One of the benefits of online retailing for consumers of color is that it allows consumers to maintain a certain degree of anonymity in terms of their racial or ethnic background. However, research is showing that certain demographic and descriptive information can reveal race and ethnicity in online shopping (e.g., neighborhood address, name), which has the potential for discriminatory treatment. A possible workaround for this problem is that online consumers might use the address of a relative who lives in a more ethnically diverse ZIP code or use a name that sounds less ethnic. The next frontiers for marketplace discrimination may shift from brick-and-mortar establishments to online retail interactions and delivery services. It will become increasingly important for the legal community to keep abreast of these developments.

## Academic Community

Looking at inequities in the marketplace has been a long-standing interest of the academic community. At least one researcher, LaPiere, a white man, examined marketplace discrimination in the 1930s. In a cleverly designed study, LaPiere traveled widely in the United States with a Chinese couple, stopping at 66 sleeping places and 184 eating places.[3] The group of three was refused service only once. However, based on a follow-up mail questionnaire asking whether these same establishments would take "members of the Chinese race as guests in your establishment," 93 percent of the restaurants and 92 percent of the hotels said they would *not* serve Chinese people. The results of this study raised questions concerning discriminatory behaviors manifested in the marketplace and accompanying attitudes.

Almost 50 years ago, marketers' attention was turned to marginalized consumers when the question was asked, "Do the poor pay more?"[4] This triggered what Andreasen (1978) has referred to as the ghetto marketing life cycle, which is the cycle of research dealing with problems of marginalized consumers. Lavidge noted that "marketing has a key role to play in the drive for increased efficiency within our economy" but also "has an opportunity to play a significant role in the drive for *social justice*."[5] He also observed that "as the impact of marketing on society increases, so does the social responsibility of marketing people."[6]

Many contemporary consumer researchers and marketing scholars also have expressed interest in social justice research and the need to put a greater emphasis on it.[7] But, as this book demonstrates, racial and ethnic minorities continue to face disparate treatment and other forms of discrimination in the marketplace. Although it is encouraging to see more and more academic researchers getting involved in transformative consumer research (TCR), it is clear that the academic literature has fallen short in this area.

In a literature search of the major academic marketing journals (i.e., *Journal of Marketing, Journal of Marketing Research,* and *Journal of Consumer Research*) from 1987 to 1992, Gilly (1993) found that minority issues received virtually no attention.[8] Only one article could be found in the *Journal of Consumer Research*, which examined Hispanics and none could be found that addressed the needs of African Americans or Asian Americans. Williams (1995) conducted a content analysis of journals emphasizing consumer research (i.e., *Journal of Consumer Research, Journal of Consumer Psychology,* and *Psychology and Marketing*) for all issues until 1994 and found that only 3.4 percent of the total number of articles had a racial or ethnic minority focus and only 2.3 percent of the total number of subjects were identified as racial or ethnic minorities.[9] Williams, Lee, and Henderson (2008) examined the 10-year period from 1995 to 2004, and reached conclusions similar to Williams' 1995 analysis of consumer research studies in the earlier period.[10] They found that only 2.5 percent of the total number of articles had a racial or ethnic minority focus compared with 3.4 percent in the earlier period, and only 2.0 percent of the total number of subjects identified in the Methods section of the articles were identified as racial or ethnic minorities, compared with 2.3 percent in the earlier period.

Within the service domain, there also have been several studies that address marketplace injustice and discrimination. For example, Baker, Meyer, and Johnson (2008) investigated the role of contextual cues in the evaluation of a service failure.[11] They found that although discrimination is a factor in the evaluation of a service failure for black versus white customers, contextual cues also play a role in the evaluation of the encounter (e.g., when a black customer experiences a service failure), the failure will be evaluated more severely when no other black customers are present. Also, Ainscough and Motley (2000) examined how a customer's visible physical characteristics influence retail service delivery.[12] They found that black and male customers wait significantly longer than white and female customers at retail customer service counters. In addition, there have been a few studies conducted that address issues beyond race and ethnicity (e.g., age, gender, physical ability, and sexual orientation).

One goal for this book is to spur other researchers to pursue a path that will bring more justice into the social justice domain of the TCR agenda by addressing issues of marketplace inequalities. As the population of the United States grows ever more diverse, academic researchers must continue to investigate marketplace inequities and identify solutions. Theories developed and tested for, by, and of the dominant consumer group (i.e., white, Euro-Americans) may not apply to ethnic minority consumer groups who perhaps differ in terms of household compositions, values, lifestyles, self-perceptions, and aspirations as was discussed in Chapter 4.[13] For a variety of reasons, members of different racial and ethnic groups may respond differently to marketplace questions and researchers' attempts to measure various consumer psychological constructs.[14] Therefore, adopting a liberation psychology perspective, research focusing on marketplace discrimination must be open to new methods and approaches to fully capture the diversity and complex behaviors associated with response to mistreatment in the marketplace.

Researchers may need to employ novel approaches to better understand marketplace discrimination. For example, behavioral and psychological studies could examine what motivates discriminatory behavior, the Implicit Attitude Test (IAT) can be used to study racial attitudes toward shoppers of various races/ethnicities, aversive racism scales and modern racism scales can capture nuances that are not reflected in more traditional scales that were tested for the most part on nonminority populations. Also, researchers should look at studying the reasons why judges and juries decide against plaintiffs in consumer discrimination cases. Multiple methods may need to be employed to get convergence on reasons for discrimination. For example, qualitative methods, along with experimental, and video matched-pair mystery shopping could be used in the same study.[15] The academic community can play a significant role in eliminating marketplace discrimination. With this insight, academic researchers can continue to develop approaches and methods for dealing with the challenges of doing so.

## Consumer Community

Although this book focuses on how consumers are treated, it is important to acknowledge that marketplace discrimination can occur in reverse. In other words, consumers can display discriminatory attitudes toward shop owners and store personnel. Research on xenophobia has shown that as diversity in the marketplace increases through immigration, examples of intolerance, confrontation, and even violence by nationals toward immigrant small business owners have increased, and there have been instances of discrimination by customers toward store owners.[16] Therefore, part of the onus for achieving equality in the marketplace rests on consumers.

What can consumers do to navigate a marketplace in which, as explained in this book, there is a likelihood of mistreatment of certain racial/ethnic consumer groups and what can they do specifically when they are victims of consumer discrimination? First, consumers should be willing to boycott products, services, and establishments whose policies or actual treatment of people is discriminatory or otherwise unjust. They also should be willing to speak out when they witness marketplace mistreatment, which may involve speaking to friends and family, to the media, and others. For instance, in 2015, protests on Michigan Avenue on Black Friday diminished store sales by 25–50 percent.[17] Second, an effective way for consumers to respond to incidents of discrimination is to know their rights when they find themselves in situations where those rights may be at risk.

Historically, communities of color have coalesced around the idea that knowledge of one's rights and privileges in a given situation works to empower not only citizens, but also the system as a whole, and this kind of proactive response can easily be applied to the retail marketplace.[18] In 2013, civil rights groups such as the National Action Network and the National Urban League worked in concert with the Retail Council of New York State and a coalition of high-end retailers to develop a "Customer Bill of Rights" whose goal was to provide knowledge to customers about their civil rights to protect them from "shop-and-frisk" practices described in Chapter 8.

The Customer Bill of Rights underscores the retail industry's zero tolerance for racial profiling in stores. It contains statements such as "profiling is an unacceptable practice and will not be tolerated" and "employees who violate the company's prohibition on profiling will be subject to disciplinary action, up to and including termination of employment." In addition to prohibiting racial profiling, the Customers' Bill of Rights also prohibits "the use of excessive force or using threatening, vulgar language when apprehending or detaining suspects." Macy's, Barneys New York, Bloomingdale's, Lord & Taylor and Saks Fifth Avenue have posted the one-page document in their stores and on their websites. By informing customers of their rights, these retailers clearly understand that it is in their best interest to become part of the solution (see Figure 10.1 for a copy of the document).

Modern know-your-rights efforts involve the use of apps that provide information and tools to improve traffic stop experiences, safety, accountability, and justice. The first app was developed by an African-American lawyer after police fatally shot her 21-year-old child during a routine traffic stop. It was designed to teach young black people how to survive being pulled over by police. It coaches drivers on what to do once they have been pulled over. It includes an alert function that allows users to program in three numbers—their mother, a friend and a lawyer, for instance. Then, when the driver is stopped by an officer, the user can press the "alert" button to immediately send a message to those three people. The app includes a record function so users can tape and log their interactions with police. It has video tutorials that show good and bad behavior during traffic stops and forms for submitting commendations or complaints against officers. It also includes a checklist for ways a driver can keep officers at ease. Another "driving while black" app developed by a pair of Portland lawyers informs users of their rights during traffic stops and what steps to take if they believe they are involved in a stop with a racial pretext.

Although a similar app or guidelines for consumers does not exist yet, the American Civil Liberties Union (ACLU) recently sponsored a smartphone app called "mobile justice" which allows users to video interactions with authorities, which are then uploaded directly to the ACLU. Perhaps this app could be used during "shopping while black" incidents just as the "Stop and Frisk Watch" app has been used since its release in New York in 2012. In these ways, technology can be used to create an environment where people of color will not be subject to discrimination.

## BOX 11.1: CUSTOMER'S BILL OF RIGHTS

### Customers' Bill of Rights

#### [Store Name] Prohibits Profiling in our Stores

"Profiling" is defined generally as the practice of judging and addressing people based on their race, color, religion, sex, sexual orientation, gender identity, national origin, age, disability, ancestry, appearance, or any personal or physical characteristics.

***Profiling is an Unacceptable Practice and will not be Tolerated***

[Store name] is committed to ensuring that all shoppers, guests, and employees are treated with respect and dignity and are free from unreasonable searches, profiling, and discrimination of any kind in our store.

[Store name] strictly prohibits unreasonable searches and/or the profiling of customers by any employee. The participation by employees in such activities or the failure to report such instances of which they have knowledge is a violation of company policy. Employees who violate the company's prohibition on profiling will be subject to disciplinary action, up to and including termination of employment.

[Store name] supports the use of internal programs to test compliance with our strict prohibition against profiling practices.

[Store name] retains security guards and/or loss prevention professional to help provide shoppers and employees with a safe and secure shopping environment. Security guards in New York State are trained and licensed pursuant to New York State's General Business Law, including pre-employment training, on-the-job training, and regular in-service training required by state law.

[Store name] requires its employees to respect the basic civil and legal rights of any person suspected of shoplifting or other crime committed on store property.

[Store name] requires all loss prevention employees to identify themselves as members of [Store name] loss prevention department when initiating any customer contact and to willingly provide his/her name to any customer upon request. The use of excessive force or using threatening, vulgar language when apprehending or detaining suspects or in the course of performing any duties as a loss prevention representative is prohibited.

A person may be detained only in a reasonable manner and for not more than a reasonable time to permit investigation or questioning, provided an authorized employee has reasonable grounds to believe that the person so detained was guilty of criminal possession of an anti-security item or was committing or attempting to commit shoplifting on the premises (New York State General Business Law, Section 218).

Nothing contained herein is intended to limit any other obligations the Store may have or rights that the shopper may have under any Court decrees or under state and federal Constitutions or the laws of the State in which the Store is located.

**To report any instance of profiling or violation in this store, please call:**

[Store to identify contact information for manager on duty.]
[Store to identify corporate contact.]
New York State Division of Human Rights: 1-888-392-3644
New York City Commission on Human Rights: 212-306-7450

*Source*: Retail Council of New York State, National Action Network, and National Urban League (2013), "Customers' Bill of Rights" (accessed January 16, 2016, [available at http://retailcouncilnys.com/customers-bill-of-rights/].

## Civil Rights Activists and Groups Concerned About Social Justice Community

The National Association for the Advancement of Colored People (NAACP) and the National Retail Federation have been crucial in providing training and direction to the business community on issues of diversity in the marketplace, but there have been far fewer interventions to inform consumers themselves as to what they can do to address discrimination. There are many avenues for this community to consider pursuing to address marketplace inequality. These actions include publishing an annual "state-of-the-nation" report on marketplace discrimination to monitor firms and identify those that are "diversity friendly;" creating a national clearinghouse to catalogue reported cases of marketplace discrimination; maintaining an ongoing database of court cases on marketplace discrimination at federal, state, and local levels, that would be publicly accessible for researchers and others; developing a "report card" for firms based on the case database; and establishing a website so that anyone can report a case and be offered suggestions on where to go to seek assistance. Already, initiatives similar in scope are being considered or implemented, such as those described below in the discussion of Congressional black caucus efforts.

The NAACP has developed a Consumer Choice Guide, commonly known as the "Business Report Card," that offers a comprehensive look at the diversity efforts of businesses in five industries: lodging, telecommunications, financial services, general merchandising, and automotive. The main goal is to determine some level of economic reciprocity between the world's leading corporations and the African-American community. Each industry is graded across five categories: employment, advertising/marketing, vendor relations (supplier diversity), and charitable giving. The fifth category is unique to each industry. The overall score is calculated from the average of the five-category scores. African-American consumers use the report card to become more educated and informed about the progress companies are making to better serve their needs as a collective community of buyers. With this report card, there is a wealth of information available to tell African-American consumers how each firm performs on dimensions that are important to them, including involvement in the community and philanthropic efforts.

The Congressional Black Caucus convened a panel on consumer racial profiling at its 33rd Annual Legislative Conference in 2003 in Washington, D.C. One of the items emanating from that meeting was a proposal to pursue a national agenda to address issues of consumer racial profiling, including the establishment of a national center for such purposes.

Some of the items that were proposed for inclusion among the scope of activities that a Center for Consumer Equality would undertake are listed below:

1. Conduct in-house research on consumer discrimination, for example, behavioral and psychological studies on the reasons employees engage in

discriminatory behavior and use the Implicit Attitude Test (IAT) to study employees' racial attitudes toward shoppers of various races/ethnicities.

2. Work in conjunction with existing commercial mystery/secret shopping study firms to conduct external studies for firms facing consumer discrimination challenges. The advantage is that the center could position itself as an outside, objective entity. In some cases, the hiring of such an entity has been part of a consent decree with a company, but it has been difficult to identify firms who are perceived as objective.

3. Work with public policy makers to develop and support legislation that addresses consumer discrimination in today's economic climate and environment since many of the current laws have limited impact of seeking relief for victims of consumer discrimination.

4. Provide fellowships and postdoctoral study opportunities for graduate students, faculty, and other researchers to work at the center and conduct research on consumer discrimination.

5. Provide scholarships for graduate students to conduct research at their respective universities—this should attract students from various disciplines, for example, business, marketing, advertising, social work, sociology, psychology, African and African American studies, law, government and public policy.

6. Coordinate the offering of training courses to assist companies facing consumer discrimination problems or wanting to avoid these issues. The center could link them with consultants who provide such courses.

7. Support conferences and other venues where sessions are held on consumer discrimination, for example, Congressional Black Caucus panel, Marketing & Public Policy Conference.

8. Develop a series of center publications on consumer discrimination.

9. Publish an annual "state-of-the-nation" report on consumer discrimination.

10. Serve as a clearinghouse to catalogue reported cases of consumer discrimination; establish a website (as well as a hotline) so that people can report a case and be offered suggestions on where to seek assistance.

11. Maintain a database of court cases on consumer discrimination to help attorneys and others in conducting legal research.

12. Serve a monitoring function by developing a report card on firms that are "diversity friendly" from a customer perspective (as opposed to most diversity report cards that report on hiring practices, promotion, percentage of upper-level management, suppliers).

Despite the large body of research on the frequency and prevalence of discrimination in major areas such as housing and employment, there is considerably less information about the consumer transaction setting. But we know that the incidents of consumer discrimination that may seem small and somewhat innocuous to some are causing harm—little by little—to many others. A goal of this book was to provide insight regarding these types of commercial encounters, and then contribute to an ongoing dialogue going forward that inspires communication among members of the various communities concerned about consumer inequality in the marketplace. Moving from the realm of speculation, accusation, and rhetoric to conclusions based on research backed by empirical findings will be the foundation needed to make real change.

It is the sincere desire of the authors that members of all the interested communities will play an active role toward the adoption of effective policies and practices to ensure that consumers are treated in an equitable fashion. This requires understanding the problem first. Business leaders who are willing to collect and analyze information about their employees' interactions with customers of all backgrounds will have the tools to manage their workforce and provide better service. As management guru Peter Drucker famously said: "If you can't measure it, you can't manage it." The problem is that many important things are difficult to measure. The quality of new hires and the ability of managers to make good decisions are not readily quantifiable, and there is no easy fix. In *Better: A Surgeon's Notes on Performance*, Dr. Atul Gawande writes: "We always hope for the easy fix: the one simple change that will erase a problem in a stroke. But few things in life work this way. Instead, success requires making a hundred small steps go right—one after the other, no slip-ups, no goofs, everyone pitching in."

This is certainly true when it comes to interactions in the marketplace. After all, human interactions can be messy. A basic principle for anyone concerned about combating racism, discrimination, and prejudice at any level and in any context, is to be an agent for positive change by treating others with dignity and respect. All of us can cultivate open mindedness in interacting with people who may respond differently to incidents than we do. All of us can promote consumer equality in the marketplace and foster an environment where everyone is treated fairly and equitably.

## Notes

1. Cleaver, 1969.
2. Rodriguez, 2014.
3. LaPiere, 1934.
4. Caplovitz, 1963.

5. Andreasen, 1978; Lavidge 1970, p. 25.
6. Lavidge, 1970, p. 28.
7. Laczniak, 1999; Laczniak and Murphy, 2008; Ferrell and Ferrell, 2008; Sirgy et al., 2008.
8. Gilly, 1993.
9. Williams, 1995.
10. Williams, Lee, and Henderson, 2008.
11. Baker, Meyer, and Johnson, 2008.
12. Ainscough and Motley, 2000.
13. Gilly, 1993; Riche, 1990.
14. Baker, Motley, and Henderson, 2004; Motley, Henderson, and Baker, 2003.
15. Bone, Christensen, and Williams, 2014.
16. Johnson, Meyers, and Williams, 2013.
17. Janssen, 2015.
18. Rengif and Slocum, 2014.

## References

Ainscough, Thomas L. and Carol M. Motley. 2000. "'Will You Help Me Please?' The Effects of Race, Gender, and Manner of Dress on Retail Service." *Marketing Letters* 11: 129–136.

Andreasen, Alan R. 1978. "The Ghetto Marketing Life Cycle: A Case of Underachievement." *Journal of Marketing* 15: 20–28.

Baker, Stacey Menzel, Carol M. Motley, and Geraldine R. Henderson. 2004. "From Despicable to Collectible—the Evolution of Collective Memories for and the Value of Black Advertising Memorabilia." *Journal of Advertising* 33: 37–50.

Baker, Thomas L., Tracy Meyer, and James D. Johnson. 2008. "Individual Differences in Perceptions of Service Failure and Recovery: The Role of Race and Discriminatory Bias." *Journal of the Academy of Marketing Science* 36: 552–564.

Bone, Sterling A., Glenn L. Christensen, and Jerome D. Williams. 2014. "Rejected, Shackled, and Alone: The Experience of Systemic Restricted Consumer Choice among Minority Entrepreneur Consumers." *Journal of Consumer Research* 41(August): 451–474.

Caplovitz, David. 1963. *The Poor Pay More: Consumer Practices of Low Income Families.* New York: Free Press of Glencoe.

Cleaver, Eldridge. 1969. *Speech.* San Francisco, CA: The Free Press of Glencoe.

Ferrell, O.C. and Linda Ferrell. 2008. "A Macromarketing Ethics Framework: Stakeholder Orientation and Distributive Justice." *Journal of Macromarketing* 28(March): 24–32.

Gawande, Atul. 2007. *Better: A Surgeon's Notes on Performance.* New York: Metropolitan Books/Henry Holt & Company.

Gilly, Mary. 1993. "Studies of Women and Minorities in Marketing Research." Paper presented at the American Marketing Association Winter Educators' Conference.

Janssen, Kim. 2015. "Michigan Avenue Black Friday Protests Cost Stores 25–50 Percent of Sales." *Chicago Tribune. Business.* November 30.

Johnson, Guillaume, Yuvay Jeanine Meyers, and Jerome D. Williams. 2013. "Immigrants Versus Nationals: When an Intercultural Service Encounter Failure Turns to Verbal Confrontation." *Journal of Public Policy & Marketing* 32 (Special Issue): 38–47.

Laczniak, Gene R. 1999. "Distributive Justice, Catholic Social Teaching, and the Moral Responsibility of Marketers." *Journal of Public Policy & Marketing* 18(Spring): 125–129.

Laczniak, Gene R. and Patrick E. Murphy. 2008. "Distributive Justice: Pressing Questions, Emerging Directions, and the Promise of Rawlsian Analysis." *Journal of Macromarketing* 28(March): 5–11.

LaPiere, Richard T. 1934. "Attitudes versus Actions." Social Forces 13: 230–237.

Lavidge, Robert J. 1970. "The Growing Responsibilities of Marketing." *Journal of Marketing* 34(January): 25–28.

Motley, Carol M., Geraldine R. Henderson, and Stacey Menzel Baker. 2003. "Exploring Collective Memories Associated with African-American Advertising Memorabilia—The Good, the Bad, and the Ugly." *Journal of Advertising* 32: 47–57.

Rengifo, Andres F. and Lee Ann Slocum. 2014. "Community Responses to "Stop-and-Frisk" in New York City: Conceptualizing Local Conditions and Correlates." *Criminal Justice Policy Review*, December 17.

Retail Council of New York State, National Action Network, and National Urban League. 2013. "Customers' Bill of Rights." Available at: http://retailcouncilnys.com/customers-bill-of-rights/. Accessed January 16, 2016.

Riche, Martha F. 1990. "Demographic Change and Its Implications for Marketing Research." *Applied Marketing Research* 30: 23–27.

Rodriguez, Dariely. 2014. "Marketplace Discrimination." In *Marketing & Public Policy Conference*, ed. Elizabeth Miller and George Milne and Easwar Iyer. Boston, MA: American Marketing Association.

Sirgy, Joseph M., Dong-Jin Lee, Stephan Grzeskowiak, Jean-Charles Chebat, J.S. Johar, Andreas Hermann, Salah Hassan, Ibrahim Hegazi, Ahmet Ekici, Dave Webb, Chenting Su, Jordi Montana. 2008. "An Extension and Further validation of a Community-Based Consumer Well-Being Measure." *Journal of Macromarketing* 28: 243–257.

Williams, Jerome D. 1995. "Book Review of Race and Ethnicity in Research Methods." *Journal of Marketing Research* 32: 239–243.

Williams, Jerome D., Wei-Na Lee, and Geraldine R. Henderson. 2008. "Diversity Issues in Consumer Psychology Research." In *Handbook of Consumer Psychology*, ed. Curtis P. Haugtvedt, Paul Herr, and Frank Kardes. Hillsdale, NJ: Lawrence Erlbaum Associates, Inc.: 877–912.

# Index

Academic community, how to help, 168–71
ACLU. *See* American Civil Liberties Union (ACLU)
Adam's Mark Hotel, 137
Adamson, Jim, 147–62
Adickes, Sandra, 6
*Adickes v. Kress,* 7
Adkins, Natalie Ross, 164
Advertising: people of color underrepresented in, 68; promotion and discrimination in, 66–70; stereotypes in, 66–68
African Americans: population numbers, 56; purchasing power and growth rate, 58; treatment in the marketplace, 7–8
Aguero, Veronica, 111–13
Ainscough, Thomas L., 178
Airbnb, 66
Alexander, Michelle, 20
Alexis, Marcus, 58, 63, 152
Alliance for Board Diversity, 150
Allstate, 161
Amazon.com, Confederate flags, 12
American Civil Liberties Union (ACLU), 137, 172
American Honda Finance, 154
American Indians: purchasing power and growth rate, 58; racial group in colonial America, 54
American Marketing Association, 167
American marketplace, race and, 4–7
*The American Non-Dilemma: Racial Inequality without Racism* (DiTomaso), 139
*Anderson and Humphrey v. Dillard's,* 41, 45
Andreasen, Alan, 7, 63

Andreasen, Amanda, 112
Annoyance vs. avoidance, 31–53
Apple Bottom, 61
Arguello, Denise, 38
Asian Americans: population numbers, 56; purchasing power and growth rate, 58
Aversive racism, 14
Avis, 116–17
Ayres, Ian, 64

Bach, Erwin, 135
Baker, Stacey Menzel, 66, 178
Baker, Thomas L., 178
Barack Ferrazzano Kirschbaum & Nagelberg, 106, 153
Barcode sensors, 93
Barneys, ix
Barneys New York, 172
Barry Leeds & Associates, 159
Baur's Opera House, 139
Beasley, Rick, 108–9
Becker, Gary S., 11
Behnken, Brian D., vii–viii
Bell, Myrtle, 161
Benskin, Tammy, 108
Benson, Sammie (Blac Youngsta), 15
Bentley, Willie, Jr., 126
Berube, Amanda, 139
Bessinger, Maurice, 11–12
Best Buy, 117
*Better: A Surgeon's Notes on Performance* (Gawande), 177
Better Business Bureau, 23
Bishop, Samaad, 117
*Bishop v. Best Buy, Co. Inc.* (2010), 120
"Black Bike Week," 129–30, 152
Black College Reunion, 137

*Black Consumer Profiles: Food Purchasing in the Inner City* (Alexis et al.), 58–59
Black consumers, in the "Jim Crow" era, 4–7
Blake, James, xxiv–xxv
Blanchard's Wine and Spirits, 31
*Blink* (Gladwell), 156
Blockbuster Music Store, xvii
Bloomingdale's, 91, 172
Bloomsdale, PA, xxiv
Bolden, Joe, 142
Bone, Sterling A., 125
Boyd, William, 68
Brewster, Zachary W., 25
Broaddus, Toni, 68
Brondolo, Elizabeth, 20–21
Brown, Michael, ix, 19
Brown & Williamson, 69
Bureau of Justice Statistics, 96
Bureau of Labor Statistics, 59
Burrell, Tom, 58
Butler, Dan, 157

Cain, Theresa, 109
Cardiovascular problems, racial discrimination and, 21
Carpenter, Richard, 142
Carter, Robert T., 18–20
CDO. *See* Chief diversity officer (CDO)
Center for Consumer Equality, 175–77
Chapman, Lynette, 105–6
*Chapman v. The Higbee Company d/b/a Dillard Department Stores, Inc.* (2003), 120
*Charles Lewis et al. v. Jill Doll, John Doll and the Southland Corporation, d/b/a Seven-Eleven*, 133
Chief diversity officer (CDO), 151
The Children's Place, 40, 139
Childs, Ted, 152
Christensen, Glenn L., 125
Christian, Lois, 114
*Christian v. Wal-Mart Stores, Inc.* (2001), 120
Civil recovery statutes, 93
Civil rights, 4–7
Civil Rights Act (1964): advertising images before, 67; Title II, 77–78, 139–40, 167

Civil Rights Act (1866), Section 1981, 76–77, 105–7, 110, 118, 126
Civil rights activists, how to help, 174–77
Civil Rights Bureau, Office of the New York State Attorney General, 148; ten best practices for retail equity, 149
Civil War (1865), advertising images, 67
Clark, Nancy, 138
Clark, Richard, 114
Clark, Thomas, 138
Clarke, Kristen, 148
Cleaver, Eldridge, 167
Cloverland Farms Dairy, 127
Coger, Emma, 1–2
Collins, Leon, 142
Colomb, Bob, 156
Colonial America, racial groups, 4
Command Performance hair salon, 128
Confederate flags, 12
Congressional black caucus, panel on consumer racial profiling, 175
Connecticut Commission on Human Rights and Opportunities, 129, 136
Conoco, 38
Consumer community, how to help, 171–74
Consumer equality, in the modern era, 8
Consumer Expenditure Study, 58–59
Consumer inequality, x
Consumer racial profiling (CRP), x, 32, 91–104
Consumer racism, vii
Consumers: coping mechanisms, 22–24; physical effects of discrimination, 20–22; psychological effects of discrimination, 18–20
Coping mechanisms, discrimination, 22–24
Cortisol, racial discrimination and, 21
Cox, Taylor, Jr., 164
Cracker Barrel Old Country Store, 106, 130–31
Crawford, John, ix, 3, 19
Creative Bridals, 136
Credit Suisse, 151
Criminal suspicion/treatment, 34, 39–40; cases, 105–21

Crocker, Jennifer, 26
Crockett, David, 26
CRP. *See* Consumer racial profiling (CRP)
Cruz, Carmen Yulin, 141
Cultural Fluency, 159
Customer Bill of Rights, x, 171–74

Dabney, Dean, 93–94
Daddato, Nancy, 75
Daniel, Renee, 130–31
*Daniel v. Paul*, 395 U.S. 298, U.S. Supreme
    Court (1969), 88
Davis, Judy Foster, 9
Degradation: of goods and services, 3;
    overt, 33–34, 37–38; subtle, 33–34,
    36–37
Delivery services, retail redlining, 168
Demangeot, Catherine, 158–59
Demographics Now, 41
Demographic test, 43
Denial: of goods and services, 33; overt,
    34, 39; subtle, 34, 38–39
Denny's Restaurants, 39, 60, 147–65;
    celebrate success and showcase it
    externally, 161–62; chief diversity
    officer, 151–52; clear, enforceable
    nondiscrimination policies, 153–55;
    committed leader, 149–50; company-
    wide ownership of diversity/inclusion,
    152–53; diverse board of directors,
    150–51; drivers of change, 148; educate
    and train your workforce, 155–56;
    monitor, measure, and report results,
    159–60; rewards and recognition,
    160–61; structures that can impede
    inclusion, 156–57
*The Denny's Story: How a Company in
    Crisis Resurrected Its Good Name*
    (Adamson), 148
DeRosa, Rochelle, 135–36
Devos, Thierry, 18
Differential treatment, 11–30
Dillard's Department Stores, ix, 37, 41–53,
    60, 82, 105–6, 107–13; demographic
    data, 44; Rules and Procedures for
    Security Personnel, 105; security code
    "44," 108
Director Diversity Initiative, 150

Discrimination: in advertising, 66–70;
    categorization of cases, 34; overt and
    subtle, 33–34; physical effects on
    consumers, 20–22; price, 63–64; product/
    service and, 60–63; psychological effects
    on consumers, 18–20; retail redlining,
    64–67, 168
DiTomaso, Nancy, 139
*Diversity in Advertising* (Williams, Lee,
    and Haugtvedt), 68–69
Diversity/inclusion, company-wide
    ownership of, 152–53
*DiversityInc* magazine, 150–51
*Diversity in Organizations* (Bell), 161
Dixon, Tom, 55
Douglas, Mary, 123
Dovidio, John F., 13
*Drayton v. Toys "R" Us Inc.* (2009), 121
Drexler, Madeline, 21
"Driving while black," 32, 35;
    know-your-rights efforts, 172
D'Rozario, Denver, 65
Drucker, Peter, 177
Dugan, Laura, 93–94
Dunbar, Cheyenne M., 18

Eberhardt, Jennifer L., 27
Economic inequality, vii, ix
Economic spending patterns, people of
    color, 59–60
Eddie Bauer, xxii
Edens, Amber, 114
Einstein, Albert, 147
Ekpo, Akon E., 23, 66
Equal employment opportunity (EEO)
    work, xx
Equal Rights Center, 116
Ernster, Cletus, 41
Ethnicity: Dillard's and Macy's customers,
    42; U.S. population, 56
Ethno-racial composition of the U.S.,
    55–59
European colonists, racial group in
    Colonial America, 4
Evett, Sophia R., 66, 88

Farrell, Amy, 35
Federal Bureau of Investigation (FBI), 96

Federal public accommodation law, 77–78
Federated Department Stores, Macy's
    West, 155
Ferguson, Nakeisha S., 164
Fight-or-flight response, racial
    discrimination and, 21
Food deserts (food-insecure areas), 64
*Framework for Intercultural Competency*
    (Demangeot et al.), 158
"Freedom Riders," 6
"Freedom School," 6
Fromm, Erich, 8
FUBU, 61

Gabbidon, Shaun L., 32, 94–95
Gaertner, Samuel L., 13
Gainey, Annie, 129
Gallup poll, racial profiling, 32
Garner, Eric, ix, 19
Garrett, John, 118–19
*Garrett v. Tandy Corp.* (2002), 103
Gawande, Atul, 177
*Gawker,* 23
General Electric Company, xxiii
Gerstner, Lou, 151–52
Ghetto marketing life cycle, 169
Gilly, Mary, 178
Gladwell, Malcolm, 156
Glanville, Doug, 142
Glass Menagerie, 140
Global marketplace diversity and
    inclusion, 68
Glover, Danny, 141
Goldsby, William, 19
*Good Housekeeping* magazine, 17, 135
Goveo, Alberto, 38
Graham, Lawrence Otis, 164
Gray, Freddie, 19
Great Clips, 129
Green, Charlan, 111–13
Green, Rodney, 111–13
Green, Victor, 5
*Green Book,* 5
Greensboro Four, 6
*Green v. Dillard's, Inc.* (2007), 121
Greenwald, Anthony G., 164
Gregory, Crystal, 107
Gregory, Kenneth, 109

*Gregory v. Dillard's, Inc.* (2007), 121
*Gregory v. Dillard's, Inc.* (2009), 121
Grier, Sonya A., 26
GroupMe app, 23
Guzmán, Francisco, 72

Hakstian (Harris), Anne-Marie G., viii,
    xix–xx, 32–33, 68, 182–83
*Halton v. Great Clips* (2000), 133
*Hammond v. Kmart Corp. and Sears
    Holding Corp.* (2013), 27
Hampton, Mrs., 37
*Hampton v. Dillard's Dept. Stores,*
    82–84, 139
Hanes Hosiery, 61
Harding, Calvin, xviii–xix
Harley Week, 129–30, 152
Harmon, Chandra, 130–31
Haugtvedt, Curtis P., 74
Henderson, Geraldine Rosa, viii,
    xvii–xviii, 23, 32–33, 66, 152,
    181–82
Henson, John, 55
Hewlett-Packard (HP), 62–63
Heyman, Jenny, 127
Hidden cameras (CCTV), 93
Higbee Company, 52, 120
Higgins, George E., 32, 94
Hill, Daron, 123
Hilton Hotels Worldwide: clear,
    enforceable nondiscrimination
    policies, 153–55; Diversity and
    Inclusion Policy, 152–53
Hirschman, Albert, 22
Hodson, Gordon, 13
Hollinger, Richard, 92–94
Holmes, Oscar, 160
Hood-Phillips, Ray, 147–48, 152–56
Huff, Lenard, 72
Humphreys, Jeffrey M., 72
Huynh, Que-Lam, 18
*Hyatt Corporation v. The Honolulu Liquor
    Commission,* 137–38

IBM, 151–52; company-wide ownership
    of diversity/inclusion, 152–53
Ifill, Gwen, 17, 23
Illinois Human Rights Act, 138

Immigration rates, U.S., 57
Implicit Association Test (IAT), 16, 155–56, 170
Implicit racism, 12
Inclusionary Housing Program, New York City, 140–41
Indigenous Americans, racial group in Colonial America, 4
Interactional Model of the Impact of Diversity on Individual and Organizational Outcomes, 161
Intercultural competence, 158–59
International Council of Shopping Centers (ICSC), 42–43
Interstate Commerce Commission, regulations prohibiting segregation, 6
Isherwood, Baron, 123

Jackson, Carol, 155
*Jannie Lewis v Dillard's, Inc., and the Higbee Company* (2005), 52
"Jim Crow" era, xxi, 4–7; *Green Book,* 5
Johnson, Guillaume, 158–59, 179
Johnson, James D., 178
Johnson, Robert, 31
*Jones v. Alfred H. Mayer Co.* (1968), 89
Joseph, Whitney, 75, 139
*Joseph v. New York Yankees Partnership* (2000), 89, 144
*Journal of Consumer Psychology,* 169
*Journal of Consumer Research,* 169
*Journal of Marketing,* 169
*Journal of Marketing Research,* 169
J&R Cab Company, 142
Juror perceptions, cases of retail discrimination, 80–81
Jury research, market discrimination, 82–87

Kantamanto, Abdur-Rahman, 142
Kenyon, Karen L., 21
Keohane, Nan, xix
Kipnis, Eva, 158–59
Kite, Mary, 13
Kleine, Rob, 124
Kmart, 15
Know-your-rights efforts, 172
Koratsky, Kim, 140

Kujawa, Peter, 136
Ku Klux Klan, 11

LaPiere, Richard T., 168
Larsen, Carl, 117
Latinos: population numbers, 56; purchasing power and growth rate, 58
Leach, Michael, 127
*Leach v. Heyman, 233 F.Supp.2d 906* (2002), 133
Lee, Spike, 69
Lee, Wei-Na, 74
Legal, regulatory, and public policy makers community, how to help, 167–68
Legal protection, 75–89
Legister, Brian, 117
Leone, Robert P., 64
Le Terrace Club, 137–38
Levi's, Curve ID campaign, 61
Lewis, Charles, 128
Lewis, Ms., 113–14
*Lewis v. Dillard's,* 41, 45–46
*Lewis v. JC Penney Co., Inc., 948 F. Supp.* (1996), 121
Liggett & Myers, 69
Lindridge, Andrew, 66
Lord & Taylor, 172
Lorillard, 69
Lubin, Paul C., 159
Lwin, May O., 66
Lynch, John R., 2
Lynn, Michael, 25

Macaluso, Todd, 115
Macy's, ix, 41–42, 172; demographic data, 44
Macy's West, 155
Magic Shave, 62
Magill, Mike, 43
Major, Brenda, 22, 33
Mandiberg, James M., 164
Marketing: 4 P's, 60; price and pricing discrimination, 63–64
Marketplace discrimination, x; classification scheme, 124–26; special occasions of, 135–45; understudied phenomenon, 7–8

Marketplace diversity, 147–65
Marketplace inclusion, business case for, 55–74
Martin, Trayvon, ix, 132
Martin-Baro, I., 89
Maryland Inn, 138
Massachusetts Attorney General's Office, Children's Place, 40
Massachusetts Commission Against Discrimination, 142
Masters, Stacey, 136
Matthews, Karen, 21
Mays, Vickie, 21
*McCoo v. Denny's, Inc.* (2000), 52
McCoy, Shannon K., 22, 33
McCrary, Linda, 111–13
McDevitt, Jack, 35
McKinney, Jefferson, 108
McLaughlin, George, 6
Mediamark Research, Inc., 41
MediaSmart computers, HP, 62–63
Merchant detention statutes, 93
Mexican Americans, treatment in the marketplace, 7–8
Meyer, Tracy, 178
Meyers, Yuvay Jeanine, 179
Microaggressions: definition, 14; racial, 14–18; three types, 14–15
*Microaggressions and Marginality: Manifestation, Dynamics, and Impact* (Sue et al.), 14
Microassaults, 14–15
Microinsults, 14–16
Microinvalidations, 14–16
Minimization/discounting perspective, discrimination, 22
Mitchell, Ojmarrh, 95
"Mobile justice" app, 172
Modern discrimination, 13
Monrot, Rose, 114
Montgomery Ward, 43
Morris, Darryl, 118
Morrison, Lloyd, 91
*Morris v. Office Max, Inc.* (1996), 121
Motley, Carol M., 66, 72, 178
Mueller, Rene Dentiste, 164
Mulhern, Francis J., 64
Multicultural marketing, xx–xxi

Multicultural plan for the marketplace, 147–65
Mundane and everyday, definition, 124
Mundane consumption cases, 123–34
Murray, Peter, 23
Murrell, Marie, 38–39, 139
*Murrell v. Ocean Mecca Motel, Inc., 262 F.3d 253* (4th Cir., 2001), 53
Mystery shopping, 159–60

NAACP. *See* National Association for the Advancement of Colored People (NAACP)
*NAACP et al. v. Shawnee Development, Inc. et al.* (2003), 134
*NAACP v. Cracker Barrel Old Country Store, Inc.* (2002), 134
Nailor, Leggitt, 118
Nardone, Patrick. *See* American Civil Liberties Union (ACLU)
Nardone, Ray. *See* American Civil Liberties Union (ACLU)
National Action Network, 171
National Association for the Advancement of Colored People (NAACP), 129, 174; Adams Mark Hotel, 137; consumer choice guide (business report card), 175; Cracker Barrel, 131–32
National Incident Based Reporting System (NIBRS), 95–98
National Research Council study, 33
National Retail Federation, 157, 174
National Retail Security Survey, 2015, 92
National Shopping Behavior Study, 59
National Urban League, 171
*The New Jim Crow* (Alexander), 20
*Newman v. Piggie Park Enterprises, Inc.* (1968), 29
Newton, Thandie, 67
New York City Taxi and Limousine Commission, 141
New York Police Department (NYPD), 99, 117
New York Yankees Partnership, 89, 144
NIBRS. *See* National Incident Based Reporting System (NIBRS)
NYPD. *See* New York Police Department (NYPD)

Obama, Barack, 1, 12, 105
Ocean Mecca Motel, 38–39, 139
Office Max, 118
Online shopping, 66, 168
Osorio, Arturo E., 73
Osowski, Manige, 16
Oyler, Randy, 106, 153–55

Page, Clarence, 29
Parks, Rosa, 5–6
Parti Quebecois, xix
*Patterson v. McLean Credit Union* (1989), 89
Penney, J. C., 113–14
PepsiCo, 159
Peter Pan Bus Lines, 142–43
Petty, Ross, 68
Philip Morris, 69
Phillips, Katherine W., 165
Piggie Park BBQ, 11
Pilgrim, David, 10
Placek, Brian, 117
Plainfield Daycare Center, 129
Planter's Hotel, 2
*Plessy v. Ferguson,* 5
Post-traumatic slave syndrome
    (PTSS), 19–20
Post-traumatic stress disorder (PTSD), 20
Price discrimination, 63–64
Price sensitivity, 64
Prince George's County Human Relations
    Commission, 138
Prisons, vii
*Psychology and Marketing,* 169
*Psychology Today,* 160
Pugh, Linda, 116–17
*Pugh v. Avis Rent-A-Car Systems Inc.*
    (1997), 121
Pullig, Chris, 158–59
Purchasing power, growth rate of
    population and, 58

Quang Loi Jewelry, 135–36
Quiles, Ricardo, 117
Quinton, Wendy J., 22, 33

Race-Based Traumatic Stress (RBTS) scale,
    19–20
Racial matching, 159

Racial microaggressions, 14–18
Racial profiling, ix; consumer (CRP), 32,
    91–104; GroupMe app, 23
Racism, vii; aversive, 14; implicit, 12–14
Radio Shack, 118–19
Ramirez, Deborah, 35
Randolph, A. Phillip, 141–42
Red Apple Kwik Fill, 126
Reno, Janet, 137
Resilience building actions, 158
Retail Council of New York State, 179
Retail discrimination, juror perceptions,
    80–81
Retail purchasing trends, 59–60
Retail redlining, 64–67, 168
Reynolds, R. J., 69
Rice, Tamir, 19
Richard, Steven, 118–19
Richeson, Jennifer A., 29
The Right Site, 41
Rodriguez, Dariely, 167–68
Roker, Al, 141
Roof, Dylan, 12
Ross, John, 17
*Ross v. Schade,* 17
Roy, Abhijit, 164

Saks Fifth Avenue, 172
Salomon, Kristen, 21
Sargent, Ron, 149–50
Saveedra, Carlos, 159
*Sawyer v. Southwest Airlines,* 143
Scarborough USA, 41
Schools, vii
Schroeder, Brad, 140
Schwanke-Kasten Jewelers, 55
Selig Center, 58–59
Selya, Bruce M., 91
Sensor tags, 93
7-Eleven, 128
S. H. Kress & Company, 6
Sharpton, Al, 31–53, 99
Shell Oil, 123, 154, 160
Sheraton Inn, 138
"Shop and frisk," 99
"Shop and frisk" practices, x
Shoplifting: behavioral variables, 94;
    consumer racial profiling and, 32,

91–104; definition, 92; official government arrest data, 95–101
"Shopping while black or brown," vii, ix
Siegelman, Peter, 64
Snell, Maren, 109
Snuggs, Thelma, 32
"So at variance" standard, Minnesota, 77
Social justice, 169
Social justice community, how to help, 174–77
Sommers, Samuel, 81
Southern Hotel, 2
Southland Corporation (7-Eleven), 133
Southwest Airlines, 143
Speedway SuperAmerica, 127
Spence, Benet DeBerry, 23
Spitzer, Eliot, 44
SS *Merril*, 1–2
Stadium Club, Yankee Stadium, 75, 139
Staples, 115–16, 149–50
Starbucks, 67
State public accommodation laws, 78–80
Stearnes, Mark, 139
*Stearnes v. Baur's Opera House, Inc.* (1992), 145
*Stearnes v. Baur's Opera House, Inc.* (1993), 145
Stereotyping, 11–30
Stewart, Potter, 75
"Stop and Frisk Watch" app, 172
Stoute, Steve, 55
Sue, Derald Wing, 14
Sullivan, Louis W., 69
Systemic restricted choice, 124–25

*Tandy Corp.*, 103, 121
*Tanning of America: How Hip-Hop Created a Culture That Rewrote the Rules of the New Economy* (Stoute), 55
TCR. *See* Transformative consumer research (TCR)
*Terry v. Ohio* (1968), 104
Thomas, David A., 165
Tisdale, Sam, 131
Toussaint, Lorraine, 136
Toyota, 67
Toys R Us, 117

Transformative consumer research (TCR), 169
Treasure Cache, 60
Troupas, Peter, 117
Trump, Donald, 16
Turner, Alberta, 107–8
Turner, Tina, 61, 135

UCR. *See* Uniform Crime Report (UCR) data
Unconscious discrimination, 12–14
Uniform Crime Report (UCR) data, 95–98
United States: immigration rates, 57; population by ethnicity, 56; purchasing power and growth rate of population, 58
*United States of America v. HBE Corporation, d/b/a Adam's Mark Hotels* (2000), 145
Uptown cigarettes, 69
U.S. Census demographic data, 41
U.S. Court of Appeals: Conoco, 38; Dillard's, 37; Ocean Mecca Motel, 39
U.S. Department of Justice: Adam's Mark Hotel, 137; Cracker Barrel, 131–32; Glass Menagerie, 140
U.S. Supreme Court: Dillard's, 37; *Plessy v. Ferguson*, 5; Section 1981, Civil Rights Act (1866), 76
U.S. Surgeon General's Report of 2001, 18
*U.S. v. Glass Menagerie, Inc.* (1988), 145

Video recording devices (DVRs), 93
Vigilance perspective, discrimination, 22

Walker, Andre, 135
Walker, Gail, 138
Walmart, ix, 3, 114–15; Confederate flags, 12
Washington Human Rights Commission, 128
Wells Fargo, 15
Wendy's, 16
West, Cornel, 20, 141
West Africans, racial group in Colonial America, 4
Whitcomb, Charles, 143
White Americans, population numbers, 56

Whitley, Bernard, 13
Williams, Christine L., 73
Williams, Jacqueline A., 26
Williams, Jerome D., viii, xx–xxv, 32–33,
    64, 65–66, 183–84
Williams, Rathea, 126
*Williams v. Cloverland Farms Dairy Inc.*
    (1999), 134
*Williams v. Staples* (2003), 121
Winfrey, Oprah, 135

Woolworth's, 6
Workplace 2000, 152

Xenophobia, 171

Yachtsman Resort Hotel, 130
Yankee Stadium, 75, 139
Yellow Cab, 142

Zhou, Fran, 21

# About the Authors

The three authors of this book are recognized leading authorities in the field and are uniquely positioned to author this book—having collaborated over a number of years in research and publications on marketplace discrimination. They have presented their research and opinions in scholarly journals, to professional and academic organizations, to national and local media, as expert witnesses in court cases and consultants to corporations and government agencies.

**Geraldine Rosa Henderson** ("Gerri"), PhD, is associate professor in the marketing department of the Quinlan School of Business of Loyola University Chicago and the former chairperson and associate professor of the department of marketing department at Rutgers Business School, Rutgers University, Newark and New Brunswick, New Jersey. She has also been on the faculty at Duke University's Fuqua School of Business, Howard University's School of Business, and the University of Texas at Austin's Department of Advertising and Public Relations. She has also taught at George Washington University, Northwestern University's Kellogg School of Management, Stanford University's Graduate School of Business, The University of Virginia's Darden Graduate School, Thunderbird: The Garvin School of International Management, and in Executive Education at both Duke University (Fuqua) and UCLA (Anderson). Courses taught include advertising and promotion, theories of persuasion, marketing management, marketing strategy, consumer behavior, brand management, advertising and society, multicultural advertising, multicultural marketing, consumer discrimination, and advertising and black representation, and the global academic travel experience (GATE) to Southern Africa. Her primary areas of research include branding, marketplace diversity, digital marketing, and consumer networks (cognitive and social). She has authored over 50 publications in outlets such as the *Journal of Business Research*, the *Journal of Advertising*, the *Journal of Public Policy &*

*Marketing, International Journal of Research in Marketing,* and the *European Journal of Operational Research.*

Dr. Henderson completed her MBA and PhD degrees in marketing from the Kellogg Graduate School of Management at Northwestern University, after earning her BS degree in electrical engineering from Purdue University. Prior to pursuing her PhD, she worked for several years at IBM in Relationship Marketing (specializing in the healthcare, insurance, and pharmaceutical industries) and briefly in Brand Management at Kraft Foods. Dr. Henderson serves or has served on several corporate and nonprofit boards including the American Marketing Association, the National Black MBA Association, the National Society of Black Engineers, the Advisory Council of the Association for Consumer Research, and as president of the Marketing Ethnic Faculty Association. In addition, she serves or has served on the Editorial Review Board for several journals including the *Journal of Public Policy & Marketing,* the *International Journal of Advertising,* and the *Journal of Current Issues and Research in Advertising.* She has also served as a special issue editor for the *Journal of Public Policy and Marketing* and for the *Journal of Business Research.* She considers herself a "Doctorpreneur" since she often serves as a marketing consultant and a research moderator.

**Anne-Marie Hakstian**, JD, PhD, is a professor at the Bertolon School of Business and Coordinator of the Legal Studies program at Salem State University in Salem, Massachusetts. She serves on the university's President's Advisory Committee on Diversity, Affirmative Action, Equity and Social Justice. In that capacity, Dr. Hakstian has collaborated with other campus members to create a community of learners that value diversity and social justice. Her research agenda includes work on marketplace discrimination, racial profiling in traffic enforcement, and jury decision-making. Her research on marketplace discrimination was cited in the NAACP's Amicus Curiae brief filed with the U.S. Supreme Court in support of the petitioners in the case of *Arguello v. Conoco.* Dr. Hakstian recently completed her doctoral dissertation in which she studied the reforms undertaken by municipal police departments in Massachusetts to address racial and ethnic disparities in traffic enforcement outcomes. She examined the extent to which police departments adopted certain reforms as well as their effectiveness in reducing racial and ethnic disparities in traffic citations. With Dr. Sophia Evett, a social psychologist, her current research seeks to understand what factors impact the perceptions of jurors in consumer discrimination cases.

In particular, they are exploring how characteristics of both the jury and the legal claims filed by plaintiffs influence the outcomes of these lawsuits brought against retail stores.

Dr. Hakstian consults with public and private organizations on issues of racial profiling in marketplace and law enforcement contexts. She has been named as an expert witness in court cases involving claims of racial profiling. She is a member of the Law and Society Association and the Academy of Legal Studies in Business. She serves on the Editorial Board of the *Business Law Review*, a publication of the North Atlantic Regional Business Law Association. Dr. Hakstian has served on the board of the Salem Award for Human Rights and Social Justice Foundation whose mission is to recognize, honor, and perpetuate the commitment of individuals and organizations working to alleviate discrimination and promote tolerance. Prior to her current career in academia, Dr. Hakstian was a consultant to federal government agencies on issues relating to Equal Employment Opportunity law and policy. In addition to investigating claims of discrimination and writing final agency decisions, she assisted in the design, development and implementation of customized training sessions for public and private client organizations. Dr. Hakstian received her PhD from Northeastern University and a JD from the George Washington University Law School. She earned a BA from George Washington University and a Certificat d'Etudes Politiques from the Institut d'Etudes Politiques in Paris, France.

**Jerome D. Williams**, PhD, is provost and executive vice chancellor of Rutgers University-Newark. He also is distinguished professor in marketing and holds the prudential chair in business. At Rutgers he previously served as director and research director of The Center for Urban Entrepreneurship & Economic Development, in the department of management and global business, and as PhD program director. Prior to joining Rutgers, he held endowed chair positions at four different universities, including the Whitney M. Young, Jr. Visiting Associate Professor in the Wharton Business School at the University of Pennsylvania, the Anheuser-Busch/John E. Jacob Professor at Howard University, the F.J. Heyne Centennial Professor at the University of Texas at Austin, and the visiting Wee Kim Wee Professor at Nanyang Technological University in Singapore. Prior to being on the Howard faculty, he was on the Penn State University marketing department faculty for 14 years. He has published extensively in the areas of multicultural marketing, Internet privacy, and public health communication.

He was a member of an Institute of Medicine Committee that authored the landmark report *Food Marketing to Children and Youth: Threat or Opportunity?* and appointed by U.S. Census Bureau to chair the 2010 Communications Contract Academic Assessment Team.

Dr. Williams is co-editor of *Diversity in Advertising: Broadening the Scope of Research Directions,* and *Advances in Communication Research to Reduce Childhood Obesity* and several volumes on marketing and public policy issues. He has been named as an expert witness in numerous court cases on marketplace discrimination. He has served as chairman of the Board of Trustees of the American Marketing Association Foundation. The foundation's Williams-Qualls-Spratlen award is named in his honor to recognize marketing scholars for mentoring students from underrepresented backgrounds. In 2009, he received national recognition by the Academy of Marketing Science as the recipient of the Outstanding Marketing Teaching Award. He currently serves as associate editor of the *Journal of Public Policy & Marketing.* He received his PhD from the University of Colorado in marketing, with a minor in social psychology. He also has an MS degree from Union College and a BA degree from the University of Pennsylvania. He is a long-time runner; he was captain of the track and cross-country teams at the University of Pennsylvania where he set several records and has completed over 20 marathons. In 2010, he was inducted into the high school athletic hall of fame in Bristol Township, Pennsylvania, for his running accomplishments.